Lieven D'hulst / Carol O'Sullivan / Michael Schreiber (eds.)
Politics, Policy and Power in Translation History

Transkulturalität – Translation – Transfer, Band 24
Herausgegeben von
Dörte Andres / Martina Behr / Larisa Schippel / Cornelia Zwischenberger

Lieven D'hulst / Carol O'Sullivan / Michael Schreiber (eds.)

Politics, Policy and Power
in Translation History

Verlag für wissenschaftliche Literatur

Umschlagabbildung: Censored information grunge concept © alexskopje – Fotolia.com

ISBN 978-3-7329-0173-9
ISSN 2196-2405

© Frank & Timme GmbH Verlag für wissenschaftliche Literatur
Berlin 2016. Alle Rechte vorbehalten.

Das Werk einschließlich aller Teile ist urheberrechtlich geschützt.
Jede Verwertung außerhalb der engen Grenzen des Urheberrechtsgesetzes ist ohne Zustimmung des Verlags unzulässig und strafbar.
Das gilt insbesondere für Vervielfältigungen, Übersetzungen,
Mikroverfilmungen und die Einspeicherung und Verarbeitung in
elektronischen Systemen.

Herstellung durch Frank & Timme GmbH,
Wittelsbacherstraße 27a, 10707 Berlin.
Printed in Germany.
Gedruckt auf säurefreiem, alterungsbeständigem Papier.

www.frank-timme.de

Table of Contents

Translation policies: What's in a name?	7
Lieven D'hulst, Carol O'Sullivan & Michael Schreiber	
Official interpreters and the foreign policy of the Chosŏn dynasty (14th–16th centuries)	15
Nam Hui Kim	
Translation as a tool in the scramble for the Americas: A case study of some 17th century English translations of the "Brevísima relación" by Las Casas	33
Marieke Delahaye	
Ethical issues of community interpreting and mediation: The case of the Lagerdolmetscher	53
Małgorzata Tryuk	
Translation zwischen Irakkrieg und intellektueller Korruption. Oder: Translatoren in der arabischen Literatur im Spannungsfeld von Politik, Macht und Berufsethik	69
Nahla Tawfik	
A systematic approach to manipulation in translation – a case study of Ye Junjian's 1958 translation of H. C. Andersen's tales	95
Wenjie Li	
Der Krieg mit den Mol(o)chen: Politik und Ideologie in der Rezeption eines tschechischen Romans in Portugal	113
Jaroslav Špirk	
Censorship of translated literature under Franco's dictatorship: Self-censorship of Czech literature	135
Petra Vavroušová	
Mute, dumb, dubbed: Lulu's silent talkies	157
Tessa Dwyer	

Politics of film translation: 187
Cinema and nation-building in China (1949–1965)
 Fan Yang & Dongning Feng

Freddi's preliminary norms: Italy's censorship bureau   211
 Irene Ranzato

The influence of policy on subtitling for the deaf and hard of hearing   229
in Poland
 Renata Mliczak

Translation policies: What's in a name?

Lieven D'hulst, Carol O'Sullivan & Michael Schreiber

1 Policy, politics, institutions

Following Longman's *Dictionary of Contemporary English*, a 'policy' may be defined as "a way of doing something that has been officially agreed and chosen by a political party, a business or another organization" (p. 1339), while the concept of 'politics' is restricted to the "ideas and activities relating to gaining and using power in a country, city, etc." (p. 1340). Both concepts are often studied in coalescence because no policy can be fully applied without recourse to politics. Even if it is tempting to consider 'policy' as a hypernym of 'politics', there is little doubt that power- or management-driven aspects of ideas and activities currently have a stronger steering capacity than interest- or problem-driven aspects. However, a theoretical distinction between policies and politics is less productive than an analytical one because the relative weight given to each always depends on specific time-space situations as well as on the specific disciplines and social practices in which the interaction between policies and politics takes form. As a matter of fact, inclusive approaches gained ground several decades ago under the umbrella denomination of Policy Studies, nowadays a full-fledged discipline with a solid basis in political science and public administration (cf. A. Wildavsky 2006), but which also extends to other disciplines in the humanities (and even far beyond). Indeed, since most cultural and social practices are to some extent subjected to policies and politics, overarching views invite the implementation of relevant expertise into disciplines that purport to study such aspects, and also invite interdisciplinary cooperation between several disciplines working on the same or adjacent domains. In many cases, this may lead to integrated models with coordinated research programs (cf. G. González Núñez 2016).

One would, for instance, expect the study of language and translation policies to meet and interact on a similar basis. At least the study of language from a policy viewpoint has become a major domain of language research since the 1970s (for the most recent period see e.g. S. Wright 2007, B. Spolsky 2009, A. Blanc 2013). Nowadays, language policy covers a vast range of topics, including planning of language learning, codification and maintenance of language use, support given to minority languages, political and governmental agents or instances such as schools, churches, media, armies, and so on. As to 'translation policy', the concept made its entry into translation studies at a later stage. According to James Holmes, it applies to "the place and role of translators, translating, and translations in society at large: such questions, for instance, as determining what works need to be translated in a given socio-cultural situation, what the social and economic position of the translator is and should be, or [...] what part translating should play in the teaching and learning of foreign languages" (1988/2000: 182). Although this definition does not seem to fully match the former one – the role of translating and the selection of works to be translated might appear to be more a purview of translation functions – there is good reason to assume that everything that makes up a language policy may also enter a definition of translation policy.

Has that potential common ground led to an interdisciplinary dialogue? This would at least suppose that the two disciplines involved share some interest in achieving one. As we know, translation studies being a rather young academic discipline, it is strongly indebted to other disciplines in the humanities, including those including policy components in their purview, such as cultural studies, economics and business studies, politics and legal studies or the sociology of literary exchange. At the same time, translation studies strives for growing autonomy, stressing the call for a specific *approach* for dealing with *translational* aspects of language. Such a viewpoint echoes an older one, against which translation studies precisely tried to take a rather firm stand a few decades ago, emphasizing that translation constitutes a proper object or field of study requiring tailor-made approaches. This debate, even if it touches at the heart of the identification and description of translation policies, nevertheless falls outside the scope of this book: our concern is not so much to contribute to a theoretical debate, because this would leave aside a perhaps equally urgent task, i.e. the reconstruction of the ins and outs of past and present translation policies without which, in the longer run, an understanding of the specifics of translation policies would remain speculative.

This being said, the wide range of possible topics to be covered does not facilitate the task of the translation historian. Should the latter break translation policies down into manageable units for the purpose of a historical description? Does it make sense to distinguish subdomains, such as translation politics at large and 'institutional translation', as understood by Christina Schäffner et al. (2014), as a sort of "translation that occurs in an institutional setting" (p. 493), being managed by an institution? Without a proper frame of research the temptation to have recourse to existing approaches is not only understandable, it is no doubt the most efficient way to date to enter the field of historical research on translation policies. The results obtained will – at least provisionally – be able to fill a number of gaps in our historical knowledge and lay bare the "variety of meanings, designing official institutional settings […] but also a wide range of relatively informal situations related to ideology, translators' strategies, publishers' strategies, prizes and scholarships, translator training, etc." (R. Meylaerts 2011: 163). But filling the gaps is not only a matter of finding and describing, it also requires historical self-awareness, and a proper methodology.

2 Historical approaches

It is a truism to state that historical approaches are first and foremost informed by the historical understanding of past translation policies, politics and institutions. In fact, this understanding includes many complex methodological issues of which only a few can be recalled here. First, metalanguage: how were 'policies' named and defined in the past? Are they defined in explicit ways, as laws or rules, or are they to be extracted from other sources (correspondences, comments, reviews, the translations themselves)? Are they culture-specific and domain-specific, i.e. are translation policies understood the same way inside and outside Europe, in literary translation, media translation, historiography and religious translation? Second, categories: it should be determined whether it is instrumental to consider publishers, critics, and patrons as managing 'agents', the translator's, subtitler's or dubber's aims and techniques as 'strategies', translation 'norms' as tokens of the codification and maintenance of literary language and genres, of audiovisual genres and the like. Third, periodization: what is the temporal status of translation policies? For instance, translation policies designed by the French revolutionaries (L. D'hulst & M. Schreiber 2014) seemed to stretch over a generation only (1795–1815), yet it is plausible that former European hegemonic regimes, such as the Spanish and the Austrian, handled similar policies that the French only had to adapt slightly (without acknowledging their debt to their predecessors). We therefore need a different understanding of time paths and continuity of traditions (an idea that has been easily accepted for the poetics of pre-modern translation in Europe). Fourth, space: where do translation policies emerge and take shape; do they stretch and cover other cultural spaces? Policies may be designed and imposed locally (by a city administration, on subgroups of inhabitants such as migrants), at a national level (through laws and decrees) in the context of nation-building (see, e.g. Kumar 2013; Dizdar, Gipper, Schreiber 2015), at an international level, with the support of military or economic forces (as may be testified by translation policies of supranational organizations (see, e.g., Hermans 2009), international publishers, film and business companies). Indeed, the study of policies benefits from the understanding of the politics (and depending other powers) that sustain it for whatever reason. This attests the need for a thorough contextualization of translation policies.

As may be clear by now, there is ample room for the exploration of domains that apparently fall outside the scope of more or less official or public policy-making such as translations of literature, religious texts, scientific texts, or of other media such as cinema. It may perhaps suffice at this stage to consider a reconfiguration and rephrasing of existing insights on such issues as particularly useful when the outcome puts forward the historical specifics of translation policies and enables them to be interconnected as well as integrated into larger research programs. At least, one may say, the following collection of papers, being one of the first of its kind, aims to pave the way, not through its consistent attachment to a single period, area or type of policy, but by offering a number of interesting and original approaches that may serve as landmarks and inspiring examples for more to come.

3 Presentation of the book

The contributions in this book are partly based on papers given at the 7th congress of the European Society for Translation Studies (EST), held at the Faculty for Translation Studies, Linguistics and Cultural Studies of the University of Mainz in Germersheim, Germany, between 29 August and 1 September 2013. For this publication, all papers have undergone a review process.

In order to illustrate the variety of contents and approaches involved in the concept of translation policy, we have organised the chapters thematically rather than chronologically. Our objective in doing so was to show how policies influence a wide array of discursive practices.

The first group of articles is concerned with the policy of translating and interpreting in power settings, including policy making, from the 14th till the 20th century (Kim, Delahaye, Tryuk, Tawfik).

Kim Nam Hui's article focuses on the history of interpreting during the Chosŏn Dynasty in Korea, especially between the 14th and the 16th centuries. It shows how the official interpreters, as "field workers for diplomatic relations with the kingdom's neighbors", contributed to the implementation of Korea's foreign policy during this period.

Marieke Delahaye presents a case study of translation policy in the 16th and 17th centuries: the English translations of the *Brevísima relación* by Las Casas. According to Delahaye, these translations reflect the political and religious powers in Europe and the colonies.

Małgorzata Tryuk describes the situation of the camp interpreters in Nazi concentration camps during World War II, the so-called *Lagerdolmetscher*. The paper shows in what communicative situations interpreters were needed in the camps, who they were, how they were recruited and how they performed their tasks under these extraordinary circumstances. Nahla Tawfik's paper can be seen as a contribution to the 'fictional turn' in translation studies. It analyses the role of fictional translators and interpreters (actually a military interpreter and a literary translator) in two Arabic novels, one situated in Iraq during the occupation by the US army and the other in 'pre-revolutionary' Syria.

A second group deals with translation policies as applied to a wide corpus of literary texts, both for children and adults (Li, Špirk, Vavroušová).

Wenjie Li's paper focuses on a translation of H. C. Andersen's tales into Chinese from the year 1958 as an example of translational manipulation. It illustrates various types of manipulation and their influence on the reception of Andersen's tales in China.

Jaroslav Špirk deals with three second-hand Portuguese translations of Karel Čapek's *War with the Newts* (1936), published in 1965, 1979 and 2009 respectively. Focusing on the paratexts of the translations, the paper analyses the political, historical and cultural circumstances under which these indirect translations were produced.

Petra Vavroušová's article deals with two Spanish translations (published in 1980 and 2008) of J. Hašek's novel *The Good Soldier Švejk*. The analysis is based on censor's reports, interviews with translators and publishers and a micro-textual analysis of the source and target texts.

A third group is devoted to the policies of media translation since the era of the silent film (Dwyer, Yang and Feng, Ranzato, Mliczak).

Tessa Dwyer's paper retraces the cultural context of the history of dubbing and presents two films by Louise Brooks. In her analysis, she compares interlingual dubbing and intralingual 'revoicing' and shows the influence of revoicing on the production and reception of a film.

Fan Yang and Dongning Feng examine the Chinese policy on film translation in the period 1949 to 1965, especially with regard to the Soviet films. The paper shows how films were selected for a translation and how they were translated and promoted.

Irene Ranzato focuses on the *Ufficio di Revisione* Cinematografica (Bureau of Film Revision), more commonly known in the Italian film industry as *ufficio censura* (censorship bureau), which was created in 1913.

Renata Mliczak outlines the development of subtitling for the deaf and the hard of hearing (SDH), from the beginnings of this type of audiovisual translation in the USA and the UK to the situation in Poland today.

References

BLANC, Agnès (2013): *La langue de la République est le français. Essai sur l'instrumentalisation juridique de la langue par l'État, 1789–2013.* – Paris, L'Harmattan.

D'HULST, Lieven & SCHREIBER, Michael (2014): "Vers une historiographie des politiques des traductions en Belgique durant la période française", *Target: International Journal of Translation Studies*, 26:1, 3–31.

DIZDAR, Dilek, GIPPER, Andreas & SCHREIBER, Michael (2015): *Nationenbildung und Übersetzung.* – Berlin, Frank & Timme.

GONZÁLEZ NÚÑEZ, Gabriel (2016): "On translation policy", *Target: International Journal of Translation Studies*, 28:1, 87–109.

HERMANS, Theo (2009): *The Conference of the Tongues.* – Manchester, St. Jerome.

KUMAR, Ravi, (ed.) (2013): *Role of Translation in Nation Building.* – New Dehli, Modilingua.

MEYLAERTS, Reine (2011): "Translation policy". In: GAMBIER, Yves & VAN DOORSLAER, Luc, (eds.): *Handbook of Translation Studies*, vol. 2, 163–168.

SCHÄFFNER, Christina, TCACIUC, Luciana Sabina & TESSEUR, Wine (2014): "Translation practices in political institutions: a comparison of national, supranational, and non-governmental organisations", *Perspectives: Studies in Translatology*, 22:4, 493–510.

SPOLSKY, Bernard (2009): *Language Management.* – Cambridge: Cambridge University Press.

WILDAVSKY, Aaron (2006): *Cultural Analysis: Politics, Public Law, and Administration.* – New Brunswick, NJ: Transaction Publishers.

WRIGHT, Sue (2007): "Language Policy and language planning". In: LLAMAS, Carmen, MULLANY, Louise & STOCKWELL, Peter, (eds.): *The Routledge Companion to Sociolinguistics.* – London & New York: Routledge, 164–172.

Official interpreters and the foreign policy of the Chosŏn dynasty (14th–16th centuries)

Nam Hui Kim
Kyungpook National University
namhuik@yahoo.de

The rules and principles of the Chosŏn Dynasty's foreign policy (1392–1910) were established in the early years of the dynasty. The official interpreters Yŏkkwans and their institution Sayŏgwŏn were the actors who put foreign policy into practice. To present the officials and illustrate their roles and positions during that time, we shall preface the introduction with a self-understanding and world view of the Chosŏn elite with their Chinese orientation, as exemplified by a high-ranking scholar. We begin with a short historical-political overview in Chosŏn during the 14th–16th centuries and its foreign policy principles. We then introduce Yŏkkwan and their institution Sayŏgwŏn, the implementing actors who were field workers for diplomatic relations with the kingdom's neighbors, though not yet esteemed and recognized as such. The findings presented here are based on the Database of Korean Classics where we can find the historical source texts translated into Korean such as T'ongmun'gwanji (Handbooks for Interpreting Officials), Kyŏngguktaejŏn (Complete Code of Law) and Chosŏn Wangjo Sillok (Annals of the Chosŏn Dynasty) as primary sources and other studies on Korean history and language as secondary sources.

Self-understanding and understanding of others and foreign policies

The Korean dynasties – especially Koryŏ (918–1392) and Chosŏn (1392–1910)[1] – adopted many customs and rites from Chinese dynasties. Their texts were almost always written in Chinese in acceptance of the Sinitic world order. Following Mongolian dominance in the late Koryŏ period, Chinese regained importance with the emergence of the Ming Dynasty (1368–1644). The newly founded Chosŏn Dynasty proclaimed a pro-Ming policy and proudly regarded itself as "little China (小中華)". After the Manchu invasions (1636/1637) and the subsequent constitution of the Qing Dynasty (1644–1912), Chosŏn even regarded itself as the authentic successor of the Han-Chinese (Chŏng 1993: 22–23). Chosŏn foreign policy fundamentally aimed to serve the Great (Han) China and to maintain amicable relations with its neighbors, meaning the Japanese, Mongolians and Jurchen. This principle of diplomacy is called Sadae (事大) and Kyorin (交隣).

The following appeal of Ch'oe Mal-li (崔萬理 ?–1445), then court deputy at the Institute for Books and Research (Chiphyŏnjŏn), makes it clear just how the Chosŏn elite thought of themselves and their neighboring states. The Institute, for example, provided moral principles and textual guides for governing the nation according to Confucian ideology, which made up the core of the politics and policies of the last dynasty of Korea. Ch'oe expressed his deep concern to King Sejong (r. 1418~1450), who invented the Korean script, Han'gŭl, together with some scholars in Chiphyŏnjŏn. Here Ch'oe comments upon the act of creating the Korean script which he finds unjustifiable:

> Since our ancestors, our land, Chosŏn, has been serving the Great Country sincerely and in conformity with Chinese regulations and without changing the Sinitic system. [...] From an-

---

[1] McCune/Reischauer system has been used for the Romanization of Korean in this paper. According to the point of division and perspective, the Chosŏn period can be divided into two or three sub-periods. It will be roughly divided into two sub-periods in this paper: the times of Japanese invasion (1592–1598) shall be a decisive point for economic, political and social changes, so that the period from the foundation of the dynasty until the end of the 16th century will be regarded as the first half of Chosŏn.

cient times, even though the local language and conditions were different [from China], there has never been an instance where a [state] within a Sinitic territory has invented its own letters. Only those like the Mongolians, Western Xia, Jurchen, Japan and West Tibet have their own letters, but it is not worth mentioning, since these are the affairs of barbarians. The classical writings say 'change the barbarians by using Cathay'. I have never heard of Cathay changing into barbarians. [...] To make coarse letters [Korean letters] at this time means that [we] are turning our back on Chinese civilization and reverting to barbarity out of our own initiative [...], what a great flaw to a civilization. (Annals of Sejong, 20/02/1444)2

It is obvious that all the others, i.e. Manchu, Japanese or Ryukyu, were regarded as barbarians, and consequently, not on the same level as Koreans. Though the spoken languages were different from Chinese, Koreans shared the use of Chinese characters. These characters are called Hanja and Hanmun (Chinese characters and Chinese texts respectively) in Korean. With the foundation of the Chosŏn Dynasty, the state religion, Buddhism, practiced during the last dynasty, was suppressed and Confucianism became the ruling ideology for moral standards. This intensified the identification with Chinese culture and defined self-awareness during the Chosŏn period. Under these circumstances, relations with the Chinese imperial court were crucial for a newly founded dynasty both politically and ideologically. From the perspective of the Chinese, they were the center of the world, and all the other races and states around the Chinese Empire were to serve the "Great Country" by regularly contributing material tributes based on the principle that there are tributes, there are rewards" (Kim Yang-soo 1996b: 6). The Chosŏn court sent tributes to China via delegations and also exchanged delegations with Japan. The delegations to Ming (1368–1644) were rewarded with gifts bestowed upon them from the Ming court in exchange for those tributes the delegations had taken with them – this was the official manner of trading with China at that time. The exchanges between Ming and Chosŏn were also of great economic importance. At the same time, these exchanges influenced the cultural and political identities of Chosŏn.

---

2 All cited historical texts which were originally written in Classical Chinese, have been translated into Korean. The Korean texts have been used as the source texts for translations into English in this paper. All the cited dates are based on the lunar calendar and will follow the format of Date/Month/Year. The leap month will be marked with the capital letter L after the month e.g. 29/08L/1433).

According to the Annals of T'aejo (19/11/1394), Sŏl Chang-su (偰長壽, 1341–1399), the supervisor of the institution of interpreters and a naturalized Uighur, presented a note to King T'aejo (r. 1392–1398) regarding the qualifications for the entrance examination for the Sayŏgwŏn as well as the number of trainees. His note clearly states the close relationship between Chosŏn's foreign policy and the foundation of Sayŏgwŏn and interpreter training:

> As others and I humbly have heard, men of ability should be regarded as the foundation for ruling a country and they should practice their knowledge. To establish schools is therefore of central importance for politics. Since we serve China, it is not possible not to acquire the language and scripts of China. That was the reason why your Majesty installed this institution when the state was founded [...]. (Annals of T'aejo 19/11/1394)

What is "this institution" which was established "when the state was founded"?

Sayŏgwŏn (1393–1894): An institution for official interpreters and their education

During the Koryŏ Dynasty, T'ongmungwan (通文館) was one of several institutions established in 1276 to teach Hanŏ (漢語) to people under forty years of age (Koryŏsajŏryo 19th chapter, 1st year of King Ch'ungnyŏl [...] 1276). Normally, the word Hanŏ (漢語) stands for Chinese, but since this is during the period of Mongolian intervention, it might instead refer to Mongolian. In the late Koryŏ period, a new institution called Sayŏgwŏn was founded in 1389. The power of the Yuan declined, and as the Ming Dynasty (1368–1644) became stronger, the importance of Chinese also grew. That might be one of the reasons why a new institution was established for interpreting during the Koryŏ Dynasty.

To fulfill the foreign policy principles in a newly founded Chosŏn Dynasty, a systematized and well-structured institution for interpreting was needed. Sayŏgwŏn was founded to teach Chinese and Mongolian in 1393 (again), a year after the Chosŏn Dynasty was constituted. Languages like Chinese, Mongolian, Japanese and Jurchen, called the Four Studies, were taught to the candidates training to become official interpreters, Yŏkkwans,³ at Sayŏgwŏn. It was at the same time the institution for official interpreters during the Chosŏn Dynasty. In the foreword to the 1720 edition of the Handbook for Interpreting Officials, *T'ongmun'gwanji* (hereafter *TMGJ*)⁴, one of the initial editors, Kim Kyŏng-mun (金慶門, ?–?), describes the tasks of the Sayŏgwŏn, which was staffed by around 600 people, including servants (*TMGJ* I 1998: 39). In Sŏl's note, mentioned above (Annals of T'aejo, 19/11/1394), he suggested allocating one of every three professors to teach Mongolian for trainees for Chinese start learning Mongolian as a second foreign language. Mongolian was already being taught in

---

[3] The syllable, Yŏk(g), stands for translating and interpreting. The Study of Interpreting (Yŏkhak, 譯學), a term used during the Chosŏn Dynasty, covers learning, teaching and research on foreign languages, and interpreting. Foreign languages were called Yŏgŏ (譯語) (Kang 1966: 326). A Yŏkkwan (譯官) is an interpreting official. Another term for an interpreting official, T'ongsa (通事), was used for people who were usually interpreters accompanying Chosŏn delegations to China or Japan, or interpreters who carried out related tasks when envoys visited. In the official diaries of Crown Prince Sohyŏn (1612–1645) who lived in Shenyang, the first capital city of the Qing Dynasty (1636–1912), he mentions interpreting officials from the Qing Dynasty also as T'ongsa. These records show that Yŏkkwan and T'ongsa were used to refer to interpreting officials in general.

[4] Kim Chi-nam (金指南, 1654–?), an interpreting official for Chinese, edited and complied TMGJ together with his son, Kim Kyŏng-mun, who was also an interpreting official for Chinese. TMGJ, handbooks, bulletins and even to some degree annals, were first printed in 1720 (46th year of Sukchong) and financed by editors with other interpreting officials. This handbook (6 volumes with 12 sections) for interpreters contains the following sections: 1. The organization of the Sayŏgwŏn and the training of interpreting officials (sections 1 & 2); 2. Regulations and procedures regarding the principle "to serve the Great" Country (referencing the Sadae diplomacy toward China, sections 3 & 4); 3. Regulations and procedures regarding the principle "to maintain amicable relations with neighbors" (relating to the Kyorin diplomacy toward Japan, sections 5 & 6); 4. Anecdotes of interpreters, whose names have been handed down to posterity (section 7); 5. Old stories relating to the Sayŏgwŏn and its assets, such as bondsmen, wooden printing blocks and books (section 8); and 6. Brief historical records chronologically ordered from 1636 (14th Year of Injo) until 1888 (25th Year of Kojong) (sections 9–12). After its first publication, TMGJ was periodically revised until the end of the 19th century. The TMGJ, originally written in classical Chinese, was translated into Korean by the commemorative organization for King Sejong the Great in 1998 (TMGJ I 1998, 28) and has been used for this paper.

these early days of Chosŏn rule. In the same record we find information about a person who was able to read Mongolian and Uighur. As such, it may be the case that an individual who studied Mongolian also studied Uighur as a second foreign language. According to the document presented in 1411 by the Ministry of Rites (which was, among other things, in charge of foreign affairs) to King T'aejong (r. 1400–1418), Mongolian seems not to have been popular (Annals of T'aejong, 02/12/1411). In respect of Japanese, there is a record in the Annals of T'aejong (26/10/1414) of teaching Japanese in the Sayŏgwŏn. With regard to the Jurchen language, according to a reference in the Annals of Sejong (25/06/1434), it was ordained that people be selected "who can understand the letters of Jurchen and train them in the Sayŏgwŏn, and appoint them as T'ongsa". Though the Ryukyu language did not belong to the Four Studies, there is, nevertheless, a record related to the teaching of that language. From the beginning of the Chosŏn Dynasty there were exchanges of delegations between Chosŏn and Ryukyu. The Ministry of Rites asked for a trainer who could teach trainees studying Japanese and the Ryukyu language. According to the Annals of Sejong (27/11/1437), it was decreed that "a person who can understand the letters of Ryukyu shall be found and appointed as a trainer."

The education in Sayŏgwŏn covered a period of about three years; the age limit for admission was fifteen years of age (Annals of T'aejo, 19/11/1394). Trainees could become interpreting officials after undergoing a complex procedure of screening and testing. They had to pass examinations in order to be promoted, retain their position or to be paid at all – as well as to be selected as interpreting officials for delegations (*TMGJ* I 1998: 73–99). Students were tested to assess their spoken and written proficiency in languages in addition to conversational and communication skills along with their knowledge of classical canons like the *Four Books* and the *Code of Governance (*hereafter the *Code)*. However, the assured track to becoming an official was by passing the Yŏkkwa civil service examination. Of the three categories of examinations, viz. literary, military and miscellaneous, 'interpreting' examinations belonged to the last. The successful candidate for the literary category – usually members from the hereditary Yangban class – would become part of an elite group in the Chosŏn Dynasty who together with the kings would shape court politics. The family background and social position of candidates were screened for qualification during the initial stages of the examinations. Yŏkkwa tested a candidate's skills in reading, reciting, commenting, and translating canonical classical Chinese texts, practical conversation and familiarity with the *Code* (*TMGJ* I 1998: 75–80). The treatment of the spoken language during the civil service examination is noteworthy since it reflects the practical aspects of the job in a society that greatly relied on written texts. In the same context, we can identify various measures introduced to enhance foreign language competence.[5]

The descending order of language significance was Chinese, Mongolian, Japanese and Jurchen. The order was subsequently changed in 1765, by advancing Manchu directly behind Chinese (Song 2001: 18; *TMGJ* I 1998: 44). In the 17th century, Manchu actually gained the power in China and founded the Qing Dynasty. However, it took Chosŏns elite more than a century to implement the shift of power from Han-Chinese to Manchu finally being reflected in the order of language significance for interpreting training. On the one hand, it was a fact that Chinese was still very important in diplomatic matters and documents, even though the dynasty was ruled by the Manchus. But to reiterate more importantly, it took a long time for the Chosŏn Dynasty to accept Manchu as the real power, since Chosŏn regarded itself as the authentic power successor of the Han-Chinese. Chinese students and, later, Chinese interpreting officials were going to serve "the Great Country" (Ming), which meant that interpreters of Chinese were generally held in higher esteem than those speaking other languages, especially during the first half of the Chosŏn Dynasty. However, the best applicant from the literary category of the state examination would be appointed two ranks higher than the best applicant for interpreting, who was always selected from among those who studied Chinese.

---

[5] King Sejong tried to send interpreting officials to China in 1433, which was not permitted by the Chinese court (Annals of Sejong, 29/08L/1433; Paek 2000: 31–32). A regulation – speaking only in foreign languages within Sayŏgwŏn – was introduced in 1442. In 1682, a department staffed by native speakers was established for conversation in the four foreign languages (*TMGJ* I 1998: 58).

Implementing foreign policies

Interpreting officials for Chinese

In spite of its pro-Ming policy, the first reigning Ming Emperor Hongwu (r. 1386–1398) mistrusted Chosŏn, and bestowed neither an imperial mandate nor a golden seal upon the Chosŏn royal court, which were important symbols of recognition by the Chinese imperial court for the newly founded Chosŏn. There were further problems. The first issue arose from improperly worded official documents sent to the Ming court. On the surface, certain 'presumptuous' expressions in the documents were singled out as troubling, although the real issue lay in the Ming Emperor's mistrust toward the Chosŏn court. Another issue concerned the genealogy of the founder of Chosŏn, Yi Sŏnggye (King T'aejo), which was incorrectly recorded in Ming history books and needed to be corrected. Following the death of the first Ming emperor relations between Ming and the Chosŏn returned to normalcy by 1400 when the second Chosŏn king, Chŏngjong (r. 1398–1400) received the imperial mandate and a golden seal (Kim, Ku-jin 1990, 3–6). Nevertheless, Ming history books were corrected not until around 200 years later after many delegations and interpreting officials had been sent repeatedly for this purpose (Annals of Sŏnjo, 28/03/1588).

Envoys to the Ming court were of vital importance and were sent on a regular basis, as many as four to five times a year. The number of regular delegations was determined settled by solicitation of the Chosŏn court (Kim Ku-jin, 1990: 6–8).[6] Chosŏn was very eager to send regular tributes frequently, since that was more or less the only way to trade officially with the Ming. Many delegations were also sent on an ad hoc basis. During the first half of Chosŏn – the last part of the 14th to the end of the 16th century – the Ming court sent envoys 125 times to Chosŏn. This is even less than once a year on average. Unlike Ming, Chosŏn sent envoys regularly, namely around 300 to 400 times and another 500 to 600 ad hoc delegations (Kim Ku-jin, 1990: 45–48). The envoy's entourage comprised between 70 and 80 people. There was an ambassador, a deputy, and a re-

---

[6] According to Kim, the Ming allowed Japan, for example, one tribute every ten years; for Ryukyu, one for every two years; and for Annam, one for every three years.

porting officer. The latter took care of regulations regarding dispatching members. Since there were very few paid positions for interpreting officials, it was hard for them to make a living. For interpreting officials it was therefore essential to join a delegation as accompanying interpreting officials, T'ongsa, as they were allowed to trade privately when they accompanied delegations to China or Japan. Needless to say, one of the principal tasks of the interpreting officials was to supervise official trading with the Chinese, Japanese and others. Officials for the Chinese or Japanese also accompanied delegations to Japan and China. There was a limit on goods which envoy members could take with them for private trading. The allowances for fabrics and ginseng were set according to the rank and position of the delegation members (the *Code*: 1998, 430). The highest official interpreter was in charge of trading at large. The second highest interpreting officer was in charge of trading with medicinal substances. Further, official interpreters were responsible for taking care of the belongings of the whole envoy delegation and for miscellaneous tasks. Interpreting officials called Pugyŏngch'ea were appointed to manage all affairs during the journey and assist the highest interpreting officer. They also assisted in trading, especially regarding medicinal substances, vegetable seeds, etc. When a Chosŏn delegation finally reached the Chinese capital, accommodation was provided at the designated guest hall. During their stay, the civil officers and official interpreters prepared to submit diplomatic documents and rehearsed a royal audience. Once in the court, they submitted the tributes and conducted official trading. To be a member of a delegation to China was – for both civil and interpreting officials – a great honor for the interpreter and his family, since China was regarded as a great civilization and the source of culture and Confucian ideology. In addition, there were also great economic advantages for official interpreters due to extensive official and private trading activities.

In the Annals from Sejong until Myŏngjong (r. 1545–1567), we find – apart from compliments and praise – also criticism aimed at official interpreters and their extensive trading habits, especially in relation to any illegal conduct. Yŏkkwans gradually became despised by civil officials. One of the reasons for this attitude towards official interpreters can be explained by the rigid social class hierarchy: scholar, farmer, artisan and merchant, and the interpreters were almost exclusively in charge of trading. Yŏkkwans were in charge of communication when the official diplomatic documents were submitted to the Ming court, but they were excluded from the preparation procedure of those documents, which was one of the most important tasks in foreign affairs.

Ultimately, then, did Yŏkkwans just interpret and trade? We can enumerate their other tasks: working as a court interpreter; accompanying the whole delegation, interpreting on the way – especially as they passed through various Chinese border posts; submitting diplomatic documents; being in charge of official trade; the legal- and illegal-purchasing of books ordered by the Chosŏn court (almanacs, Four Books, books on arithmetic, etc. Not every book was allowed to be bought by the Chinese court); buying medicinal ingredients, horns of water buffalos for bows, and other commodities for the royal court and for Yangban; collecting valuable information on the Chinese court; or even acquiring new skills and technologies.[7] The Ming court sent delegations to Chosŏn too, but much less than Chosŏn to the Ming court.[8] To welcome a Chinese delegation, a welcoming messenger was sent to the near border posts prior to its arrival in the Capital. Sometimes, official interpreters attended as welcoming messengers. Upon arrival in Seoul, a reception was given by the King, and he himself went over to the guest hall of the Chinese envoy, where a court interpreter was needed. The duties of the official interpreters include being near the envoys and acting as intermediaries bringing forward their requests; taking care of the members and working as interpreters at the court. Apart from working as court interpreters, the Yŏkkwans attended receptions and took care of Chinese delegations during their stays in Chosŏn. During receptions officials also collected information on diplomatic affairs. Further, they took part in the selection of young girls as ladies-in-waiting at the Chinese imperial court and boys who were to be made eunuch as a tribute. Interpreting officials worked near the borders of Chi-

---

[7] Annals of Sejong (02/03/1431), also see Kim Ku-jin (1990: 34–45), Kim Yang-soo (1996b: 7–8), Paek (2000: 97–131).

[8] According to Kim Yang-soo (1996a: 36) the first Chinese delegation came to Chosŏn in the 5th Month of 1393 (2nd Year of T'aejo), i.e. one year after the foundation of Chosŏn. They visited most frequently during T'aejong, Sejong and during the Japanese invasions (1592–1598) for setting up diplomatic relations with Chosŏn and expediting issues like sending and supporting military forces during Japanese invasions and post war negotiations.

na, or Japan, and were also in charge of interrogating stranded people and educating local trainees.

Interpreting officials for Japanese

What about relations with the Japanese and official interpreters for Japanese? In the early Chosŏn era, the Japanese Shogunate dispatched a delegation in reply to a delegation sent from Chosŏn to Japan. Besides this, there were powerful Japanese local families who visited the three ports of Pusanp'o, Jep'o and Yŏmp'o (now called Pusan, Jinhae and Ulsan). These exchanges took place on more than a thousand occasions. In the first half of the Chosŏn period, around 65 delegations were sent to Japan, most of them headed for Tsushima. From 1423 (5th Year of Sejong) onwards, people from Tsushima were allowed to come and go to Pusanp'o and Jep'o; from 1426 (8th year of Sejong), Yŏmp'o was opened to them too. These ports were subsequently closed for the Japanese as the result of riots by some Japanese in the three ports. (cf. Yi Jin-hee, 1986: 98–99, Kim Yang-soo 1996a: 78–82). Delegations to Japan were sent for various reasons: to congratulate the King on ascending the throne, to commemorate the installation of a new kampaku, to return the visit of Japanese delegations, etc. In the chapter 'Reception of Foreign Delegation' of the *Code* (1998: 236), we find, for instance, that the Japanese (倭人) and Jurchen (野人) should also be received according to traditional rules and rites. According to the ranking of the dispatched Japanese delegations, the Chosŏn court sent the receiving envoy together with the diplomatic documents and ritual gifts to Pusan. If an envoy was sent by a provincial governor, say, of Tsushima, then a local Yŏkkwan from Pusan or nearby city would receive him. From the moment the Japanese envoys got off their ship to re-embarking for the return journey, various rituals were performed and receptions given. Lower ranking interpreters called Sot'ongsa (小通事 [little interpreter]), who normally assisted the interpreting officials, and an interpreter from Japan were in charge of communications during the rituals and receptions (*TMGJ* I, 268–290).

The general duties of an interpreting official for Japanese do not differ from those of Chinese interpreting officials, e.g. accompanying the delegation, taking care of the usual interpreting matters on the way and of all the trade related issues, checking and collecting new (secret) information and knowledge, bringing back the captives or stranded, etc. The Annals of Sŏngjong (25/03/1479) contain instructions for delegation members to Japan. They were to collect geographical, climatic and military information, observe and record the four ceremonial occasions, namely coming of age, weddings, funerals, and ancestral rites in Japan and in Ryukyu. They were also to collect information regarding the genealogy of the Japanese royal family, their customs and the rules of the court. Apart from these instructions, there were also lists of precautions. We can see also that the Chosŏn court was worried about information leaks by interpreting officials, and thus questioning their loyalty. However, the mistrust towards Yŏkkwans was not limited to the Japanese interpreters, but also extended to Chinese interpreters (Annals of Sŏngjong, 13/04/1482, Annals of Chungjong, 19/01/1521, Annals of Myŏngjong, 02/03/1553). Although delegations to Japan were less frequent than to China there was a special feature in diplomatic relations with Japan: Waegwan (倭館) was a place where people from Japan (those who had permission) could stay and trade for longer periods and which was also used to accommodate delegations from Japan. By modern standards, it could be thought of as a kind of consulate. The Japan House hosted trading activities: Japanese envoys were received here. It also served as accommodation for interpreting officials, envoys and administrative members and traders. *TMGJ* contains short biographies of 51 interpreting officials, including 8 interpreters of Japanese (*TMGJ* II 1998, 13–51) who were praised for their loyalty during the Japanese invasion, excellent language competence and their highly respected personality. Official court records, however, criticize the official interpreters of Japanese. In the Diary of the Royal Secretariat (13/10/1648), they were described as having "only profits in mind", presumably because of their extensive (and sometimes illegal) trading and commercial activities. Since the exchanges between Korea and Japan had actively taken place after the 16th century, most of the historical records were related to the second half of the Chŏsun period.

Challenging tasks and low status

One of the first court interpreters among interpreting officials was Wŏn Minsaeng (元閔生 ?–1435). One of the tasks given to him was to gather information on the method of refining gold and silver. While accompanying a delegation to China, he was to collect market information regarding gold and silver in order to prepare the exemption of gold and silver tributes from the regular gifts to the Ming Dynasty (Annals of Sejong, 26/06/1428). The Korean delegations had to bring gold and silver as tributes, but these were not common local products, and were proving to be a great financial burden on the Chosŏn court. In 1429, gold and silver were replaced by gifts of horses and this was praised as an achievement of the deputy envoy and official interpreter, Wŏn Min-saeng. His obituary records a statement by the King himself: Wŏn

> ...trekked ten thousands of lis, and reported to the emperor [of China] in detail. Since his words [...] were genuine [...], the Emperor praised his loyalty and integrity. [Won enabled] to save [from making] tributes of gold and silver, the joy overflowed in the East [Korea] and [the King] awarded him a costume to show his grace [and his] honor moved the whole country. (Annals of Sejong, 29/09/1435)

As a court interpreter, he was once in considerable difficulty after he expressed the wish of a Chinese ambassador who wanted to see the King's sword, but who then took it away with him. Civil officers criticized Wŏn for not reacting properly (e.g. filtering out the request). However, King Sejong defended Wŏn with the following words:

> The task of an interpreter is <u>only to render the words</u>. [...] How could he have reacted differently with tact in such a sudden situation; and even if that would have been possible, how could he know that [the ambassador] then would take it with him finally". The King supported the interpreter, and he was going to settle this case by dismissing Wŏn from further action. (underlined by KNH, Annals of Sejong, 18/08/1430)

Thereupon an appeal was raised as follows:

> The task of a court interpreter is not just to render the words, but to comprehend the degree of seriousness and urgency of words carefully; and he shall not be neglectful at any point. Even during the reception, when the ambassador wanted to see the sword, it is so clear, that the occasion was not at all proper to express such a wish, so it was not difficult at all to prevent [the outcome]. Wŏn Min-saeng – just an official interpreter – had reached [even] the position of the second rank, but on that occasion he was still not able to anticipate such event at his own discretion, and may just have rendered it as is, spontaneously. [...] We hereby ask you [the King] to let us decide on his misdemeanor. (underlined by KNH)

During the early Chosŏn era, many kings showed their favor towards capable interpreting officials bestowing higher ranks upon them or awarding them prizes (e.g. Sejong and Sŏngjong), and they were patrons to Yŏkkwans, as we witness the case with Wŏn and King Sejong. However, for civil officers, Wŏn was "just an interpreting officer, who has reached [even] the position of the second rank, […]." Ironically, the civil officials valued more the interpreting task ("not just to render the words") than the patrons of interpreters. However, the actors performing the tasks were not highly esteemed by the civil officials. Even though the task of interpreting is the responsibility of interpreting officials, interpreting for kings was not the sole mission for interpreting officials. The position of a court interpreter was occupied by sometimes by a civil officer based on the argument that one is well educated and fluent in Chinese (also in written texts). Here we can find a record from the Annals about court interpreters (Annals of Chungjong, 01/12/1536):

> <u>The reason why we select a court interpreter from civil officers is that they are very good at written and spoken languages,</u> but at this time, [I, the King] have no idea whom I shall select from the Mandarins. Ch'oe Se-jin [who is not a civil officer, but an interpreting officer] is now in mourning, and he is [quite] old. Even though he may not be able to advance and retreat firmly as he did before, he may [still] be very good at Chinese. […] A selected court interpreter must be one who is very skilled, and only then, will he be suitable to honor our state. (underlined by KNH)

Those who had excellent language competence and were well educated also worked as court interpreters, like Ch'oe Se-jin (崔世珍 1468–1542) mentioned above. According to his obituary (Annals of Chungjong, 10/02/1542), he was "from a lowly status, but he studied very hard since childhood. He was especially well versed in the Chinese language. After he stated working as an official interpreter, he was in charge of all the diplomatic documents related to Sadae and Kyorin and achieved the 2nd rank". He was even involved in the drafting of diplomatic documents, which was actually the task of civil officials, while writing and editing several Chinese textbooks for interpreters.

Civil officials had a pretext for being critical of promotions and rewards given to interpreting officials, since Yŏkkwans were from a class lower than they were. The highest position for interpreters was the lower third position, but there were interpreters who reached positions even higher than the upper third rank, as did Wŏn and Ch'oe. Also, their "lack of education in Arts and Classics" was massively criticized by the Minister of Culture (Annals of Sejong, 06/09/1429). Nevertheless, in the Wŏn-case, indeed a scandal, a valuable sword of the Chosŏn King had been taken by a mere ambassador and that needed to be resolved. This was why the court interpreter Wŏn was almost made a scapegoat, in spite of being previously highly praised for his diplomatic achievement of reducing the state's expenses. During the Chosŏn Dynasty, Yŏkkwans were easily exposed to danger, since they were dealing with delicate political and diplomatic issues, and were not in a sufficiently strong social position of power to protect themselves.

Closing

Records from *Koryŏsajŏryo* and *Tongsagangmok* show that interpreters during Koryŏ dynasty accompanied delegations to and from China. They were charged with receiving delegations and, in some cases, solving diplomatic difficulties such as border conflicts, and also reducing cultural influences of the Yuan Dynasty on Koryŏ traditional customs. According to historical records, interpreters were rewarded for their achievements but also accused of wrongdoing – e.g. illegally accumulating a fortune by depriving others of land or assets. Unlike Chosŏn, however, there was no mention of interpreters who traded with China and others.

During the first half of the Chosŏn period, there was a limitation on promotion but some of the skilled official interpreters transcended the rigid system reaching higher positions than allowed. With the exception of writing diplomatic documents, their tasks varied considerably including negotiation, trading, and collecting information legally (and illegally) in addition to receiving and taking care of their guests. This is essentially what we understand today to reflect as the typical conduct of diplomats, which they were in effect. However, many of the official interpreters came from a middle or lower class, and some were sons of concubines, or low-ranking local bureaucrats. Chosŏn functioned according to Confucian ideology, which highly valued knowledge of classics and literature as well as rites, ethics and morals. The interpreters, however, mostly used non-written texts in their profession. Professional tradesmen were not yet an entity during the first half of the Chosŏn era; official interpreters filled the future role of the merchants. Interpreters were therefore much less esteemed. Official interpreters, and their institution Sayŏgwŏn, as implementing actors who fulfilling the role of field workers for foreign policy towards the kingdom's neighbors, were sometimes valued and recognized for what they were and did by their patrons, but hardly ever by the civil officials. Whether they gain recognition or struggle for social respect and political power shall one day be illuminated through further research on the history of interpreters in Korea.

References

Historical sources

The Code of Governance (Sinp'yŏn'gyŏngguktaejŏn). Translated and annotated by Yun, Guk-il. (1998) – Seoul: Sinsŏwŏn.

Diaries of Crown Prince Sohyŏn in Shenyang (Sohyŏnseja simyangilgi) (1637–1643). Institution for lecturing the crown prince. Translated (2008). – Seoul: Minsokwŏn.

T'ongmun'gwanji (1720–) Translated and edited by Kim, Kujin/Yi Hyun-suk (1998). I, II. – Seoul: The Commemorative Organization of King Sejong the Great.

Historical internet sources

The Annals of the Chosŏn Dynasty. http://sillok.history.go.kr/main/main.jsp (30.09.2014).

Diaries of the Royal Secretary [Sŭngjŏngwŏn ilgi], Koryŏsajŏryo, Tongsagangmok. In: Korean Classics Database. http://db.itkc.or.kr (30.09.2014).

Other references

CHŎNG, Ok-cha (1993): *Chosŏnhugi yŏksaŭi ihae* [Understanding of the history of the second half of the Chŏsun] – Seoul: Ilchisa.

KANG, Sin-hang (1966): "A Research on the foreign language scholars during the early Joseon Period (ijoch'ogi yŏkhakchae taehan koch'al)", *Jindan Journal* (29, 30). 324–338.

KIM, Ku-jin (1990): "Introduction to the Relationships between China and Korea during the first half of Joseon – Envoys of the Joseon and Ming Dynasty and their meaning", (chosŏnjŏn'gi hanjunggwan'gyesaŭi siron – chosŏn'gwa myŏngŭi sahaenggwa kŭ sŏnggyŏk), *Hongik Sahak* (*hongik sahak*) 4, 3–62.

KIM, Yang-soo (1996a): "Activities of Yeokgwan during the first half of Joseon", I (chosŏnjŏn'giŭi yŏkkwanhwaltong sang), *Silhaksasangyeonggu* (*sirhaksasangyŏn'gu*) 7, 33–86.

KIM, Yang-soo (1996b): "Activities of Yeokgwan during the first half of Joseon", II (chosŏnjŏn'giŭi yŏkkwanhwaltong ha), *Silhaksasangyeoggu* (*sirhaksasangyŏn'gu*) 8, 5–66.

PAEK, Ok-kyŏng (2000): *A study on interpreting officer during the first half of Joseon*. Doctoral Dissertation at Ewha Women's University.

SONG, Ki-joong (2001): *The Study of Foreign Languages in the Chosŏn Dynasty (1392–1910)*. – Seoul: Somerset Jimoongdang.

YI, Jin-hee (1986): "Tongsinsa during the second half of Joseon Dynasty". In: *T'ongsinsa during the Joseon Dynasty (chosŏnwangjohuban'giŭi t'ongsinsa, chosŏnsidaet'ongsinsa)*. – Seoul: Samhwa, 98–117.

Translation as a tool in the scramble for the Americas: A case study of some 17th century English translations of the "Brevísima relación" by Las Casas

Marieke Delahaye
KULeuven HU Brussel
marieke.delahaye@kuleuven.be

The question whether political authorities in the past developed active translation policies or not, and to what purposes, is a rather "neglected topic" in translation history studies.

This essay deals with the role of policy and power in translation history by means of a case study of the English translations of the Brevísima relación *by Las Casas between 1583 and 1699, against the background of European politics. It reconstructs the genealogy of the English tradition of the text, based on a thorough study of bibliographical data. It then presents the results of a comparative analysis of selected topics and/or fragments in the versions under study, along with a brief discussion on their political and religious context.*

The results of this analysis contain strong evidence of the existence of steering translation policy by the authorities. The successive English translations of this one text seem to navigate the waves of the political and religious powers, and their ever changing equilibrium in Europe and in the colonies.

These findings appear to confirm the results of research by translation studies scholars like Lambert (2013) or Van Doorslaer (2013) on contemporary issues in translation policy: rather than building bridges between people(s), translation policy aims at conservative purposes as well as at constructing the own identity by the manipulation of texts and their authors through translation.

The consequences hereof for historiography and the constitution of the (national) canon are huge.

Introduction

The question to what extent and with which objectives past political authorities developed active translation policies, is a topic which has received comparatively little attention in translation history studies.

The present essay attempts to provide an answer to both parts of this question by means of a comparative and descriptive analysis of the 17th century English translations of the *Brevísima relación* by Las Casas (Sevilla, 1552). It elaborates upon a chapter, dealing with the European traditions of the text in a doctoral research on the topic of the discovery and colonization of America by the Spanish Crown, conducted to explore the relation between translation and historiography. From a theoretical perspective, it builds on ideas of scholars such as (a) White (1973, 1981 and 1987), who emphasizes the importance of the linguistic form and the narratological character of historical and historiographical texts; (b) Bakhtin (1971 and 1981), Kristeva (1969), Genette (1982) and Venuti (2009), who draw attention to the multiplicity of voices in discourse; (c) Veyne (1971), O'Gorman (2006) Mudimbe (1988) and Saïd (1978), who explore the relation between the "self" and the "other" and the retrospective character of historical investigation; (d) Ong (1993), who sheds light on the essential differences between oral and literate societies.

This research shows how a variety of problems emerges when one studies the system of references to sources and citation strategies with regard to the languages mentioned and/or used, as well as the unmarked (or "invisible") and indirect translations in contemporary historiographical discourse – scientific as well as popularizing – on the subject. The reasons for these problematic reference and citation systems were found to be due to the trajectories of historical and historiographical texts through time and space. Accordingly, a case study was conducted on the above mentioned *Brevísima relación*, an emblematic text that has been translated into several European languages (Spanish, Dutch, French, English, German, Latin and Italian) during the last 500 years. The corresponding genealogy was drawn up on the basis of bibliographical research, resulting in three overall text families, the second of which comprehends several English translations, mostly based on the first French translation of 1579, hence translated indirectly.

All in all, the present essay aims to clarify the role of policy and power in translation history by means of a close analysis of the English translations of the *Brevísima relación* by Las Casas between 1583 and 1699 – broadly speaking, the 17th century – against the background of European politics and, more specifically, in the context of the relations between England and Spain in Europe and in the American territories.

The topic is more relevant than ever: during the recent Bangor Conference in September 2013[1], Van Doorslaer raised the question whether translation is used by policy makers for conservative purposes, or rather to build bridges between people(s), realizing integration and pacification or constructing a new world. Although by its very nature, one would expect translation to be a matter of building bridges between cultures, it is not inconceivable that it is often meant to maintain a status quo or to confirm one's own cherished ideas, such as strengthened nationalistic feelings, affirmation of identity, strong emphasis on differences with other territories or the rigid pursuit of one's own (political) objectives.

Case study

The *Brevísima relación de la destrucción de las Indias* by Bartolomé de las Casas, first published in Seville in 1552[2], is in fact a long list of atrocities perpetrated by the Spanish colonists against the indigenous population in the Americas, directed to the Spanish Crown as a plea to stop authorizations for further conquest and exploitation of the natives. In this respect, the text can be considered as a political and historiographical discourse, although it has frequently

---

[1] "Did anyone say Power?" – Conference Bangor, 5–6th September 2013. http://power.bangor.ac.uk/videos.php.en?subid=0

[2] The text was published along with several other texts which fall out of the scope of this essay.

been branded contemptuously as a mere pamphlet. On the other hand, the text has also been classified as a literary discourse, entirely in accordance with the European tradition that does not distinguish between historiographical texts and literary ones until the 19th century. It has even been labelled a religious text due to the fact that the author was a monk who never questioned the legitimacy or even the necessity of the conquest for the purpose of evangelization.

Between 1583 and 1699, the text of Las Casas has been published in English in probably five different translations (1583, 1625, 1656, [1663?], 1689, 1699). The reconstruction of the genealogy of the text[3] has shown that there are three large "translation families" – *viz* F1, or the Dutch branch, named after the first translation of this family, F2, or the so-called French branch, and F3, or the Italian family – and that geopolitics have played an important role in its publication and translations. The first English translation (1583) pertains to the F2 family on account of the fact that it was translated indirectly, through the first French translation (1579) by Jacques de Miggrode (Alden & Landis, 1980: 172 and Hanke & Giménez, 1954: 209)[4].

The question why it took 31 years before the text was translated in English may be due to the fact that England, as a colonizing power, initially wanted to avoid drawing attention to models of bad governance and exploitation, to let sleeping dogs lie with respect to its own behaviour in its overseas dominions. But in the eighties of the 16th century, when the hostile relationship with Spain had intensified[5], the animosity was in need of firm support. England stood by

---

[3] See DELAHAYE, Marieke (Forthcoming UFSC, Brasil). *Viaje de exploración hacia la lengua de la historiografía: las Crónicas de Indias en su trayectoria europea*. The genealogy of the *Brevísima relación* has been reconstructed on the basis of a thorough study of bibliographical sources and a comparative analysis of macrotextual elements and paratexts.

[4] It seems important to underline this affiliation because a recent publication (2004) presents the translation of the book as an original work by M.M.S., affirming that "in 1583 a traveller known only as M.M.S. had written *The Spanish Colonie: or a Brief Chronical of the Acts and Gestes of the Spaniards in the West Indies*". The assertion is even confirmed on the next page, when the author states that "The first translation of him [Las Casas, M.D.] was by Purchas in 1625, *A Briefe Narration of the Destruction of the Indians by the Spaniards*" (Kelly, 2004:5/9 and 6/9).

[5] See the Anglo-Spanish war of 1585–1604.

the Netherlands in their struggle for emancipation from Spain: both in the political (rivals in expansionism) and religious (Protestantism versus Catholicism) sphere, both England and the Netherlands were the antithesis of Spain. The translation of the *Brevísima relación* thus came at the right moment to strengthen the foreign policy of the English Crown against the growing power of Spain in Europe and overseas.

It is true that the Las Casas text has been translated more often into French than into English. But we must not forget that French used to be a language of culture in English intellectual circles. The text was thus not unknown to the English elite before 1583, when the publication of its first English translation made it possible to reach a much wider audience.

The 1583 English translation

The source text of the English version published in 1583 is a first-hand French translation (1579) of the Spanish text of 1552, directed towards the French speaking part of the Dutch population in the Netherlands. Although the target audience has clearly shifted[6], from the political (and religious) point of view there is but one and the same camp. And since the mysterious translator M.M.S. remains unknown, unlike the translator of the French version (Miggrode), one can hypothesize that his work may have been backed by a specific translation policy of the English Crown, aimed at supporting its political decisions in helping the Dutch against Spain in the war with the Spanish Armada of Philip II, and in the Dutch Declaration of Independence.

What is more, the Miggrode translation had apparently transformed the text into a bite-sized version for the purposes of the English. Indeed, despite the large concordance between the source text and the Miggrode translation with respect to terminology and phrasing[7], there are significant differences resulting from the added texts and the omissions. In fact, Miggrode published in one vol-

---

[6] The addressee in the title, "Pour server d'exemple et advertisement aux XVII Provinces du pais bas", has been transposed to the preliminary "To the Reader", otherwise a faithful translation of Miggrode's "Au Lecteur".

[7] See the results of the descriptive comparative analysis between the source text (1552) and its first French translation (1579) in Delahaye, M. (forthcoming UFSC, Brasil).

ume the text of the *Brevísima relación* followed by a partial letter, as is the case in the 1552 edition, plus three treaties that Las Casas also published in 1552, though in separate volumes, namely *Huitième remède* (*Entre los remedios*), the *Traité justificatif* (*Octavio remedio*) and *Controverse* (*Aquí se contiene una disputa o controversia entre Las Casas y Sepúlveda*). And it is precisely in these additional texts that the translator omits the elements which do not serve his purpose, since he only publishes "les choses qui ont semblé servir à notre propos." Saint-Lu (1978) notes that Miggrode omits those parts of the three additional texts that clearly establish the exclusive rights of Castile to evangelize the native peoples in the West Indies, while selecting others that denounce the greed of the (Spanish) conquerors[8]. Therefore, even though it is true that Miggrode respected the source text in his translation, we can state that his "infidelity" is to be found at the level of the omitted elements in the additional texts. The careful selection of materials allows him to realize his goal, i.e. to show the cruelty and greed of the Spaniards in the New World as an example and a mirror of what they might do in the Netherlands. The moralistic tone replacing the complaint is perhaps the greatest infidelity of Miggrode, and sets the tone for the whole translation family F2, which includes the English translations. Similarly, we find in this indirect translation a fidelity to its source text (the translation by Miggrode), with identical omissions that, however, can no longer be considered as omissions, since those (parts of) texts are already lacking in the French translation of 1579.

A comparison on the micro level between the French (1579) and the English (1583) translations shows an almost servile imitation, leaving aside some slight changes in the title, a shift in the addressee, and the addition of a new epigraph, which however reflects perfectly the essence of the dedication ("Au lecteur") by Miggrode regarding the exemplary function of another man's harm[9]. The dedication in the English version itself is again a nearly literal translation of the French one. There are but a few deviations, consisting in the occasional insertion

---

[8] "Des vingt 'raisons' développées par Las Casas, la première et la neuvième, qui proclamaient le droit exclusif de la Castille à assumer sa mission aux Indes, brillent par leur absence, [...]" (Saint-Lu, 1978: 443).

[9] "Happie is hee whome other mens harmes doe make to beware" (The Spanish Colonie, [...], 1583).

of a descriptive term such as "friendly Reader" for "lecteur", or "there have been so many spaniardes procreated into this worlde" for "il y a eu tant d'Espagnols au monde". However, the sonnet echoing the warning for the provinces of the Netherlands in the Miggrode version has not been withheld in the English translation of 1583, while the subsequent texts of the "Argumento" and the "Prólogo" have entirely been reproduced in quite literal translations from the French version. Then follow the chapters of the *Brevísima relación* in a translation that clearly echoes the Miggrode text, but with frequent omissions of fragments in which the same cruelties are repeated over and over (perhaps for stylistic reasons?). Furthermore, the "cristianos" of Las Casas are systematically translated into "spaniardes" – English protestants being Christians, not Spaniards –, the syntax repeats the French sentence structure, as it sections the same long sentences into smaller ones; certain word classes are replaced by others [i.e. a verb for a preposition as in "s'ingérant aussi (de mettre)"/"pressing also (to lay)" for "hasta (poner)"],...; "l' ile espagnole" becomes "the Ile of Hispaniola", using the Latin form when the first Latin translation has not yet been published; obviously the translator, M.M.S., is influenced by other texts on the discovery of the West Indies, possibly that of Pedro Martyr d'Anghiera[10]. In short, the first English translation of the *Brevísima relación* seems to address the people of the Netherlands; however, the publication comes at a time when the Anglo-Spanish relations reach rock bottom: the religious and political differences are so profound that the field is ripe for the spread of the famous Black Legend, and the publication of this text in English is only adding fuel to the fire.[11]

---

[10] "When Columbus took possession of the island, he named it as *La Española*, meaning 'The Spanish (Island)'. When d'Anghiera wrote in Latin about this island, he translated the name as *Hispaniola*, a new word. Because Anghiera's literary work was translated into English and French in a short period of time, the name "Hispaniola" is the most frequently used term in English-speaking countries regarding the island in scientific and cartographic works", (http://www.websters-dictionary-online.org/definitions/Hispaniola).

[11] For a summary of the situational background, see Dadson, 2004: 127–175, "The image of Spain in England in the sixteenth and seventeenth centuries".

The English translation of 1625

The next edition in English appears with an interval of 40 years, in 1625. The translation is apparently anonymous, and is included in the fourth volume (p. 1567–1603) of the collection of Samuel Purchas, *Hakluytus Posthumus*, or *Purchas, His Pilgrimes*, published in London.

The dedication of Miggrode ("To the Reader") in the 1583 edition has been replaced by a new text with the same heading, in which the editor praises the intentions of Las Casas when pleading that the King of Spain intervenes in favour of the Indians to enable their conversion to Christianity. The author of the dedication puts into perspective and clarifies the cruel acts of the Spanish, Portuguese and Dutch, noting that they also commit good deeds, and that the English themselves are not exempt from "evil acts". In a commentary on his translation, he admits to have shortened the text omitting much of the verbal abuse that Las Casas uses to give expression to his zeal and passion, without therefore losing the essence ("the flowre") of the story. He refuses to name the captains muted by Las Casas but points out that the curious reader will find them in the text of Antonio de Herrera, included in the same book *Purchas His pilgrimes*. He concludes his dedication by saying that the translation follows the English version of 1583 (Purchas, 1625, p. 1567)[12].

The comparative analysis shows that the 1625 translation has actually omitted certain parts of the 1583 version, namely the "Argument", the "Part of a let-

---

[12] "For my part I honour vertue in a Spaniard, in a Frier, in a Iesuite: and have in all these voluminous stories not been more carefull to show the evil acts of Spaniards, Portugals, Dutch in quarrels twixt them and us, then to make knowne what soever good in any of them, when occasion was offered. And so farre am I from delighting to thrust my finger in sores (which yet I doe in necessitie, even with the English also) that I have left out many many inventives and bitter Epithetes of this Author, abridging him after my want, and lopping of such superfluities, which rather were the fruit of his zeale, then the flowre of his History. I could also have added the names of those which he calleth Tyrants, the Captaines in those Expeditions; but he spared them, as the living, and in Herera before you have them, [...] This Booke is extant in Spanish, Latine, Dutch and in English also printes 1583, when as peace was yet betwixt England and Spaine, which English Copie I have followed." (Purchas, 1625, p. 1567).

ter, written by one which saw things mentionede" and "The Summe of the disputation between Fryer Bartholomevy de las Casas or Casaus, and Doctor Sepúlveda". Moreover, the micro analysis reveals relatively frequent omissions of text fragments, generally corresponding to the repeated description of atrocities committed against the Indians. To mention just one example, at the end of the introductory chapter, the translator has eliminated certain paragraphs that polarize the goodness of the Indians and the cruelty and greed of the Spaniards.

Summarizing, we can conclude that the letter to the reader by Purchas mitigates the demonization of the Spaniards, while acknowledging that the English also are to be blamed. Here again, Dadson (2004: 147–150) informs us on the climate of the Anglo-Spanish relations of the time. With the enthronement of James I in England in 1603, and given the disastrous state of the finances, the king was forced to seek peace with Spain. The period from 1603 to 1625 – the year that England joins the Thirty Years War in Europe (1618–1638) – turns out to be a time of relative peace and tranquillity in the relations between both countries, although English citizens are strongly averse to their monarch's new friendship with Spain. In this climate, it is easy to understand the rather long "silence" of the *Brevísima relación* in English, and the reconciling tone – or at least the tone of restrained passions – in Purchas's letter to the reader.

The English translation of 1656

The international situation changes completely, and reaches a new climax by the mid-seventeenth century. It is the era of the interregnum of Cromwell, who with his "Western Design" seeks to control certain islands before the shores of the West Indies that are in the hands of Spain. The Anglo-Spanish War has just broken out when a new English translation of the *Brevísima relación* is published by John Phillips, the nephew of Cromwell's minister of foreign languages John Milton, author of *Paradise Lost*. The title[13] uses more dramatic expressions than

---

[13] The Tears of the Indians: Being an Historical and true Account of the Cruel Massacres and Slaughters of above Twenty Millions of innocent People; Committed by the Spaniards in the Islands of Hispaniola, Cuba, Jamaica, etc. As also, in the Continent of Mexico, Peru and other Places of the West-Indies, To the total destruction of those Countries.

those of previous translations; it emphasizes the contradiction between the suffering of the defenceless Indians ("innocent") on the one side, and on the other, the extreme cruelty of the Spaniards; this polarization is reinforced by the use of lexical items such as "true", "massacres and slaughters", "total destruction", as well as by references to figures ("twenty millions") and places ("Hispaniola, Cuba, ..."). These elements show the exasperation and the fanaticism of the anti-Spanish hatred. And the incorporation of five engravings of Theodore De Bry drawn from the 1598 Latin translation adds even more drama to the story. The effect of these gruesome illustrations cannot be underestimated, particularly because they appear here for the first time in an English edition of the text. And although it is more than likely that the illustrated Latin edition had also been circulating on British territory, its audience must have been necessarily limited to a restricted group of highly educated people.

In principle, a new title does not automatically imply a different text. But the mention of both the Spanish and the English versions suggests that this translation could be a direct one from the Spanish 1552 version, or even an indirect one based on the Latin translation.

A brief comparison of the English editions shows that Phillips introduces his translation with a new dedication, addressed to Cromwell ("To His Highness, Oliver, Lord Protector of the Commonwealth...",) followed by a letter to "all true Englishmen". He does not reproduce the letter to the reader by Miggrode that appears in the English translations of 1583 and 1625, nor does he incorporate the "Argument" and the "Prologue" by Las Casas. In his dedication, Phillips advances two topics: the just war for revenge, and religion. He passes the text off as a long lament about the massacres of the Indians who will be avenged by Cromwell in a just war against the bloody and Catholic Spanish nation. Spaniards are – according to Phillips – even worse than the Irish, as their killings exceed the popish cruelties of Ireland. The letter addressed to "all true Englishmen" comprises a first part in which the innocent Indians[14] are diametrically op-

---

Written in Spanish by Casaus, an Eye-witness of those things; And made English by J.P....

[14] "Innocent blood", "so many Millions of poor innocent Heathens", "the poor Indians", "the poor innocent Heathens", "the poor creatures", "so many departed souls".

posed to the terrible Spaniards[15], followed by a call to all "men of England" to fight against their "old and constant enemies, the Spaniards, a proud, deceitful, cruel and treacherous nation"; it ends pointing to the right of England over the territories of Spain in the Indies ("his Golden Regions") by virtue of the conviction that the American continent had been discovered by Sebastian Cabot at the service of Henry VII of England, not by Columbus by order of the Spanish Crown. Phillips outlines thus a very English framework within which he appropriates the text of Las Casas. Indeed, both the dramatic title and the dedication to Cromwell, as well as the letter to the "true Englishmen" contextualize the *Brevísima relación* anew in a contemporary scene of English nationalistic tendency, transforming the objective of Las Casas into a moral lesson against the Spaniards, and ignoring the plea of the author for a new legal organization of the colonies.

Regarding the structure of the text, we note that Phillips partially rearranges the division into chapters. He even shortens the text, as the chapters "From the island of Cuba" and "De la Tierra Firme" (*About the mainland) are compressed into one single chapter called "Of the Island of Cuba", and comprises a selection of paragraphs from both chapters. As a consequence, all references to the American mainland disappear from the text. Phillips suppresses "de la tierra firme" again in another title; "De las provincias de la Tierra Firme por la parte que se llama la Florida" is replaced by "Of the Provinces of the Country of Florida." The double omission ties in with the above mentioned conviction of Phillips about the discovery of the "continent" (or the mainland) by Sebastian Cabot in the service of the Crown of England: he only recognizes the discovery by Columbus of some islands offshore the American continent, not of the mainland. This is precisely the reason adduced by Phillips, why the "Protector", Cromwell, in representation of the English, must defend "the right of the English to the West Indies".

The comparison of a few fragments has shown that the changes made by Phillips have far-reaching political consequences. He magnifies the polarization

---

[15] "the Iesuitical Spaniards", "the wicked Spaniards", like the Pestilence", "those that called themselves Christians", "Christians, the Professors of a Religion grounded upon Love and Charity", "Devils".

between the cruelty of the Spanish conquerors and the innocence and helplessness of the Indians, and dehumanizes thus the Spaniards, denying them any (moral) right to preach the gospel among the Indians. As an illustration, just one example.

In the following excerpt, the (Spanish) "santo varón" (*holy man) ceases to be holy in English; he is reduced to a neutral "Monk". The parallelism between the words of the Franciscan about heaven and hell ("iría al cielo […], ir al infierno") is lost, as is the dialogue towards the end of the scene, while indirect speech replaces the direct style. These interventions throw a very different light on the monk, who loses his human nature in this already horrifying scene. Even his offer of free choice between heaven and hell has disappeared, not only in the summary of the monk's words (in italics in both versions), but also in the transformation from indirect to direct speech of the cacique's text (italics), resulting in a magnified, more resounding and brutal dialogue. All trace of Christian piety that is readily perceived in the Spanish text disappears in this translation.

Brevísima relación, 2006, p. 126	The Tears of the Indians, 1656, p. 23
Atado al palo decíale un religioso de San Francisco, santo varón que allí estaba, algunas cosas de Dios y de nuestra fe (el cual nunca las había jamás oído), lo que podía bastar aquel poquillo tiempo que los verdugos le daban, y que si quería creer aquello que le decía que iría al cielo, donde había gloria y eterno descanso, y si no que había de ir al infierno a padecer perpetuos tormentos y penas. Él, pensando un poco, preguntó al religioso si iban cristianos al cielo. El religioso le respondió que sí, pero que iban los que eran buenos. Dijo luego el cacique, sin más pensar, que no quería él ir allá, sino al infierno, por no estar donde estuviesen y por no ver tan cruel gente.	While he was tyed to the stake, there came to him a Monk of the Order of St. Francis, who began to talk to him of God and of the Articles of our Faith, telling him, that the small respite which the Executioner gave him was sufficient for him to make sure his salvation if he believed. Upon which words after Hathvey had a little while paus'd, he asked the Monk if the door of heaven was open to the Spaniards, who answering, Yes, to the good spaniards. Then replyed the other, Let me go to Hell that I may not come where they are.

Figure 1

Finally, the Phillips translation does not reproduce the "pedaço de una carta…;" nor "entre los remedios", two texts in which Las Casas proposes "remedios" or solutions to improve the situation of the Indians in the Americas, including the abolition of the *encomienda*, a legal system by which the Spanish Crown granted the conquistadors of a number of natives, who paid tribute (gold, labour) to the *encomendero* in return for religious instruction. Obviously Phillips did not intend to mention that the Spaniards sought to remedy the mistakes made by his countrymen.

The English translations of 1689 and 1699

By the end of the 17th century, two new English translations of the *Brevísima relación* had been published, one in 1689 and a second one in 1699. It is the eve of the European struggle for the Spanish Crown because of the lack of a direct successor. Indeed, King Charles II of Spain is childless, and pretenders to his heritage are to be found in several ruling houses in Europe, as family ties bind the Habsburgs of Spain and Austria, and the Bourbons of France. Since a future union between two of these monarchies could disrupt the precarious political and military balance in Europe, the continent prepares for the so-called War of the Spanish Succession, dividing the continent into two axes: Spain and France versus Austria and England. A new balance will be struck in the Peace of Utrecht (1713), by which the new king of Spain, Philip V (from the House of Bourbon), is compelled to relinquish the throne of France in order to prevent the future union of the two kingdoms. In this climate of international tension, the tone rises, the hatred grows. No wonder then that the title[16] becomes even more dramatic than the one by Phillips.

But above all, it strikes the reader that the native peoples of America disappear steadily from the core of the discussion. If the translation of 1656 still had the decency of mentioning them in the title ("The Tears of the Indians"), by the end of the century there is no trace of them left. Instead, it is the anti-papist mood that now occupies the foreground. Although different, the title seems to echo the previous one (1656) (see also footnote 13) in the lexical pairs "true" and "truly", "true account" and "faithful narrative", "massacres and slaughters" and "unexampled massacres, butcheries", "in the islands of Hispaniola, Cuba, etc." and "several kingdoms". The cover further mentions that the text was

---

[16] Popery Truly Display'd in its Bloody Colours: Or, a faithful Narrative of the Horrid and Unexampled Massacres, Butcheries, and all manner of Cruelties, that Hell and Malice could invent, committed by the Popish Spanish Party on the inhabitants of West-India Together with the Devastations of several Kingdoms in America by Fire and Sword, for the space of Forty and Two Years, from the time of its first Discovery by them.

"composed first in Spanish by Bartholomew de las Casas, a Bishop there, and Eye-Witness of most of it in Original Barbarous Cruelties; afterward Translated by him into Latin[17], then by other hands, into High-Dutch, Low-Dutch, French, and now Taught to Speak Modern English". This text seems to indicate that it has been translated directly from Spanish, although the parallelism between the titles suggests that the version of 1656 has at least been consulted.

But here ends clearly the parallelism. From the macro structure point of view, the comparison between both translations reveals that the 1689 version has substituted the dedication to Cromwell by Phillips with "The Argument of this Narrative by way of Preface to the Reader", and that the succession of chapters has been restored including the one entitled "of the Continent". The political objective of support for Cromwell's "Grand Design" is no longer on the agenda. The shift to the religious design as expressed in the new title is confirmed by the translator himself at the end of his new "Preface to the reader", when he marks that

I earnestly beg and desire all Men to be perswaded, that this summary was not published upon any private Design, sinister ends or affection in favor or prejudice of any particular Nation; but for the publick Emolument and Advantage of all true Christians and moral Men throughout the whole World. (Las Casas, 1689, "The Argument...")

What is more, the author of this "Argument" even clears the King of Spain of guilt ("his Caesarian Majesty moved with a tender and Christian compassion towards these inhabitants...") referring to the "Council at Valedolid, Anno Dom. 1542" that was called by the monarch in response to the pleading of Las Casas. He then states clearly his own agenda, consisting in the use of the Las Casas text as a mirror to warn the reader against "unlimited and close fisted Avarice" that he considers to be "the predominant and chiefest motive to the commission of such inexpressible Outrages". This explains "the Popish Spanish Party" in the title: the enemy of Christianity is not the Spanish Monarchy, it is that fragment of Spanish society that follows the Pope of Rome.

The last English translation of the 17th century appears in 1699. There is a little confusion here: Bibliographical sources mention the existence of two Eng-

---

[17] This contradicts other information found about the author of the Latin translation: he would be unknown.

lish translations that year, but analysis has shown that there is probably but one translation, published with slightly different titles.[18] There is bibliographical evidence[19] to sustain the claim that the translation of 1699 is inspired by the French one of the year before (1698) by l'abbé Bellegarde, whose strategy consists in "softening" the most cruel fragments of the text in order to preserve the sensitive readers feelings[20]. However, a close analysis of some fragments has shown that this assertion is at least questionable; some descriptions ultimately prove to be even more cruel than their counterparts in the Las Casas text, and the insertion of a number of engravings by Th. De Bry makes the horror even more direct and graphic.

Furthermore, the English translation of 1699 has a new preface in which the translator surprisingly talks about the "Europeans", whereas others previously used the term "Spanish" (for "Christians"). In this way, England explicitly distances itself from Europe, creating an own identity in opposition to anything Europe may stand for in the context of the translated Las Casas discourse. It soon becomes clear that the same idea is at stake as found in Phillips (1656), namely that England claims to have discovered the American mainland, while Columbus is supposed to have reached only some islands offshore. This would entitle the British to all the rights to the colonization and exploitation of the American mainland[21], putting them in a situation diametrically opposed to all other nations with colonizing pretensions, particularly France for its "annoying" presence in North America and its hegemonic aspirations in Europe facing the imminent change of dynasty in Spain. The preface further comments almost exclusively on the religious opposition between Catholicism and Protestantism, and on the air of honesty, sincerity and charity of Las Casas as an eyewitness of the events in

---

[18] This is a known phenomenon in the history of the book industry, since the typesetting was done by hand.

[19] See Hanke & Giménez, 1954, p. 242: "Traducción ilustrada del francés, aparentemente de la edición de Ámsterdam de 1698, que contiene la *Brevísima relación* y trozos de la mayoría de los demás tratados de 1552...".

[20] "On a adouci en quelques endroits des choses qui paroissoient trop cruelles, et qui auroient pû faire de la peine aux personnes délicates".

[21] "The Europeans Had No sooner Entered on this vast Continent and the Islands about it, ..." (*An Account* ..., 1699, p. 1).

the Indies. Because of his defence of the natural right of everyone to freedom and property, Las Casas is seen to come closer to the standards of Mohammedans than to the principles of Christianity and its Inquisition; and his praise of the Pope of Rome inspires nothing but pity. The author of the preface then expresses his admiration for the fact that the text has been published in France *cum privilegio*, considering the lack of liberties granted to its subjects. In the last part, the translator refers to the French translation of Paris ("lately received a new dress in Modern French in Paris"), emphasizing the fidelity with which he has rendered into English the French translation ("i have done it Justice"). In doing so, he confirms the bibliographical evidence on the French filiation of the present translation. The preface finally brings to mind the historical massacres perpetrated by the papists, namely the bloody Crusades of the 12th and 13th centuries, and the persecutions and massacres following the Reformation.

As to the text itself, the comparative analysis shows that the English version bears an important concordance with the French translation of 1698. No chapters have been suppressed, the engravings of Th. De Bry are equally present, but now at the beginning of the booklet, and the raw wording in describing the atrocities is sometimes even magnified.[22]

Conclusion

In conclusion, the (comparative) study of the English translations of the *Brevísima relación* in the 17th century shows that Las Casas is used as ultimate proof of the truth about the discovery and conquest of America by the Spanish crown. He is a privileged eyewitness, who accuses his own countrymen of cruel behaviour towards the Indians; hence his words must be true. Gradually his role gets more important in the prefaces to the translations. He eventually awakens both admiration for his courage and pity because he is not "one of a better Religion than that in which he had the unhappiness to be educated"[23]. At the same time, the natives disappear gradually from the scene. Ultimately, the focal point

---

[22] E.g. "devour" (1699) instead of "consume" (1656) as a translation of "comer" in the context of Spaniards eating the food of the Indians.

[23] "An Account ... ", 1699, Preface, p. 2.

is no longer the fate of the Indians, but the right of England to the American mainland. The contrast between the Protestant and Catholic Christian churches is connected with the "cruel and barbaric" behaviour of the Spaniards – Catholics – which implies by antinomy that the Protestant church must be characterized by goodness and civilization.

The observations in this analysis highlight the important role of the English translations (and their manipulation) of the lascasian text as well as the engravings added by Th. De Bry in the growing animosity against Spain and the magnification of the black legend. The essence of the text is long forgotten. Instead, these translations seem to empower the dominant political and religious forces in (national) society. They support the urge for territorial expansion among the political class through the rousing of public sentiment aimed against the immediate rival, using political and religious arguments. Translation in this setting becomes clearly a tool in the scramble for the Americas, and even in the struggle for hegemony in Europe.

Contrary to what one would expect from a translation, these 17th century English translations do not build bridges between peoples. They mainly aim at conservative purposes, trying to maintain the status quo of the precarious international equilibrium between European monarchies.

As for the consequences on the longer term, it seems not inconceivable that historiography and the (national) canon both bear the effects of text manipulation through translation in the service of pragmatism. A closer analysis of the most recent translations of the text could illuminate us on this matter.

References

Corpus

CASAS, Bartolomé de Las (2006/1552). *Brevísima relación de la destruición de las Indias.* Sevilla: Sebastián Trujillo, in: TORREJÓN Martínez & MIGUEL, José (eds.), "Edición crítica, estudio preliminar y notas de Martínez Torrejón, J. M." – Alicante: San Vicente del Rapseig, Universidad Alicante.

CASAS, Bartolomé de Las (1552) in English, before 1700: EEBO (Early English Books Online, Bell & Howell): access full text through http://eebo.chadwyck.com.

[B]1583 *The Spanish Colonie, or Briefe Chronicle of the Acts and gestes of the Spaniardes in the West Indies, called the newe World, for the space of XL. Yeeres: written in the Castilian tongue by the reverend Bishop Bartholomew de las Casas or Casaus, a Friar of the order of S. Dominicke. And now first translated into English, by M.M.S.* – London: Thomas Dawson, for William Bro(o)me.

[B]1625 "A briefe narration of the destruction of the Indies by the Spaniards: written by a frier Bart. De las Casas a Spaniard, and bishop of Chiapa in America". In: Purchas, Samuel, *Purchas his pilgrims. In five books...* – London: Printed by William Stansby for Henrie Fetherstone. 1567–1603.

[B]1656 *The Tears of the Indians: Being An Historical and true Account of the Cruel Massacres and Slaughters of above Twenty Millions of innocent People; Committed by the Spaniards in the Islands of Hispaniola, Cuba, Jamaica, etc. As also, in the Continent of Mexico, Peru and other Places of the West-Indies, To the total destruction of those Countries. Written in Spanish by Casaus, an Eye-witness of those things; And made English by J.P....* – London: Nathaniel Brook.

[B]1689 *Popery Truly Display'd in its Bloody Colours: Or, a faithful Narrative of the Horrid and Unexampled Massacres, Butcheries, and all manner of Cruelties, that Hell and Malice could invent, committed by the Popish Spanish Party on the inhabitants of West-India Together with the Devastations of several Kingdoms in America by Fire and Sword, for the space of Forty and Two Years, from the time of its first Discovery by them.* – London: Printed for R. Hewson at the Crown in Cornhil, near the Stocks-Market.

[B]1699 *An Account of the First Voyages and Discoveries Made by the Spaniards in America. Containing the Most Exact Relation hitherto publish'd, of their unparallel'd Cruelties on the Indians, in the destruction of above Forty Millions of people. With the Propositions offer'd to the King of Spain, to prevent the further Ruin of the West-Indies...* – London: Printed by J. Darby for D. Brown (J. Harris and Andr. Bell.).

General

BAKHTIN, Michael, (1970): *La poétique de Dostoïevski*. Traduit du Russe par Isabelle Kolitcheff, présentation de Julia Kristeva. – Paris: Editions du Seuil.

BAKHTIN, Michael, (1981): "Discourse in the Novel". In: HOLQUIST, M. (ed.) & EMERSON, Caryl and HOLQUIST, Michael (trans.): *The Dialogic Imagination: Four Essays*. – Austin: University of Texas Press, 259–422.

DADSON, Trevor J. (2004): "La imagen de España en Inglaterra en los siglos XVI y XVII". In: DE ABIADA, López, MANUEL, José & LÓPEZ BERNASOCCHI, Augusta (eds.): *Imágenes de España en culturas y literaturas europeas (siglos XVI-XVII)*. – Madrid: Verbum, 127–175.

DELAHAYE, Marieke (forthcoming in UFSC, Brasil): *Viaje de exploración hacia la lengua de la historiografía: Las Crónicas de Indias en su trayectoria europea*.

GENETTE, Gérard (1982): *Palimpsestes. La littérature au Second Degré*. – Paris: Editions du Seuil.

KELLY, Louis G. (2004): "Translators, chocolate and war." *HISTAL* enero 2004. http://www.histal.ca/ (19.08.2014).

KRISTEVA, Julia (1978/1969): "Sèméiotikè". In: VAN GORP, Hendrik (ed.), *Literature and Translation*. – Leuven: Acco, 101–116.

LAMBERT, José & Hendrik VAN GORP (1985). "On describing translations". In: DELABASTITA, Dirk, D'HULST, Lieven & MEYLAERTS, Reine (eds.): *Functional approaches to Culture and Translation. Selected papers by José Lambert*. – Amsterdam/Philadelphia: John Benjamins Publishing, 37–47.

LAMBERT, José (2013). "Universities, Languages and Translations: another chapter on Power". http://power.bangor.ac.uk/programme.php.en?menu=4&catid=11512&subid=0

MUDIMBE, V.Y. (1988): *The Invention of Africa. Gnosis, Philosophy and the Order of Knowledge*. – Bloomington: Indiana University Press.

O'GORMAN, Edmundo (2006): *La invención de América. Investigación acerca de la estructura histórica del Nuevo Mundo y del sentido de su devenir*. – México: Fondo de Cultura Económica.

ONG, Walter J. (1993): *Orality & Literacy: The technologizing of the word*. – London: Routledge.

SAÏD, Edward (1978): *Orientalism.* – New York: Pantheon.

SAINT-LU, André (1978): "Les premières traductions françaises de la 'Brevísima relación' de Las Casas. In: 'VV.AA., Hommage à Marcel Bataillon', *Revue de Littérature comparée* 52, 2–4, avril–décembre, 438–449.

TYMOCZKO, Maria & GENTZLER, Edwin (eds.) (2002): *Translation and Power.* – Amherst/Boston: University of Massachusetts Press.

VAN DOORSLAER, Dirk (2013): "Did anyone say Power?" Conference Bangor, 5–6th September 2013. http://power.bangor.ac.uk/videos.php.en?subid=0

VENUTI, Lawrence (2009): "Translation, Intertextuality, Interpretation", *Romance Studies* 27 (3), 157–173.

VEYNE, Paul (1971): *Comment on écrit l'histoire. Essai d'épistémologie.* – Paris: Seuil.

WHITE, Hayden (1973): *Metahistory. The Historical Imagination in Nineteenth-century Europe.* – Baltimore/London: The Johns Hopkins University Press.

WHITE, Hayden (1981): "The value of narrativity in the representation of reality". In: MITCHELL, W.J.T. (ed.): *On Narrative.* – Chicago: University of Chicago Press, 1–24.

WHITE, Hayden (1987): *The Content of the Form. Narrative Discourse and Historical Representation.* – Baltimore: The Johns Hopkins University Press.

Ethical issues of community interpreting and mediation: The case of the Lagerdolmetscher

Małgorzata Tryuk
University of Warsaw
m.tryuk@uw.edu.pl

In the research into community interpreting, especially during crises, war, or in situations of armed conflict, the ethical dimension of the tasks undertaken by interpreters has been broadly analysed in numerous studies. The aim of the present article is to study the records of Nazi concentration camps, and in particular the recollections of former prisoners, in order to analyse the situations the Lagerdolmetscher, or camp interpreters, were faced with during World War II. As will be shown, the generally accepted ethical norms for interpreting in community settings were not applicable to interpreting in the concentration camps, which was clearly justified by the extreme and extraordinary circumstances (e.g. interpreting under duress). In particular this paper investigates why the interpreters were needed, who they were, how they were recruited for the job, what their duties were, how they performed their tasks, and what their roles were.

Introduction

In his latest book on ethics in translation and interpreting, Anthony Pym wrote that "[w]e should translate in certain circumstances only, investing variable effort, in order to promote long-term cooperation between cultures. In all other cases, it would probably be better not to translate" (2012:12). In his book, the author tends to first investigate *why* people translate, and then tries to deduce *how* they execute their translation tasks. In this paper I concentrate not only on the question *why*, but also on the circumstances under which a translator or an interpreter has to provide linguistic mediation. As shown by numerous testimonies and recollections, from both the past and present, translators not only ask themselves the questions put by Pym: "Why should I translate?", "Under what conditions?", "In what circumstances?", but also and perhaps above all: "What if I choose not to translate?", "What will be the consequences of my act? For me, for others, for my loved ones?". These are crucial ethical questions which should be deliberated upon not only from the viewpoint of translation and interpreting studies, but also from a sociological and historical perspective. I therefore try to highlight questions such as: "What if a person has no choice but to interpret?"; "What does it mean to carry out the activity of interpreting in such circumstances?"; "Is it a situation which brings profits or gains to the interpreter or, by contrast, it exposes the interpreter and his/her relatives to danger?"; "How is the interpreting perceived and assessed by the other participants of the communication act?"; and finally, "What does the interpreter actually do?".

Interpreting and ethics

It is generally agreed that community interpreting is that type of interpreting which takes place in the public service sector in order to facilitate communication between officials and laypersons, e.g. at the police station, in immigration offices, in refugee and social welfare centres, medical and mental health institutions, schools, prisons, etc. (Hale 2007). This type of interpreting is bidirectional and is carried out in consecutive mode. It covers interpreting in face-to-face situations and is probably the oldest and best known type of interpreting worldwide. Sometimes it is performed by volunteers, untrained bilinguals, friends, relatives, and occasionally by children. In these different settings, the mediation provided by the interpreter is more vital to successful communication than in any other situation in which the presence of a translator is needed.

Studies on the work of interpreters in extreme situations have been undertaken by numerous researchers since 1980 and have produced valuable insights into this subject. They include various types of research – of an empirical, observational, and interactive character as well as works of an analytical and theoretical nature. The latter includes, *inter alia*, reports on interpreting at the trials of the Nazi war criminals in Nuremberg (Bowen, Bowen 1985, Gaiba 1998, Behr, Corpataux 2006); at Eichmann's trial in Jerusalem (Morris 1998); and in recent times, reports on the role of interpreters at the hearings conducted by the Commission of Truth and Reconciliation in South Africa (Wiegand 2000); at the UNO peace missions in Lebanon and the countries of the former Yugoslavia (Thomas 1997); and in the humanitarian missions of NGOs in Iraq and Afghanistan (Guidère 2008, Szymczukiewicz 2005) or at the hearing before the International Criminal Tribunal for Rwanda (Haas 2011). The studies on interpreting at public prosecutor offices and at all stages of court hearings and refugee interrogations are equally extensive (Pöllabauer 2004). Researchers of both the empirical and theoretical aspects of court-based community interpreting have tried to reveal the ethical norms binding on an interpreter in his or her work (Andres, Behr 2011, Tryuk 2004). These norms are deontological and *sui generis* and include: reliability, morals beyond reproach, linguistic competence and expertise, faithfulness in interpreting, impartiality and neutrality, acting in an unassuming way (as if 'in the background' 'on the margin', or even like 'a non-person'), awareness of social and cultural particularities, a high resistance to stress and observance of the rules of professional ethics. Among the norms described, impartiality and/or neutrality are usually assigned primary importance and most studies emphasize that, above all, an interpreter is expected to be accurate and impartial (Hale 2007). This means the interpreters are expected to be neutral with respect to the discourse and the persons for whom they interpret.

Nowadays, we know that in circumstances, such as war or armed conflict, the tasks undertaken by the interpreter, mediator or 'fixer' significantly exceed the transmission of messages from one language to another. What is more, it sometimes happens that interpreters, when taking on their duties, are not aware of all the possible consequences of their activities. This discordance between the principles of neutrality, impartiality, non-involvement and professionalism laid down in codes of professional ethics, on one hand, and actual activities of the interpreter in conflict situations, war, prison, and courtrooms, on the other hand, is commonly known. Numerous media publications offer accounts of such situations, which are moreover the object of the research conducted within contemporary translation and interpreting studies. Ethical issues, consistently hidden behind a screen of rules formulated in the codes, are today one of the crucial problems of translation and interpreting studies. They will also constitute the main focus of the present paper, which is dedicated to interpreters in the extreme situations imposed by the events of the Second World War. My aim is to study the records of Nazi concentration camps, and in particular the recollections of former prisoners, in order to analyse the activities of the *Lagerdolmetscher*, the camp interpreters. As I will show, the generally accepted ethical norms for interpreting in community settings were not applicable to the concentration camps as there were neither norms nor standards of any kind applicable in such circumstances. In particular, I will investigate why the interpreters were needed, who they were, how they were recruited for the job, what their duties were, how they performed their duties, as well as what their roles were.

This paper is based mainly on the authentic recollections of former concentration camp inmates which have been collected in the archives of the camps: in the Auschwitz-Birkenau Memorial and Museum Archives, the Majdanek Museum Archives as well as the archives of the Memorial Museum in Dachau. The documents in the Auschwitz-Birkenau Memorial and Museum Archives constitute a unique collection of material encompassing 134 volumes of recorded statements (3000 separate statements regarding various incidents), 200 volumes of recollections, and 76 volumes of the trial of Rudolf Höss, the first Commandant of the camp. This material is a unique example of the ontological narratives which relate the experiences of the victims of the Nazi regime. It presents accounts of the inmates' arrest, their life and the possibility of survival in the camps, their relationships with fellow prisoners, and their fear of the SS and other camp functionaries. Many accounts point to the 'good chap' who would help one survive, who would be willing to share his meager rations as well as any information he had obtained which could be crucial to survival. The 'good chap' could also be, and not infrequently was, the interpreter.

Despite the massive amount of material, it should be noted that references to interpreting *per se* are rather scant, and when they do occur they tend to be random and laconic, usually consisting of dry facts. In addition, inmates sometimes offer differing versions of the same event. For these reasons obtaining an objective, empirical account of events is virtually impossible. My research in the archives was therefore of an explorative nature and focuses mainly on the profiles of camp interpreters.

Interpreting in the concentration camps

In each Nazi concentration camp the inmates represented between 35–40 different national or ethnic groups, each with their own language. All the inmates lived in extreme conditions, with the German language ever present and dominating. The communication, if any, with the German guards or a *kapo* (a prisoner functionary) had to be in German. If any postal services were allowed at all, all the paperwork had to be in German. In the barracks and work blocks all rules, orders, and directions were delivered in German. In KL Auschwitz the use of the languages of the inmates (such as Polish, Czech, Russian, Italian or French) was forbidden. There was one official language in all the concentration camps, and that was German. The General Commandant of the Auschwitz Camp, Rudolf Höss, issued an order on July 30 1940, forbidding the camp staff to use any foreign language they might know, in particular forbidding their use of Polish or Czech. This order was directed toward the Silesians and *Volksdeutsche* (ethnic Germans) who performed various functions in the camps. In addition, every inmate was required to memorize some basic phrases in German: their camp detention number, their block (barracks) number, and the texts of songs they were required to sing for the amusement of their guards. Only in a few instances were certain signs posted in both Polish and German, for example "Halt! Stój!", as can be seen below:

By the courtesy of the Archives of the Auschwitz-Birkenau Memorial and Museum

Survival in the concentration camp without some knowledge of German was practically impossible and there are many statements proving that this was an every-day reality, as described by Primo Levi (1989: 93):

> The greater part of the prisoners who did not understand German – that is, almost all the Italians – died during the first to fifteenth day after their arrival: at first glance, from hunger, cold, fatigue, and disease; but after a more attentive examination, due to insufficient information. If they had been able to communicate with their more experienced companions, they would have been able to orient themselves better: to learn first of all how to procure clothing, shoes, illegal food, how to avoid the harsher labour and the often lethal encounters with the SS, how to handle the inevitable illness without making fatal mistakes. I don't want to say that they would not have died, but they would have lived longer and had a greater chance of regaining lost ground.

However, in reality two languages were used in the camps: German and the 'unofficial' language called *lagerszpracha,* which was created out of Polish, Yiddish, the Silesian dialect, Hungarian or other languages spoken in a particular camp. It was camp *jargon* – a way for the inmates to communicate among themselves, although occasionally it also occurred that some German functionaries and even SS troops would use some expressions from *lagerszpracha* (Gramling 2012). It should be stressed that there were different varieties of this sociolect. Levi (1960) recalls that a *lagerszpracha* used in the men's barracks was different from that in the women's camps.

There was also another 'language' in widespread use in the camps: beatings and the whip, as evidenced in the quote by Lore Shelley (1986: 363) who recalls the sadistic SS-Unterscharführer Karl Broch saying that: "Die Peitsche ist der beste Dolmetscher, sie spricht alle Sprachen" ('The whip is the best interpreter; it speaks all languages').

As in any other multilingual social situation, interpreters were needed in the concentration camps. KL Auschwitz was no different. Upon arrival in the camp a number of inmates listed their profession as 'interpreter' (*Dolmetscher*). These declarations can be found in the registration documents of new arrivals to the death camps. In the majority of cases the persons declaring themselves to be interpreters were Jews born in Poland or Russia, often transported to the camps from France or Belgium. Very few of them survived.

The function of the *Lagerdolmetscher*, or camp interpreter, was not introduced in all the camps in the same way. In KL Auschwitz interpreters functioned from the very beginning of the camp's existence in 1940. It was different in the camps situated in Germany or Austria. In Dachau, the camp interpreters were appointed only after 1942 (Musioł 1971, Malak 1961, Dobosiewicz 2000). In the Majdanek concentration camp, there was a large group of interpreters sent there from the other concentration camps in Dachau, Buchenwald, Mauthausen and Neuengamme (Muszkat, APMM VII-135/251).

It is not easy to present a general picture of those who were chosen to act as interpreters in the concentration camps, which constituted a very specific type of multilingual conglomerate with German as the dominant language. In the KL Auschwitz three groups of people acting as interpreters can be differentiated. The first group consisted of the SS men from the *Politische Abteilung* (Political Department or camp administration and Gestapo) in the camp, often *Volksdeutsche* or Silesians fluent in Polish and employing Polish during the initial interrogations. Shelley (1986) quotes the following SS members who were used as interpreters in KL Auschwitz: Klaus Dylewski, Gerard Lachman, Johann Schindler, Joseph Stetnik, Karl Broch, Alois Lorenczyk, Joseph Pach as well as

Witold Witkowsky and Georg Woznitza. A second large group consisted of female inmates working in the *Politische Abteilung* as messengers or scribes/registrars. Owing to space restriction, I would like to mention only one of them, namely, Raya Kagan, who years later testified as a witness at the Eichmann trial in Jerusalem in 1960 (Shelley 1986: 280). These interpreters were mostly Slovakian or Hungarian Jews, and owing to the nature of their duties Lore Shelley notes that they later referred to themselves as "*Secretaries of Death*". They worked in different sections of the camp administration, i.e. the Secretariat, Interrogation, Civil, Legal and Reception Sections. The third group of interpreters that can be distinguished was made up of prisoners who declared they knew German (or another language necessary in the camp, such as Russian in the KL Majdanek). They were singled out as camp interpreters, i.e. *Lagerdolmetscher*. Stanisław Skibicki (APMA-B vol. 149: 99) wrote: "The camp Commandant communicated with us using interpreters as intermediaries"[1]. In fact, these interpreters often had to perform their function despite the fact they were treated like all other inmates, i.e. in addition to the other murderous work activities forced upon them. Their interpreting did not guarantee them any privileges in terms of how they were treated, for example, they received no additional food rations. Nor did it guarantee them survival. Their knowledge of German did, however, give them access to information and enabled them to communicate better with other inmate functionaries, and in addition simply allowed them to help others. Like other functionaries in the camp, the camp interpreters wore an arm-band on their striped prison uniforms. Jerzy Poźmiński (APMA-B, vol. 82: 2) recalled it as a white brassard with black letters reading: "Dolmetscher". However, Tadeusz Paczuła (APMA-B vol.111: 155) wrote: "The Lagerdolmetscher wore a black arm-band".

In the KL Auschwitz the function of interpreter was fulfilled by the following persons:
- Władysław Baworowski (camp registration number 863) – a Polish aristocrat, often cited in the recollections and statements of former inmates as the first camp interpreter, who died in 1942 of hunger and exhaustion;

---

[1] All the quotations from statements and recollections of former inmates have been translated by the author.

- Leonard Belewski (camp registration number 11586), released from the camp in 1942;
- Franciszek Galus/Kalus (camp registration number 1000), not well regarded in the memory of former inmates, released from the camp;
- Józef Baltaziński/Balasiński (camp registration number 749), who zealously carried out all the orders of the guards; his inhumane treatment of young inmates is recalled in many records found in the Auschwitz Archives;
- Kurt Machula (camp registration number 12355), from Katowice, released from the camp in 1944;
- Egbert Skowron (camp registration number 8036), from Warsaw and with a perfect command of German, who was helpful to the inmates;
- Łukasz Łukawiecki (camp registration number 80231), who was the last interpreter in Auschwitz at the time of the final evacuation of the camp.

The names of interpreters in other concentration camps are mentioned in numerous recollections and memoirs of former inmates. In KL Dachau, the camp interpreters were Ryszard Knosała, who died of typhus in February 1945, a few months before the liberation of the camp, and Jan Domagała. In KL Mauthausen, the camp interpreters were Paweł Jasieczek, Stanisław Nogaj and Kazimierz Odrobny. In the concentration camp of Majdanek, which was designed primarily as a camp for Russian prisoners of war (*Kriegsgefangenenlager der Waffen SS Lublin* or *KGL Lublin*) also called as *Russenlager*, the interpreters were Krzysztof Radziwiłł, Iwan Bielski, Bargelski, Brzezowski, Janusz Wolski, Czesław Kulesza, Żurawski and Michał Gumiński (Tryuk 2012).

Camp interpreters were assigned and designated *ex officio* or were chosen from the prisoners. There is little hard evidence concerning the process for choosing them, although there are some references in the inmates' recollections. For example, Józef Kret (APMA-B vol. 4: 431–433) wrote:

I remember during my stay in the Auschwitz camp that in the early days of October there was an announcement during the roll call for all inmates knowing Russian and German to gather in front of barrack block nr. 25 following the roll call. About 100 inmates showed up and were organized into a line, after which they were led in, several at a time, to one of the rooms in the building. There they were examined in German and Russian by a "Lagerdolmetscher" committee, consisting of two inmates and one SS officer.

When the exam was over the results were announced and 25 inmates, including me, were deemed to have 'passed'. We were told to remain in the camp. During this time I heard that we were to join the transport of Russian prisoners of war and act as interpreters.

The designation of interpreters could also be done in a different, more direct way. Antoni Wolf (2011: 76), interpreter and *Blockschreiber* (registrar) in the KL Majdanek recalls that:

On 18 January 1943 at about 9 p.m. the door opened suddenly and four male figures with torches and whips rushed in. They were the kapos Schmuck and Wyderka, accompanied by a small boy, the so-called interpreter known by the name of Bubi. They were boozed up. They came to announce the rules and regulations to be followed in the camp. They requested the interpreter, who, after the first incorrectly interpreted sentence, was slapped on his face, and warned: 'I'll knock you into the next world for such interpretation.' Then they requested another interpreter. 'I will interpret,' I declared in German. [...] I put a lot of effort in interpreting as simply and comprehensibly as possible. I presented our 'Lords of life and death' and summarized the provisions of the rules and regulations. They accused me of making the sentences shorter than they actually were in German but I answered them that we, the Poles, do not need long explanations, we instantly understand our situation and presume that we can adapt to these conditions. The kapo Schmuck liked my answer and announced, 'You will be a dolmetscher here and responsible for the order in the block'.

In KL Auschwitz, there were primarily German-Polish interpreters and a group of multilingual, young Jewish girls who interpreted during the interrogations of Polish, Czech, Slovakian, and Hungarian inmates and Russian or Ukrainian POW. Inasmuch as the inmates were predominantly Polish, the primary need was for interpreters working from German into Polish. Nevertheless, a review of the records contained in the archives also shows references to other language combinations, for example, from German into French or Czech. Jakub Maestro, a young Jew from Thessaloniki interpreted from German into Greek, French, Romanian and Spanish, and to Polish which he learned in the camp.

The situation in KL Majdanek was different. From the very beginning the camp's existence, i.e. in November 1941, groups of prisoners were being transported to Majdanek from other concentration camps such as Dachau, Sachsenhausen, Buchenwald, Dora, Neuengamme, Mauthausen, Gusen and Gross Rosen. Up until the autumn of 1943, these groups were small, consisting in the early stages mostly of prisoner functionaries, among which were physicians and translators/interpreters. In particular, interpreters were needed for German into Russian. Most of them were Polish or German. The first interpreters were sent to Majdanek from the camps in Buchenwald, Sachsenhausen or Neuengamme and Auschwitz during the winter of 1941/1942. As reported by Plewik (2001: 67):

> Already during the first phase of the organization of the Lublin camp, i.e. from November 1941, prisoners from other concentration camps were sent to Majdanek: doctors and those who knew German and Russian. They became the prisoner functionaries in the newly established camp. The large majority were selected from among German criminals and Polish political prisoners.

The duties of the interpreters included assisting at hearings, acting as camp *Schreiber* (registrar) or *Läufer* (messenger), and other tasks such as translating the letters of inmates into German. The interpreters were required during the arrival of new prisoners at the camp, when prisoners were punished, during the 'management' of inmates and others. But most importantly, the *Lagerdolmetscher* had to interpret the 'welcoming speech' given to the new inmates by the camp Commandant. As recalled by one of the former inmates of KL Auschwitz, Czesław Rychlik (APMA-B, vol. 26a: 57):

> First there was a speech by the Commandant of the camp. His speech was translated by Baworowski. Pointing to the crematorium chimney, he explained to us that that was the only way out of the camp. Whether we lived longer or shorter depended on how hard we worked and our strict obedience to camp regulations.

At this particular moment, standing in front of terrorized prisoners, the interpreter was the only one who understood exactly what was meant by 'the only way out was through the chimney'. Interpreters were present in all the commando buildings where the prisoners worked, in each block, and even in the quarantine area or the *Revier* (camp hospital). In addition to their interpreting duties and their the function of camp or block registrar, they were responsible for order in the respective block. Sometimes, the interpreter's help was invaluable, even to the point of saving the lives of other inmates. As Alfred Wilk (APMA-B vol. 78: 1078) remembered:

> The day after Christmas Eve (or maybe it was another day) an inmate appeared at the gate, wishing to speak with the Lagerführer. The interpreter who was present, the inmate Baworowski – quickly realized that the matter was of great importance. He tried to get the inmate to

explain to him why he so badly wished to see the Lagerführer. The inmate did not want to reveal his reasons; he even became threatening. I don't know what arguments Baworowski used, but in the end he learned the truth of the matter. The inmate was wandering around near the kitchen on Christmas Eve and heard other inmates singing the Polish national anthem – and this is what he wanted to report to the Lagerführer. He was counting on a favour in return. When Baworowski learned the truth, he told the appropriate person and the denunciator was finished off during the night by Brodniewicz [the Lagerältester – MT] or the kapo Arno. It was a very sad incident, and if Baworowski hadn't intervened, many inmates would have lost their lives, not excluding such prominent camp functionaries such as Brodniewicz and the kapos Arno and Diego.

Another example of a courageous act by the *Lagerdolmetscher* was recalled by Stanisław Charulski, (APMA-B vol. 79: 132):

We also rode to Industriehof, and later to the warehouses on Bauhof. The inmate employed there as a registrar was Egbert Skowron, who had been transported to the camp with me. Before being assigned the function of registrar he had been a camp interpreter, since he was fluent in German. Skowron shielded a number of inmates from the dangerous kapo of Industriehof, August. He managed to keep sick inmates away from hard physical labour. In addition on several occasions I was able to organize additional coal supplies using the same delivery receipt. I would exchange the coal with the other blocks in exchange for bread and second helpings for my French and other starving colleagues

Julian Grabski (APMA-B vol. 65: 137) recalls in his statement:

In 1942 I came down with spotted typhus and was taken to the hospital. I managed to get out early and escape the line-up for selection to the gas chamber. I learned about the line-up from Kurt Machula – the camp interpreter.

The interpreters helped other inmates without knowledge of German in their communication with their families, as described by Nikodem Pieszczoch (APMA-B vol. 72: 14):

They [the musicians – MT] were brought to the Blockführerstube, where the interpreter, count Baworowski dictated to the candidates for the orchestra a letter they were to send to their families with a request for musical instruments.

The women inmates from the Political Section also took part in the interrogations of the prisoners. Hermine (Herma) Markovits née Hirschler remembers:

Erber [SS-Oberscharführer working in the Political Section of the camp – MT] employed me frequently as an interpreter for the Polish or Czech prisoners, although he himself, being a Czech citizen, probably understood just as much of what they said as I did. On these occasions I tried to frame the answer to favour the defendants. "Is your translation accurate?" Erber once suddenly asked me. "As far as I understand Polish it is. I am Czech, not Polish", I answered. He looked at me, frowning. "Your translation is incorrect, so shut your mouth." (Shelley 1986: 120)

In light of the sparse data available, we know little about the techniques employed by the interpreters. Kazimierz Halgas (APMA-B vol. 89: 174) writes that: "Lagerführer Fritzsch spoke to us from the steps of our barracks. His words were translated word for word by Count Baworowski". Most likely the translation consisted in short and brusque military-like orders being rendered into Polish one sentence in a time. In his recollections, Henryk Malak (1961: 304–5) describes Ryszard Knosała, interpreting at an interrogation by a SS captain in KL Dachau, as someone speaking "with a broken, colourless voice" [...]. And he adds, bitterly: "How many orders, how many sentences he had to interpret from the SS tongue into Polish or other languages."

Conclusion

In this short presentation I have described how interpreting in an aggressive monolingual environment involving terror rendered impossible the application of the norms commonly used in community interpreting. In a concentration camp, the interpreter was not simply 'a disembodied container of others' messages' (Wadensjö,1998: 279). The recollections of former inmates illustrate the complex role a camp interpreter had to assume, faced with tasks which went far beyond the neutral transfer of information from one language to another. Instead it was often a matter involving the survival of an inmate or even the interpreter him/herself. Surviving in the Nazi concentration camps without any knowledge of German was practically impossible, as information was crucial for obtaining – even illegally – the bare necessities such as food and clothing, and for avoiding illness, overworking and the brutality of SS guards. It can be seen that those who acted as *dolmetscher* performed a critically important role. They found himself at the heart of a crisis, at the centre of interaction, which had a direct impact on their life and that of their fellow prisoners. The *Lagerdolmetscher* received no additional privileges or exemptions from work, but they had access to information which could be used to help others in the camp. This uneasy position as a go-between, acting in a space between the oppressors and the oppressed, used as an instrument to convey horrific information related to life and death in the camp, or as a mouthpiece to issue degrading insults and humiliating orders, could bring out both the best and the worst in human behaviour. The *Lagerdolmetscher* was required not only to interpret camp orders, rules and directions, but also to interpret at hearings and interrogations when new prisoners arrived at the camp. As Cronin (2006) notes, the *Lagerdolmetscher* was a hostage to his own skills. He had no choice but to execute the task. At the same time, he could use his knowledge to influence his own life as well as that of others. This degree of influence, fraught with danger, has no parallel in the history of interpreting. Camp interpreters were not, and could not be, unbiased, neutral observers of the reality to which their translations pertained. In no other situation has an interpreter played such a deeply human role. By reflecting on the work of the *Lagerdolmetscher*, the complexities of community interpreting and the dilemmas that interpreters have faced can be seen in a new light.

References

APMA-B: *The Auschwitz-Birkenau Memorial Museum Archives. Statements*: volumes 4, 8a, 9, 20, 21, 26b, 29, 33, 35, 36, 39, 45, 46, 47, 50, 61, 64, 65, 66, 67, 72, 73, 74, 75, 76, 77, 78, 79, 80, 82, 83, 84, 86, 87, 88c, 89, 89b, 91, 94, 96, 97, 100, 101, 111, 114, 115, 122, 124.
APMA-B: *The Auschwitz-Birkenau Memorial Museum Archives. Recollections*: volumes 131, 133, 136, 139, 145, 148, 149, 154, 167.
APMM: *The Majdanek State Museum Archives. Statements*: vol. VII-135.
ANDRES, Dörte & BEHR, Martina (2011): *Interpretes Mundi – Deuter der Welt.* – München: Martin Meidenbauer.
BEHR, Martina & CORPATAUX, Maike (2006): *Die Nürnberger Prozesse. Zur Bedeutung der Dolmetscher für die Prozesse und der Prozesse für die Dolmetscher.* – München: Martin Meidenbauer.

BOWEN, David & BOWEN, Margareta (1985): "The Nuremberg Trials. Communication through Translation", *Meta* 30 (1), 74–77.

CRONIN, Michael (2006): *Translation and Identity*. – London/New York: Routledge.

DOBOSIEWICZ, Stanisław (2000): *W obronie życia i godności ludzkiej*. – Warszawa: Wyd. Bellona.

GAIBA, Francesca (1998): *The Origins of Simultaneous Interpretation: The Nuremberg Trial*. – Ottawa: University of Ottawa Press.

GEVE, Thomas (2011): *Un survivant d'Auschwitz*. – Paris: Jean-Claude Gawsewitch.

GRAMLING, David (2012): "Another Unspeakability: Levi and *Lagerszpracha*", *New German Critique* 117, vol. 39(3), 165–187.

GUIDERE, Mathieu (2008): *Irak in translation. De l'art de perdre une guerre sans connaître la langue de son adversaire*. – Paris: Édition Jacob-Douvernet.

HAAS, Nicole (2011): *Dolmetschen am Ruanda-Tribunal*. – München: Martin Meidenbauer.

HALE, Sandra (2007): *Community Interpreting*. – Hampshire: Palgrave Macmillan.

LEVI, Primo (1958): *Se questo è un uomo*. – Torino: Guilio Eimaudi editore s.p.a/ (1960) *Is this a man*. Abacus. Transl. by Stuart Wolf.

LEVI, Primo (1986): *I sommersi e i salvati*. Torino: Guilio Eimaudi editore s.p.a./(1989) *The drowned and the saved*. – New York: Vintage International. Transl. by Raymond Rosenthal.

MALAK, Henryk M. (1961): *Klechy w obozach śmierci*. – Londyn: Veritas.

MONACELLI, Claudia (2002): "Interpreters for Peace". In: GARZONE, Gabriela & VIEZZI, Maurizio. (eds.): *Interpreting in the 21st century. Challenges and opportunities*. – Amsterdam/Philadelphia: John Benjamins Publishing, 181–193.

MORRIS, Ruth (1989): "Court Interpretation: The Trial of Ivan Demjanjuk. A Case Study", *The Interpreters' Newsletter*, 2, 27–37.

MORRIS, Ruth (1998): "Justice in Jerusalem – interpreting in Israeli legal proceedings", *Meta* 43 (1), 110–118.

MUSIOŁ, Teodor (1971): *Dachau 1939–1945*. – Opole: Instytut Śląski w Opolu/Katowice: Wyd. Śląsk.

PLEWIK, Grzegorz (2001): "Więźniowie funkcyjni w obozie koncentracyjnym na Majdanku" [Prisoner Functionaries in Majdanek Concentration Camp], *Zeszyty Majdanka* t. XXI, 29–70.

PÖLLABAUER, Sonia (2004): "Interpreting in Asylum Hearings. Issues of Role, Responsibility and Power", *Interpreting*, 6, 2, 143–175.

PYM, Anthony (2012): *On Translator Ethics. Principles for Mediation between Cultures.* – Amsterdam/Philadelphia: John Benjamins Publishing.

SHELLEY, Lore (1986): *Secretaries of Death. Accounts by former prisoners who worked in the Gestapo of Auschwitz.* – New York: Shengold Publishers, Inc.

SZYMCZUKIEWICZ, Magdalena (2005): "L'inteprétation communautaire dans l'armée. Étude de cas: missions polonaises de paix". Unpublished M.A. Thesis, University of Warsaw.

THOMAS, Roy (1997): "United Nations Military Observer Interpreting in a community setting". In: CARR, Silvana E., ROBERTS, Roberta P., DUFOUR, Aideen & STEYN, Dini (eds.): *The Critical Link: Interpreters in the Community.* – Amsterdam/Philadelphia: John Benjamins Publishing, 249–257.

TRYUK, Małgorzata (2004): *L'interprétation communautaire. Des normes et des rôles dans l'interprétation.* – Warszawa: Wyd. TEPIS.

TRYUK, Małgorzata (2010): "Interpreting in Nazi concentration camps during World War II", *Interpreting*, 12, 2, 125–145.

TRYUK, Małgorzata (2012): *'Ty nic nie mów, ja będę tłumaczył'. O etyce w tłumaczeniu ustnym.* – Warszawa: WLS.

WADENSJÖ, Cecilia (1998): *Interpreting as Interaction.* – London/New York: Longman.

WIEGAND, Chriss (2000): "Role of the Interpreter in the Healing of a Nation: An emotional view". In: ROBERTS, Roberta P., CARR, Silvana E., ABRAHAM, Diana, & DUFOUR, Aideen (eds.): *The Critical Link 2: Interpreters in the Community.* – Amsterdam/Philadelphia: John Benjamins Publishing, 207–218.

WOLF, Antoni (2011): "Więźniowie funkcyjni". In: GRUDZIŃSKA, Marta (red.) *Majdanek, Majdanek. Obóz koncentracyjny w relacjach więźniów i świadków.* – Lublin, Państwowe Muzeum na Majdanku, 76–81.

Translation zwischen Irakkrieg und intellektueller Korruption. Oder: Translatoren in der arabischen Literatur im Spannungsfeld von Politik, Macht und Berufsethik

Nahla Tawfik
Universität Ain Shams, Ägypten
nahlanagi@hotmail.com; DR.nahlatawfik@alsun.asu.edu.eg

Der facettenreiche Zusammenhang von Translation und Politik in den verschiedenen Kulturgemeinschaften und Epochen stößt vor allem in letzter Zeit auf großes Interesse. Das findet seinen Niederschlag u. a. in der zunehmenden und vielfältigen literarischen Verarbeitung des Themas. Translatoren, ob in Kriegszeiten oder unter autoritären Regimen, avancieren mehr und mehr zu Hauptfiguren in verschiedenen epischen und dramatischen Werken. Seit der Jahrtausendwende werden diese literarischen Werke mit dem sogenannten „fictional turn" ein deutlich sichtbarer Gegenstand translatologischer Forschung. Diese Studie untersucht die literarische Verarbeitung des Zusammenhangs von Translation, Politik, Macht und Berufsethik anhand zweier Gegenwartsromane der arabischen Literatur, die 2009 für den internationalen arabischen Buchpreis nominiert wurden und deren Hauptfigur ein Translator ist. Der 2008 erschienene Roman „Alhafida alamerikia" (Die amerikanische Enkelin) von der Irakerin Inaam Kachachi handelt von der amerikanischen Besatzung im Irak ab 2003 und schildert diese Zeit mit den Augen einer jungen amerikanisch-irakischen Frau, die in ihre Heimat, den Irak, als „transitional" Migrantin zurückkehrt, um als Translatorin für die US-Armee im Irak zu arbeiten. Die Hauptfigur im 2006 erschienenen Roman des Syrers Fawwaz Haddad ist hingegen ein Literaturübersetzer im „vorrevolutionären" Syrien, der durch seine Arbeit als Übersetzer die Korruption und Gewissenlosigkeit der intellektuellen Elite, die im Dienste des Regimes steht, und die Instrumentalisierung seiner Sprach- und Übersetzungskompetenz am eigenen Leibe erfahren muss.

Die Studie verfolgt das Ziel, anhand beider Werke das Bild des Translators und die Fiktionalisierung translatorischer Thematik in der arabischen Literatur im Spannungsfeld von Politik, Macht und Berufsethik zu investigieren, und geht dabei von der Hypothese aus, dass in diesem Spannungsfeld das Stereotyp vom innerlich zerrissenen Translator und daher potenziellen Verräter erfasst wird. Anhand der behandelten Werke wird auch überprüft, inwieweit die Darstellung des Translators in der arabischen Literatur mit den drei entwickelten Grundmustern von Dörte Andres vereinbar ist, die den Zusammenhang von Dolmetschen und Macht in der Literatur beleuchten.

Fictional Turn in der Translationswissenschaft

In den vergangenen Jahrzehnten ist die Tendenz feststellbar, dass in literarischen Werken verschiedenster Kulturgemeinschaften zunehmend translatorische Thematik verarbeitet wird. Translatoren avancieren mehr und mehr zu Hauptfiguren in den verschiedenen Gattungen der Literatur, welche nach Dörte Andres die Figur des Translators in den letzten Jahrzehnten für sich entdeckt zu haben scheint, um anhand dieser als Person „dazwischen" komplexe Probleme des modernen Menschen in der entgrenzten, weil globalisierten, Welt und in den hybriden Kulturen fiktional anzusprechen. Andres erklärt diese Tendenz damit, dass vor allem seit den 1990er Jahren Translation als eine Chiffre für Globalisierung, Migration, Multikulturalität, gesellschaftliche Hybridisierung, Sprache und Identität (Andres 2008:18) begriffen wird. Um sich ein Bild davon zu machen, wie hoch die Anzahl literarischer Werke mit translatorischer Thematik und Translatoren als Hauptfiguren ist und wie unterschiedlich und gegensätzlich Translatoren in der Gegenwartsliteratur dargestellt werden, ist es angebracht, einen Blick auf die Monographie von Dörte Andres (2008) zu werfen: *Dolmetscher als literarische Figuren. Von Identitätsverlust, Dilettantismus und Verrat;* sowie auf die drei Sammelbände, die von Klaus Kaindl und Ingrid Kurz herausgegeben wurden: Kaindl/Kurz (2005): *Wortklauber, Sinnverdreher, Brückenbauer: ÜbersetzerInnen und DolmetscherInnen als literarische Geschöpfe*; Kaindl/Kurz (2008): *Helfer, Verräter, Gaukler? Das Rollenbild von TranslatorInnen im Spiegel der Literatur*; Kaindl/Kurz (2010): *Machtlos, selbstlos, meinungslos?: Interdisziplinäre*

Analysen von ÜbersetzerInnen und DolmetscherInnen in belletristischen Werken. Es werden insgesamt mehr als sechzig Werke unterschiedlicher Gattungen besprochen. Die Werke schildern verschiedene Narrationen der translatorischen Praxis und unterschiedliche Wirklichkeitsmodelle. Die diversen Rollenvorstellungen vom Translator oszillieren „zwischen Helfer und Verräter, Gaukler und gewissenhaftem Mittler, einflussreichem Kommunikator und ohnmächtigem Kommunikationsinstrument, Opportunisten und Altruisten usw." (Kurz/Kaindl 2008 : 12).

Diese literarischen Werke mit translatorischer Thematik werden im Zuge des sogenannten *Fictional Turn* in der Translationswissenschaft systematisch als Quelle herangezogen und im Hinblick auf die Darstellung der Berufsgruppe der Translatoren und deren Tätigkeit (Kaindl/Kurz 2005: 9) analysiert. Der Begriff *Fictional Turn* geht auf die brasilianische Kulturwissenschaftlerin Else Ribeiro Pires Vieira zurück, die in den neunziger Jahren einen *Fictional Turn* innerhalb des Faches bemerkte, „where fiction has both provided theoretical parameters for translation and offered itself as an alternative source of theorization" (Curran 2007: 234). Pagano verweist in diesem Kontext auf „a twofold movement concerning the trial fiction-theory-translation": auf der einen Seite die Fiktionalisierung der Translation durch Schriftsteller, auf der anderen Seite die Beschäftigung der Theoretiker und Forscher mit Fiktion als Quelle für theoretische Reflexionen über Translation. Dabei werden Romane, Novellen und Kurzgeschichten herangezogen, die Translation und Translatoren thematisieren (Pagano 1995:81).

Kaindl/Kurz sprechen hier von einem jungen „Forschungsfeld mit vielfältigen Ansätzen, Themen und Fragestellungen" (Kaindl/Kurz 2010: 11), wobei an dieser Stelle zu betonen ist, dass das Interesse an diesen literarischen Werken nicht primär literaturwissenschaftlicher Natur, sondern translatologisch fokussiert ist. Denn in erster Linie werden die translatorischen Arbeitsweisen und -bedingungen beschrieben und die Wechselbeziehung zur tatsächlichen Berufsrealität untersucht. Die dahinterstehenden Vorstellungen vom Übersetzen und Dolmetschen werden ebenfalls eruiert. Translationswissenschaftliche und praxisbezogene Erkenntnisse werden dabei herangezogen, um das in der literarischen Fiktion vorhandene Bild von der Translation und den Translatoren zu untersuchen. Neben den oben genannten drei Bänden von Kaindl/Kurz und der Monographie von Andres soll hier auch auf folgende Titel verwiesen werden: Delabastita, Dirk/

Grutmann, Rainer (2005) (Hg.): *Fictionalising Translation and Multilingualism*; Salama-Carr, Myriam (2007) (Hg.): *Translating and Interpreting Conflict. Approaches to Translation Studies*; Steiner, Tina (2009): *Translated People, Translated Texts. Language and Migration in Contemporary African Literature*; Strümper-Krobb, Sabine (2009): *Zwischen den Welten. Die Sichtbarkeit des Übersetzers in der Literatur.*

Das Interesse am *Fictional Turn* fand auch Eingang in die kulturwissenschaftlich orientierten Studiengänge der Translationswissenschaft. Als Beispiel wird hier das fächerübergreifende Seminar zum Diskurs über Dolmetscher in der Literatur und publizistischen Texten genannt, das im Sommersemester 2007 von Andreas Kelletat und Dörte Andres am FTSK Germersheim/Mainz angeboten wurde. Auch auf internationalen Konferenzen wurde dem Thema verstärkt Beachtung geschenkt. In diesem Rahmen wurde im September 2011 am Zentrum der Translationswissenschaft der Universität Wien die internationale Konferenz *First International Conference on Fictional Translators in Literature and Film* veranstaltet. Die Beiträge erschienen in dem 2014 von Kaindl/Spitzl herausgegebenen Band *Transfiction. Research into the realities of translation fiction.* Auch die Bedeutung des *Fictional Turn* für die Translationsdidaktik ist mittlerweile Gegenstand translationswissenschaftlicher Untersuchung. In seinem Beitrag *Das Potential des Fictional Turn für die Translationsdidaktik* beleuchtet Klaus Kaindl, wie durch den Einsatz von literarischen Werken mit translatorischer Thematik wissenschaftliche Theorien, Handlungstheorien und Alltagstheorien im Übersetzungsunterricht vermittelt werden können (Kaindl 2013: 143–158).

Zu diesem jungen Forschungsfeld leistet die Monographie von Andres einen großen Beitrag. Die Dolmetschwissenschaftlerin orientiert sich bei ihrer Analyse an den Ansätzen der komparatistischen Imagologie und begnügt sich dabei nicht damit, die Dolmetscher und das Dolmetschen in den behandelten Werken zu beschreiben und die Darstellung zu bewerten (Andres 2008: 20), sondern sie differenziert – nach eingehender Analyse der zwölf behandelten Werke und abgesehen von einigen Ausnahmen – drei Grundmuster der literarischen Darstellung des Zusammenhangs von Dolmetschen und Macht. Bei dem ersten Grundmuster, das sie „Spiel mit der Macht" nennt, ist die Intention des Translators darauf gerichtet, seine eigenen Interessen, die nicht unbedingt materiell sind, durchzusetzen. Der Dolmetscher manipuliert die Kommunikationspartner durch die Sprache, daher wird sein Verhalten als unmoralisch bewertet, wobei er sich in keinem Loyalitätskonflikt befindet (Andres 2008:372). Das zweite Grundmuster „Kampf um die Macht" kennzeichnet Dolmetscher, deren Verhalten auch als unmoralisch bewertet wird, denn das Eigeninteresse bestimmt deren primär materiell orientiertes Handeln. Der Dolmetscher wird literarisch als Opportunist dargestellt, wobei er sich der Zensur bedient, um Macht ausüben zu können. Der Dolmetscher genießt kein bedingungsloses Vertrauen seitens der Kommunikationspartner (Andres 2008: 377). Bei dem dritten Grundmuster differenziert Andres zwischen Verhalten aus Eigennutz und Verhalten aus Emotionalität. Im ersten Fall geht es dem Dolmetscher darum, die Absicht des Gesprächspartners aus Eigennutz zu unterlaufen, im zweiten Fall kann der Dolmetscher keine neutrale Position wegen emotionaler Verbundenheit mit einem Kommunikationspartner einnehmen. Ihm geht es darum, den Kommunikationspartner durch seine Tätigkeit zu schützen (Andres 2008: 385).

Translation und Politik in der arabischen Gegenwartsliteratur

Die vorliegende Studie[1] widmet sich der Untersuchung des Zusammenhangs von Translation, Politik, und Berufsethik in der arabischen literarischen Fiktion anhand zweier Gegenwartsromane und versteht sich dabei als ein Beitrag zum *Fictional Turn* in der Translationswissenschaft, der den Blick des Forschungsstands um die arabische Gegenwartsliteratur zu erweitern versucht. Die Studie verfolgt das Ziel, anhand beider Werke das Bild des Translators und die Fiktionalisierung translatorischer Thematik in der arabischen Literatur im Spannungsfeld von Politik, Macht und Berufsethik zu investigieren und geht dabei von der Hypothese aus, dass dieses Spannungsfeld das Stereotyp vom in sich zerrissenen Translator und daher potenziellen Verräter erfasst. Anhand der behandelten Werke wird auch untersucht, inwieweit die Darstellung des Translators in der arabischen Literatur

---

[1] Die Studie ist Teil eines breit angelegten Forschungsprojekts, das das Bild des Translators in der arabischen Gegenwartsliteratur anhand unterschiedlicher literarischer Werke untersucht.

mit den drei entwickelten Grundmustern von Dörte Andres vereinbar ist, die den Zusammenhang vom Dolmetschen und Macht in der Literatur beleuchten.

Die amerikanische Enkelin

Zum Werk

Der 2008 erschienene, 195 Seiten umfassende Roman *Alhafida alamerikia* (Die amerikanische Enkelin)[2] von der Irakerin Inaam Kachachi[3] handelt von der amerikanischen Besatzung im Irak ab 2003 und schildert diese Geschehnisse mit den Augen einer jungen amerikanisch-irakischen Frau, die in ihre alte Heimat, den Irak, als „transitional" Migrantin zurückkehrt, um als Translatorin für die US-Armee im Irak zu arbeiten. Durch ihre vorläufige Rückkehr in die alte Heimat werden Fragen der Identität und Migration literarisch verarbeitet. Diese Thematik wirft ein Licht auf das Berufsbild in Konfliktzonen und die damit verbundenen Fragen der Loyalität und Neutralität sowie des Selbst- und Rollenbilds des Translators.

Die Hauptfigur Zeina (die Hübsche) ist eine christliche Irakerin aus Bagdad, deren Familie wegen politischer Verfolgung ihres Vaters vor Jahren aus dem Irak in die USA geflohen ist. Dank ihrer hohen Sprachkompetenz, was das Arabische betrifft, bewirbt sie sich nach dem 11. September für eine lukrative Tätigkeit als Dolmetscherin für die US-Armee im Irak. Nachdem sie einige Ausbildungsseminare besucht hat, darf sie in den Irak reisen. Zeina kehrt in ihre „Heimat" in amerikanischer Uniform zurück und sieht alles Alte mit neuen Augen. Sie trifft ihre Großmutter Rahma, die an ihren Wurzeln und Traditionen festhält und Zeinas Weltanschauung zu ändern versucht. Durch ihre Arbeit zwischen beiden Fronten, aber auch durch ihre Liebe zu ihren irakischen Verwandten, gerät sie in tiefe Konflikte und hinterfragt ihre eigenen Werte, ihre Identität und Rolle als Translatorin

---

[2] Die englische Übersetzung erschien 2010 von Nariman Youssef unter dem Titel *The American Granddaughter* und die französische 2009 von Ola Mehana und Khaled Osman unter dem Titel *Si je t'oublie, Bagdad*.

[3] Inaam Kachachi wurde 1942 im Irak geboren. Sie studierte Journalistik, bevor sie 1979 nach Paris reiste, um zu promovieren. Seither ist sie Journalistin und freie Autorin in Frankreich. Von ihr sind bisher drei Romane erschienen, darunter „Die amerikanische Enkelin".

im Irak. Die Geschichte endet mit ihrer Rückkehr in die USA nach dem Tod ihrer Großmutter, wobei sich ihre Identitätsbestimmung und Weltanschauung wesentlich verändert haben.

Literarische Fiktionalisierung translatorischer Thematik

Berufsbild

Die Handlung spielt vor dem brisanten politischen Hintergrund des Irakkriegs und des amerikanischen Eingreifens im Irak. Der 11. September und die darauffolgende Kriegsentscheidung werden als Auslöser für die starke Nachfrage nach arabischen Dolmetschern in den USA dargestellt. Die Hauptfigur Zeina nutzt die Chance und meldet sich bei einer der Agenturen, um als Translatorin für die US-Armee im Irak zu arbeiten. Zeina zeichnet sich durch eine hohe Sprachkompetenz aus, sie ist zweisprachig aufgewachsen, ihr Bekanntenkreis besteht fast ausnahmslos aus Arabern (S. 20ff). Zu Hause darf nur Arabisch gesprochen werden, während das Englische in den USA die Sprache der Straße, der Arbeit und der Nachrichten geblieben ist. Zeina kann mühelos von der einen Sprache in die andere wechseln. Sie spricht dank der Bemühungen ihres Vaters ein fehlerloses Hocharabisch . Er ist Poet und übt mit ihr fortwährend das Dichten (S. 21). Auf dieses Hocharabisch ist ihre Mutter besonders stolz. Als sie von der starken Nachfrage nach arabischen Dolmetschern erfährt, will Zeina aus ihrer Mehrsprachigkeit Nutzen ziehen, sie will mehr Geld verdienen, um ihrer Familie bessere Lebensverhältnisse zu ermöglichen. Als sie sich für die Tätigkeit meldet, wird zunächst am Telefon ein kurzer Test durchgeführt. Zeina soll einen Satz ins Arabische übersetzen. Es folgen einige Fragen über das Alter, die Qualifikationen, den Gesundheitszustand, den Sozialstatus und ihre finanzielle Lage. Ihre Sprachkompetenz sowie ihre Ruhe bei diesem kurzen Test am Telefon haben den Prüfer überzeugt, dass sie für die Tätigkeit die erforderliche emotionale Standfestigkeit aufbringt (S. 25).

Verschiedene Textstellen[4] im Roman vermitteln ein Bild von der sprachmittlerischen Tätigkeit im Krisenherd Irak und zeugen davon, dass diese ein Bündel an unterschiedlichen Aufgaben umfasst. Die Palette translatorischer Tätigkeiten

---

[4] Die deutsche Übersetzung der zitierten Textstellen stammt von der Verfasserin.

in dieser Konfliktzone beschränkt sich nicht nur darauf, eine Botschaft aus einer Sprache in die andere zu übertragen, sondern es handelt sich auch um eine Art „kultureller Beratung" für die amerikanische Armee, bei der die Kulturkompetenz des Translators stark gefragt wird:

> Ich arbeitete in Tikrit als Dolmetscherin, die nicht nur zwischen den Sprachen übersetzte, sondern auch den Soldaten Traditionen erklärte. Man darf Gebetsräume nicht mit Schuhen betreten, man muss warten, bis die Frauen ihre Kopftücher tragen, dass die Leute Abneigung haben gegen Polizeihunde, die als unrein gelten, ich erklärte das alles den Offizieren und Soldaten, die manchmal zuhörten, manchmal nur mit halbem Ohr hinhörten... (S. 95).

Eine weitere Aufgabe besteht darin, den Einheimischen, die zur US-Armee kommen, um etwas zu beantragen oder sich über etwas zu beschweren, zu begegnen, mit ihnen zu reden, sie zu beruhigen und zu beraten: „Meine Dolmetscherrolle bestand darin, die Menschen zu empfangen und zu beruhigen..." (S. 72); „Die Menschen kamen, um sich zu beschweren, ich hörte zu, übersetzte, schrieb es nieder und gab gute Ratschläge" (S. 96). Auch Kollaborateure muss Zeina empfangen und ihre Informationen aus dem Arabischen ins Englische übersetzen: „Kollaborateure kamen zu uns mit wichtigen Informationen, ich sollte auch das übersetzen" (S. 97).

Im Rahmen ihrer Arbeit muss Zeina auch die US-Soldaten nachts in die Stadt begleiten und an lebensgefährlichen Missionen teilnehmen, an Polizeistreifen, die umherziehen und Häuser stürmen, von denen man vermutet, dort seien Terroristen versteckt (S. 98). Diese mit der Arbeit gekoppelte potenzielle Lebensgefahr macht den Beruf besonders lukrativ, das jährliche Gehalt beträgt wegen des harten und schwierigen Charakters der Mission sowie der potenziellen Lebensgefahr 186 Tausend Dollar. Zeina scheint sich der Lebensgefahr, die mit dem Beruf verbunden ist, bewusst zu sein: Schon am Anfang des Romans bringt sie ihre Angst bezüglich der Arbeit zum Ausdruck: „186 Tausend Dollar. Das ist der Preis für meine Sprache, ja für mein Blut" (S. 18). Mit der Angst meldet sich bei ihr auch schon vor ihrer Reise in den Irak ein Gefühl der Skepsis gegenüber ihrer Rolle. Sie muss zunächst nach Washington zur CIA, wo mehrere Treffen veranstaltet werden, sie muss dort Seminare besuchen, wo sie etwas über die von ihr erwartete Rolle erfährt, Landkarten und Filme über das Land werden auch gezeigt()S. 25 (. Die Seminare bei der CIA haben Zeina von Anfang an skeptisch gegenüber der von ihr erwarteten Tätigkeit gemacht. Sie macht sich Gedanken über das Wesen ihrer Tätigkeit, ob sie nur eine sprachmittlerische Tätigkeit ausüben wird oder ob auch anderes von ihr gefordert wird, sie sagt sich danach: „Ich bin doch eine Dolmetscherin, kein Geheimagent" (S. 25). Als sie im Irak eintrifft, muss sie erfahren, dass es einige Einschränkungen gibt, die sie befolgen muss, sie darf nicht mit den Einheimischen sprechen oder Kontakt zu ihnen herstellen: „Meine Worte sind leeres Geschwätz, das mich und meine Kollegen gefährden kann. Ich selbst muss laut Anweisungen eigentlich stumm sein" (S. 15). Eine weitere Einschränkung besteht in dem wegen der Lebensgefahr für Translatoren verhängten Ausgehverbot. Translatoren dürfen nicht allein in die Stadt gehen, denn: „Dolmetscher wurden verfolgt und wie Schafe geschlachtet." (S. 126).

Nach einigen Monaten im Irak ist Zeina alles andere als zufrieden mit ihrer Tätigkeit. „Meine Arbeit ist aufregend, aber führt zu einer Art depressiver Stimmung" (S. 152). Sie hinterfragt ihre Rolle als Translatorin bei der US-Armee: „[...] wozu hat mich mein Vater die arabische Hochsprache gelehrt? Um schließlich bei der US-Armee als anerkannte Übersetzerin zu arbeiten?" (S. 145). Die Fragwürdigkeit der Arbeit als Translator bei der US-Armee im Irak und Berufsunzufriedenheit teilen auch andere Kollegen mit ihr. Einer sagt ihr: „Zeina, wir essen nur Mist" (S. 123), ein anderer, Dolmetscher in Mosul, nimmt sich das Leben, er konnte höchstwahrscheinlich die Belastung und den psychischen Druck nicht mehr ertragen.

Neben dem Befehl zum Stummsein gibt es ein weiteres Gebot, es wird von Zeina erwartet, das sie als Translatorin Neutralität wahrt. Zeina bringt das an einer Stelle zum Ausdruck: „[...] ich darf kein Mitleid empfinden oder Empathie zeigen" (S. 96). An zwei Szenen wird aber klar, dass ihr der Versuch, emotionslos zu bleiben, völlig misslingt. Die erste Dolmetschszene spielt sich im Haus eines irakischen Lehrers ab, das von den Amerikanern gestürmt wird, weil man dort Terroristen vermutet. Beim Vernehmen wird der Lehrer auf den Boden geworfen und das Gewehr wird gegen seinen Kopf gerichtet. Zeina, die bei der Befragung dolmetschen muss, kann nicht einfach machtlos und emotionslos zuschauen. Sie handelt spontan, indem sie das Gewehr, das gegen den Kopf des Mannes gerichtet ist, wegzuschieben versucht (S. 106 ff).

Das zweite Mal ist Zeina beteiligt an einer Polizeistreife in der Stadt. Sie kommen an einigen schiitischen Frauen bei einem religiösen Fest vorbei. Die amerikanischen Soldaten machen sich dabei über die Frauen und ihre Riten lustig. Zeina mischt sich in das Gespräch ein, nimmt die Frauen in Schutz und verteidigt sie. Sie übertreibt es, indem sie sich aus Rache an ihren amerikanischen Kollegen über jüdische Riten bei der Klagemauer lustig macht. Ihr Verhalten bringt bei ihrem amerikanischen Vorgesetzten sofort Skepsis hervor. Spontan reagiert ihr Vorgesetzter mit der Frage, auf die Zeina nicht antworten kann: „Auf wessen Seite bist Du?" (S. 121). Zeina schweigt, aber die Frage „Auf wessen Seite bin ich?" lässt sie bis zum Ende der Geschichte nicht in Ruhe und offenbart ihre Zerrissenheit und ihr Dilemma zwischen beiden Seiten: Die Amerikaner, bei denen sie arbeitet, erwarten von ihr, dass sie auf ihrer Seite steht, vertrauen ihr aber nicht ganz und sehen in ihr ein Potenzial an Illoyalität und Verrat. Die Iraker sehen Zeina anders. Schon in den USA sind sich die irakischen Migranten nicht einig, was diese Tätigkeit im Irak betrifft: Während die einen in dem Beruf die Chance des materiellen und sozialen Aufstiegs sehen und daher darum ringen, dafür angenommen zu werden, betrachten andere ddiese Arbeit als Hochverrat am Irak und warnen davor, darin verwickelt zu werden. Auch für die Mehrheit im Irak ist Zeina eine Kollaborateurin, der Illoyalität vorzuwerfen ist. Sie kommt „auf den Panzern der Besatzer" (S. 77) und trägt die „Uniform der Schande" (S. 119), im Gegensatz zu ihrem verstorbenen irakischen Großvater, dessen Offiziers-Uniform die Großmutter jedes Jahr am Nationalfeiertag herausholt. An mehreren Stellen des Romans bringt Zeina zum Ausdruck, wie die Gesellschaft ihre Rolle beurteilt: „Sie sehen in mir den Sprecher des Feindes" (S. 155). Zeina ist für die Iraker sogar schlimmer als die US-Soldaten: „Die Iraker sehen die Soldaten als Besatzer, Soldaten, die den Dienst verrichten und Befehle ausführen. Sie können nichts dafür, genauso ging es den irakischen Soldaten im Iran- und Golfkrieg. Aber mich sehen sie als Kollaborateurin" (S. 160). Nur für ihren Halbbruder Haider, der sich erhofft, dass Zeina ihm bei der Auswanderung nach Amerika, in das Land der Freiheit, hilft, ist sie keine Verräterin, sondern „ein Mädchen, das von Beruf Übersetzerin ist und nichts von der Politik versteht" (S. 77). Zeina fürchtet für sich daher ein tragisches Ende, sie glaubt, dass sie entweder von ihrem Halbbruder Mohaimen oder einem seiner Genossen bei der Almahdi-Armee ermordet (S. 139) oder von den Amerikanern wegen Verdachts auf Verrat liquidiert wird:

> Die Autorin wird am Ende dieser Geschichte den schwarzen Sack auf meinen Kopf legen, und es wird aus kurzer Entfernung losgeschossen, so, wie Verräter ihre Strafe verdienen. Werde ich als Feigling sterben, ohne mich verteidigen zu können? (S. 104)

Die Rolle der Translatorin sowie ihr Dilemma werden in diesem Roman mit einigen Vergleichen und Metaphern beschrieben. Reagierend auf einen Vorwurf aus ihrer Familie, dass sie „ihre Haut wechselt", sagt Zeina: „ich habe nur eine Haut, deren Farbe sich aber rasch ändert" (S. 144). Zeina sieht sich selber als ein „Chamäleon"[5]. Auch ihre Verwandten benutzen diese Metapher, um Zeinas Rolle zu beschreiben (S. 178). Noch dazu wird sie als „Hund mit zwei Hütten" bezeichnet. Ihre Verwandten beschreiben damit ihre Haltung zwischen beiden Lagern: zwischen den Irakern als ihren Leuten und den Amerikanern, für die sie arbeitet und von denen sie Geld bekommt. Sie will beiden Herren dienen und gefallen, muss aber daran scheitern, weil es unmöglich ist. Anhand dieser Metaphern wird die Ausweglosigkeit ihrer Situation zutreffend dargestellt und zugleich an ihrer Loyalität gezweifelt.

Der untreue Übersetzer

Zum Werk

Die Hauptfigur in dem 486 Seiten umfassenden, 2006 erschienenen Roman des Syrers Fawaz Haddad[6] ist hingegen ein Literaturübersetzer im „vorrevolutionären" Syrien, der durch seine Arbeit als Übersetzer die entscheidende Macht der Politik, die Korruption und Gewissenlosigkeit der intellektuellen Elite, die im Dienste des Regimes steht, und die Instrumentalisierung seiner Sprach- und Übersetzungskompetenz am eigenen Leibe erfahren muss. Der Übersetzer Hamed

---

[5] Die Metapher des Chamäleons scheint besonders beliebt zu sein, wenn es um die Beschreibung von Translatoren geht. Verwiesen sei hier auch auf Michael Wallners *April in Paris*, in dessen Mittelpunkt der Wehrmachtsoldat Roth steht, der als Translator in der SS-Zentrale im besetzten Paris 1943 eingesetzt wird, ein Doppelleben führt, und am Ende Verrat begeht. Seine Haltung wird mit dem Chamäleon verglichen, das die Farbe wechselt und sich der jeweiligen Umgebung anpasst (S.185).

[6] Fawwaz Haddad wurde 1947 in Damaskus geboren, hat erst Rechtswissenschaft studiert, als Apotheker und Kaufmann gearbeitet, bevor er sich entschloss, sich ganz dem Schreiben zu widmen. Zwei seiner bisher neun Romane wurden für den arabischen Booker-Price nominiert, darunter „Der untreue Übersetzer". Auf Deutsch ist von ihm „Gottes blutiger Himmel" erschienen.

Selim wird am Anfang des Romans als ein ruhiger, höflicher und gutherziger junger Mann charakterisiert. Zu Beginn seiner Karriere arbeitet er als Übersetzer in der Abteilung für internationale Angelegenheiten einer Tageszeitung. Nach vier Monaten wird ihm gekündigt, weil er den Aufsatz eines berühmten amerikanischen Schriftstellers übersetzt, in welchem dieser sich negativ über die syrische Haltung bei den Friedensverhandlungen mit den Israelis unter amerikanischer Schirmherrschaft äußert. Der amerikanische Schriftsteller behauptet, die Syrer hätten Zugeständnisse an die Israelis gemacht. Vorsichtigerweise hätte Hamed, so meint der Chefredakteur, diesen Abschnitt nicht übersetzen sollen, denn die syrischen Tageszeitungen haben stets betont, dass das so nicht der Fall sei. Aber Hamed blieb dem Original treu und übersetzte den Artikel vollständig. Daraufhin verliert er seine Stelle, auch der Chefredakteur wird aus seinem Amt entlassen.

Danach versucht Hamed sein Glück damit, Rezensionen von weltberühmten Romanen zu übersetzen. Er wird durch die Übersetzung zweier englischer Romane bekannt. Die Qualität seiner Übersetzungen hat aber den großen Literaturkritiker Sharif Hosny nicht überzeugt, und daher schreibt er einen Artikel, in dem er seine Zweifel äußert und die freien Übersetzungen von Hamed kritisiert. Darauf antwortet Hamed mit einem Gegenartikel, in dem er seine Übersetzung verteidigt und den großen Intellektuellen als jemanden anprangert, der nichts von der Übersetzung und dem Übersetzungsprozess versteht, ohne ihn namentlich zu nennen. Hamed siegt bei dieser Debatte, aber erntet dadurch den Hass und die Feindschaft des Literaturkritikers, der nun auf einen Fehler von ihm lauert. Als Hamed danach eine englische Novelle eines afrikanischen Schriftstellers übersetzt und die Novelle berühmt wird, da der Autor den Britisch Poker Award gewinnt, wird der Literaturkritiker auf die Übersetzung von Hamed aufmerksam, die er zu untersuchen beginnt. Es stellt sich heraus, dass Hamed es dabei mit seinem Verständnis der freien Übersetzung und der Treue gegenüber der Leserschaft übertrieben, und dabei das Ende des Romans völlig verändert hat. Der afrikanische Held entscheidet sich im Original dafür, nach Abschluss seines Studiums in London zu bleiben bei seiner weißen Geliebten. Hamed, dem das Ende nicht gefällt, macht daraus, sein eigenes Vaterland im Sinn, ein positives Ende: Der Held geht in seine afrikanische Heimat zurück und verlässt seine weiße Geliebte. Der große Literaturkritiker nutzt die Gelegenheit und führt gegen Hamed eine Kampagne in der Presse unter dem Titel „Der untreue Übersetzer". Es folgen Intellektuelle aus dessen

Kreis mit ebenso heftiger Kritik und mit der Aufforderung, dass Hamed keine Romane mehr übersetzen dürfe. Um seine Karriere nicht aufgeben zu müssen, will sich Hamed verteidigen und seine Entscheidung rechtfertigen, indem er einen Gegenartikel mit seiner Antwort auf die Kritik an dieselbe Zeitung schickt. In den darauffolgenden Tagen erscheint der Artikel nicht, stattdessen wird Hamed in die Sicherheitsdienstzentrale vorgeladen. Nach einem scheinbar harmlosen und interessanten Gespräch, in dem sich der Sicherheitsbeamte überraschenderweise scharfe Kritik an dem Regime und der Partei erlaubt, wird Hamed darum gebeten, seinen Artikel zurückzuziehen und den großen Intellektuellen nicht mehr zu stören. Hamed, der von der Haltung des Sicherheitsbeamten zutiefst enttäuscht und deprimiert ist, bleibt lange arbeitslos, muss aber danach aus finanziellen Gründen Übersetzungsaufträge annehmen, die unter Pseudonymen erscheinen und von deren Qualität er nicht überzeugt ist. Der Gedanke an Rache für seine verlorene Karriere hat ihn aber nicht verlassen. Davon zeugt die Abmachung, die er mit dem Schriftsteller Samir Farout getroffen hat: Hamed soll seine Sprachkompetenz in den Dienst dieses Schriftstellers stellen und ihn durch Plagiat mit Material für neue arabische Romane beliefern. Im Gegenzug soll ihn der Schriftsteller unterstützen, damit er einen Roman übersetzen kann. Jener verspricht ihm auch, ein Gremium von großen Namen aus der Literatur- und Kritikszene zu bilden, welches die zuvor scharf kritisierte Übersetzung von ihm neu beurteilen soll. Farout würde dabei mitwirken und Einfluss ausüben, damit die Entscheidung positiv ausfällt. So könnte sich Hamed an dem großen Literaturkritiker rächen, der durch die Kampagne gegen ihn seinen Ruf als Übersetzer ruiniert hat. Nach anfänglicher Bejahung will Hamed die Abmachung nicht weiterführen. Der Schriftsteller lehnt dies aber ab und droht Hamed. Als Ausweg aus dieser Lage entscheidet sich Hamed dafür, den Schriftsteller bei einem nächtlichen Treffen zu ermorden. Gerade noch rechtzeitig erscheint in diesem Moment ein Passant auf der Straße, wird der schockierte Schriftsteller gerettet und geht Hamed daraufhin für immer aus dem Weg. Hamed entscheidet sich für einen neuen Anfang, nicht als Übersetzer, sondern als freier Schriftsteller.

Fiktionalisierung translatorischer Thematik

Berufsbild

Der Übersetzer Hamed Selim hat ein Studium der Anglistik abgeschlossen. Seine Reflexionen über ein übersetzerisches Vorgehen und übersetzerische Entscheidungen offenbaren eine gewisse Metakompetenz und eine Vertrautheit mit diversen Übersetzungsprinzipien.

Neben seiner Sprach- und Kulturkompetenz wird Hamed durch eine Reihe von Charaktereigenschaften beschrieben: Hamed ist ein ruhiger, höflicher und gutherziger junger Mann, er ist ein nachdenklicher Typ, der mit niemandem gern redet (S. 11.), hartnäckig und manchmal rechthaberisch (S. 13). Hamed wird auch als ängstliche Person dargestellt, die einen tiefen Drang hat, sich hinter anderen zu verbergen (S. 23). Deshalb könnte sein übersetzerisches Vorgehen ein Versuch sein, seine Gedanken durch ein bereits geschriebenes Werk auszudrücken und damit seinen Ideen und Wünschen freien Lauf zu lassen, ohne Angst haben zu müssen, mit Kritik konfrontiert zu werden. Zu seiner Angst kommt auch seine Schüchternheit hinzu (S. 262). Der Autor vergleicht den Übersetzer in diesem Kontext mit einer Maus, die nicht an den Büchern nagt, sondern sich dahinter versteckt (S. 92). Eine weitere Charaktereigenschaft Hameds ist sein Hang zum Perfektionismus. Das offenbart sich in einem inneren Monolog, in welchem Hamed sein Leid beim Übersetzen und bei der Wahl des richtigen Wortes klagt und sich selber fragt, ob es sich lohnt und ob der Leser eine Ahnung von seinem Mühsal hat und die Arbeit entsprechend zu schätzen weiß. Bei der Übersetzung einer Textstelle sucht Hamed nach dem richtigen Äquivalent: düsterer Himmel, bewölkter, bedeckter oder verhangener? Es ist ein langes Hin und Her, bei dem er sich immer daran erinnert, dass er viele Aspekte beachten muss: die Bedeutung, den Klang, die Funktion. Am Ende beklagt er den hohen kognitiven Aufwand, den ihn die Übersetzung eines einzigen Satzes kostet. Er fragt sich, ob die Leser von seinem Leid eine Ahnung haben und ob sie die Mühe entsprechend schätzen können. Er glaubt aber, dass seine Leserschaft staunen würde, wenn sie von diesem Mühsal erfahren würde, sie würde sich über diejenigen wundern, welche die großen Probleme der Menschheit nicht beachten und sich stattdessen mit kleinen Problemen plagen, mit Wörtern, die keinen großen Einfluss haben, aber viel Zeit und Denken in Anspruch nehmen (S. 14f).

Das übersetzerische Vorgehen

Das übersetzerische Vorgehen wird in diesem Roman an mehreren Stellen[7] literarisch eingearbeitet. Übersetzen wird zunächst als eine anstrengende, anspruchsvolle und belastende Tätigkeit bezeichnet, die einen hohen kognitiven Aufwand mit sich bringt:

> [...] eine Arbeit, die Anstrengung und Flexibilität erfordert [...], dass man auch manchmal auf Distanz geht, vielleicht auch von dem Richtigen abrückt, in Wörterbüchern nachschlägt, mit vulgären Ausdrücken der Fremdsprache umgeht, vielleicht sie aus dem Kontext tilgt, die Bedeutungen und Synonyme untersucht, um davon das Zutreffende auszuwählen. Es ist eine Arbeit, die sich des Verstandes bedient, oder klarer gesagt: Es ist das sorgfältige Abwägen aller Möglichkeiten. (S. 13)

In mehreren Textstellen sind Äußerungen Hameds zu seinem Übersetzungsbegriff und zur Aufgabe des Übersetzers zu finden. Durch seine Reflexionen, die ein übersetzungswissenschaftliches Interesse offenbaren, wird vor allem der Begriff der Treue am Roman kontrovers diskutiert: In dem Gegenartikel, den er verfasst hat, wehrt sich Hamed gegen die Wort-für-Wort-Übersetzung und bezeichnet die wahre Übersetzung als eine, die den Sinn des Originals erfasst und es zugleich nach den Regeln „unserer schönen arabischen Sprache schmückt" (S. 19). Die Wort-für-Wort-Übersetzung kritisiert er als eine trockene Übersetzung, die es nicht wagt, das Original anzutasten, als sei es ein heiliges Buch. Das Produkt sei ein kalter, geschmackloser Text, der den Sinn verfehlt (S. 20). Nur der maßvolle Eingriff des Übersetzers in das zu übersetzende Werk kann den Lesern dieses nahebringen und verständlich machen (S. 20). Nur so könne der Übersetzer seine Aufgabe als Brückenbauer zwischen zwei verschiedenen Sprach- und Kulturgemeinschaften wahrnehmen. Nur so könne die Sprache der Verständigung dienen und nicht der Verwirrung. Denn der Autor adressiert seinen Text an einen ihm bekannten Empfängerkreis. Er hat keine Ahnung von Lesern aus anderen Kulturgemeinschaften, denen durch die Übersetzung erst ermöglicht wird, das Buch wahrzunehmen. Im Kommunikationsprozess könnte durch eine Wort-für-Wort-Übersetzung genau das Gegenteil bewirkt werden, weil diese Verwirrung beim Empfänger hervorruft. Der Übersetzer hat aber in Hameds Augen einen Vorteil gegenüber dem Autor, der darin besteht, dass er den Empfänger der Übersetzung

---

[7] Die deutsche Übersetzung der zitierten Textstellen stammt von der Verfasserin.

kennt. Daher sieht Hamed die erste Aufgabe des Übersetzers darin, die bestehende Kluft zwischen dem Autor und dem Empfänger der Übersetzung dadurch zu überwinden, dass er in den zu übersetzenden Text eingreift (S. 22).

In seinem Gespräch mit dem Verleger einer Reihe kitschiger Romane, bei dem Hameds Übersetzungen unter Pseudonymen erschienen, treffen zwei unterschiedliche Auffassungen vom Begriff der Treue aufeinander: Treue gegenüber dem „heiligen" Original versus Treue gegenüber der Leserschaft. Im folgenden Gespräch versucht Hamed, sein freies übersetzerisches Vorgehen zu rechtfertigen, indem er sich auf den Begriff der Treue stützt:

Was hat das alles mit der Übersetzung zu tun: Treue und exakte Wiedergabe... der richtige Ausdruck?
Ich vernachlässige sie nicht, aber das Erzählen nimmt mich mit, und die Charaktere überwältigen mich, neue Ideen kommen auf, ich drücke alles, was mir durch den Kopf geht, in der Übersetzung aus... Ehrlich gesagt, der reine Übersetzungsprozess hat für mich seinen Reiz und seine Schönheit verloren. Das ist das einzige, was ich davon habe.
Das sind keine überzeugenden Gründe: Der Übersetzer übersetzt das, was vor ihm auf dem Papier steht, ohne sich einzumischen, ohne etwas hinzuzufügen oder auszulassen. Das, was Sie machen, ist ein Angriff gegen den Autor und das Werk
Aber das trägt Früchte für die Leserschaft. Sie bekommen ein zweifach geschriebenes Werk.
Sie betrügen die Leserschaft, denn diese liest nicht das Original
Aber ich biete ihnen ein Werk an, das ihnen nähergeht.
[...] ein entstelltes, verfälschtes Werk. Können Sie dessen Beziehung zum Original leugnen, es baut darauf. Ihr Vorgehen schadet nicht nur dem Übersetzungsbegriff, es schafft ihn ab. (S. 87f)

Hamed spricht auch von einem „dritten Raum" zwischen Realität und Fiktion, wo ein Austauschprozess zwischen den Charakteren und ihm stattfindet, dem er nicht widerstehen kann:

Sie (die Figuren) sind zu stark, ich kann ihnen nicht aus dem Wege gehen und ihnen nicht widerstehen, sie kommen aus dem Buch heraus, und ich verlasse die Wirklichkeit, wir gehen in einen dritten Raum über die Grenze ins Dazwischen, sie legen ihre Masken ab und stehen nackt vor mir, ich dringe in ihre Tiefen vor und entdecke einige meiner Geheimnisse und Mysterien, die Gewitter schicken mich dorthin, wo es kein Zurück gibt. (S. 85)

Im Roman äußert sich Hamed auch zur Aufgabe des Übersetzers. Sie besteht seiner Meinung nach in der Pflicht, die Mängel des Originals auszugleichen, zu beseitigen, und damit das Original zu verschönern:

Ich versuche, einiges auszugleichen. Weil ich den Charakteren sehr nah stehe, nehme ich ihre Schmerzen wahr[...] ich möchte ihnen eine zweite Chance geben, daher muss ich den gesamten Roman nochmals überprüfen: den Stil, die Geschehnisse, ich verbessere einiges, das der Autor nicht beachtet hat, und ergänze einiges, das er vergessen hat[...] (S. 86f)

Anhand des für diesen Roman zentralen Begriffs der Treue bzw. Untreue, der schon im Titel des Romans vorkommt sowie in unterschiedlichen Gesprächen zwischen Hamed und einigen Intellektuellen im Mittelpunkt steht, wird der Begriff der Treue zum Original mit Treue bzw. Loyalität des Intellektuellem zum Regime in Verbindung gebracht. Das kommt zum Ausdruck im Gespräch von Hamed und dem Sicherheitsbeamten in der Sicherheitszentrale, der nichts von Treue bzw. Verrat am Kunstwerk hören möchte, sondern nur an die Loyalität bzw. Illoyalität zum Vaterland denkt: „Der einzige Verrat ist der Verrat am Vaterland. Sind Sie dessen nicht schuldig, kann Ihnen ansonsten nichts passieren" (S. 57). Die autoritäre Machtkontrolle des Regimes, durch die Hamed seinen Beruf als Übersetzer am Anfang seiner Karriere verloren hat, veranlasst ihn dazu, der Politik aus dem Wege zu gehen und sich sicherheitshalber der Übersetzung von Literatur zu widmen. Hier erlaubt sich Hamed eine starke Machtausübung gegenüber den zu übersetzenden Werken, die er damit rechtfertigt, dass er in der Übersetzung u. a. ein Mittel sieht, fremdes Gedankengut nicht nur zu vermitteln, sondern sich mit diesem auseinanderzusetzen, Irrtümer zu erkennen und die Menschen aufzuklären, vor allem, wenn die vermittelten Gedanken nicht zur Gesellschaft passen. In seinen Augen hat die Übersetzung damit eine „konstruktive" und keine „destruktive" Aufgabe. Aus diesem Verständnis heraus muss der afrikanische Held in der arabischen Übersetzung von Hamed London verlassen und in die Heimat zurückgehen. Das originale Ende wäre, so dachte Hamed, ein Verrat am Vaterland und würde mit der Politik des Regimes unvereinbar sein, das seit Jahren über die Auswanderung der besten Wissenschaftler klagt. Hamed ist sich sicher, dass er damit etwas Konstruktives für sein Land tut, das vom Regime und von Literaturkritikern, denen die Treue zum Vaterland wichtiger als die Treue zum Kunstwerk ist, aus grenzenlosem Nationalstolz begrüßt und bewundert wird (S. 38ff).

Die heftige Kritik der Intellektuellen an der freien Übersetzung von Hamed zeigt die Abhängigkeit der Intellektuellen vom Regime und ihre Heuchelei. Denn die heftige Kampagne, der sich mehrere Intellektuelle anschließen und bei der die Untreue des Übersetzers als eine zu „verachtende Sünde und ein Hochverrat" (S.

107) angeprangert wird, wird nicht wegen des Prinzips der Treue gegenüber dem Original und dessen künstlerischem Charakter durchgeführt, sondern sie dient den Intellektuellen als Chance, dem Regime ihre Gewissenhaftigkeit zu beweisen: Die Kampagne gegen die Untreue wirdzum Zeugnis davon, dass die Intellektuellen das Prinzip der Treue im Allgemeinen hochhalten, vor allem der Treue gegenüber dem Regime (S. 101). Denn wer sich wegen der Untreue an einem Kunstwerk so engagiert, könne beim Regime nicht unter Verdacht auf Verrat kommen, denken sie.

Als Hamed den Eigennutz und die Korrumpiertheit der Intellektuellen sowie die Gleichgültigkeit des Regimes an seinem Schicksal, verkörpert durch den Sicherheitsbeamten, am eigenen Leibe erfahren muss, vollzieht er einen kompletten Gesinnungswandel. Jetzt ist er nicht mehr dem Original und nicht mehr der Leserschaft treu, sondern sich selbst. Er stellt seine Bedürfnisse in den Mittelpunkt und handelt eigennützig, ohne sich Gedanken zu machen über berufsethische Fragen. Hamed lässt sich „auf Raten verkaufen" (S. 446), er lässt seine Kompetenz von anderen instrumentalisieren und missbrauchen. Das zeigt sich an zweierlei. Zunächst akzeptiert Hamed, eine Reihe kitschiger Romane zu übersetzen und deren einseitige Darstellungsweise zu ertragen unter der Bedingung, dass er seine Übersetzungsexperimente fortsetzen kann, er darf frei übersetzen, wie er möchte, nur muss das Ende identisch bleiben. Er kann Stellen hinzufügen, verändern, abstreichen, ohne dabei die Angst haben zu müssen, mit harter Kritik konfrontiert zu werden (S. 152). Dann kommt seine Abmachung mit dem skrupellosen Schriftsteller Samir Farout: Hamed soll diesem Schriftsteller, dem es an literarischer Kreativität mangelt, durch Plagiate literarische Stoffe für neue arabische Romane liefern, bis seine Geschichte mit der untreuen Übersetzung mithilfe eben dieses Schriftstellers positiv geklärt wird (S. 371). Auch verspricht ihm der Schriftsteller, dass seine Übersetzungen in der Zukunft nicht mehr zensiert würden: „Ich verspreche dir, wenn dir ein Roman gefällt, den du übersetzen möchtest und an dem ich kein Interesse habe, dann werde ich dafür sorgen, dass dir keine Zensur oder Kritik im Wege steht, auch wenn du den Roman auf den Kopf stellst!..." (S. 440). Als Hamed die Sache nicht weiterführen will, droht ihm der Schriftsteller damit, dass er alles verlieren wird: „In den kommenden Monaten bekomme ich monatlich vier Ideen. Wenn du dich nicht an unsere Abmachung hältst, dann wirst du alles verlieren, deine Arbeit im Verlag, in der Zeitung, und der Rest kommt noch..." (S. 444). Am Ende bereut Hamed seine Situation und macht sich Vorwürfe, da er sich instrumentalisieren ließ. Er steht vor dem Spiegel und spricht zu sich:

> Dieser Mann ist nichts anders als die Überreste eines Mannes, der jedem, der Interesse hat, gegen einen mageren Lohn, der zum Überleben reicht, seinen Dienst anbietet, ... Er hat sich auf Raten verkauft, dreimal, es bleibt noch einiges zu verkaufen, und er trachtet danach, mit einem sauberen Gesicht und glänzender Maske den Schein zu wahren. (S. 446).

An einer anderen Stelle im Roman führt er seine Selbstkritik weiter. Er bereut, dass er Aufträge angenommen hat, die der Berufsethik widersprechen, und bedauert, von seinen Kompetenzen keinen richtigen Gebrauch gemacht zu haben: „er hätte sie besser einsetzen können, auf eine erhabene, nützliche und förderliche Weise. Aber es war schon zu spät, die Reue nützte nichts, ... er war nicht immun genug" (S. 452).

Hamed erscheint im Roman als in drei Übersetzerpersonen aufgespalten. Da Hamed infolge der heftigen Kampagne gegen ihn nicht übersetzen darf, muss er Übersetzungsaufträge unter den drei Pseudonymen Halfawy, Halfany und Haflawy annehmen. Diese Gespaltenheit in drei Übersetzer hat Hamed schon früh geplagt. „Was ist das für ein Übel? Ich bin drei geworden; wann habe ich Zeit für mich selbst?" (S. 195). Am Ende des Romans bewältigt Hamed diesen Konflikt positiv und überwindet seine Zerrissenheit: „es ist an der Zeit, ... zu sich selbst zurückzukehren, ohne Masken. Er wird Halfawy, Halfany und Haflawy loswerden, so schnell wie möglich..." (S. 451).

Translationswissenschaftliche Diskussion

Das Thema der Translation und die Figur des Translators eröffnen vielfältige Möglichkeiten, um das Spannungsfeld von Politik, Macht und Berufsethik literarisch zu verarbeiten, vor allem, wenn es sich um Translatoren in Konfliktzonen oder in autoritären Regimen handelt. Im ersten Roman „Die amerikanische Enkelin" geht es um die Identitätskrise einer *„transitional* Migrantin" im Irak, die zwischen zwei Identitäten und zwei Welten pendelt und daher zerrissen ist, was besonders in den beiden Metaphern des „Chamäleons" und des „Hundes mit zwei Hütten" zum Ausdruck kommt. Die Analyse des Romans zeigt, dass es sich hier bei der Translation um eine facettenreiche Tätigkeit handelt, die sowohl das Dolmetschen und Übersetzen als auch interkulturelle Informationen für US-Soldaten und die Beratung der Einheimischen umfasst. Diese heikle Rolle der Translatorin lässt die Hauptfigur nicht emotionslos und unbeteiligt, sondern diese findet sich in einigen Fällen gezwungen, gegen die professionelle Ethik zu handeln, vor allem, was das Zeigen von Mitgefühl oder Empathie bei der Ausübung ihrer Tätigkeit angeht. Sie überschreitet die Grenze der Neutralität und zeigt Gebundenheit an ihre Ursprungskultur, indem sie versucht, den irakischen Lehrer zu schützen und die schiitischen Frauen zu verteidigen, was ihr gegenüber Skepsis und den Verdacht der Gespaltenheit und Illoyalität hervorruft. Die Überschreitung der Neutralitätsgrenze in beiden Fällen entsteht vor allem dadurch, dass der Translator kein Sprachautomat ist, sondern ein Mensch, der manchmal aufgrund seiner Emotionalität diesen Teil der Berufsethik nicht vollständig respektieren kann. Das Überschreiten der Neutralitätsgrenze bleibt nicht ohne Folgen für Zeina. Anhand der Frage „Auf wessen Seite bist Du?" wird die Möglichkeit der Einhaltung von Neutralität in Konfliktzonen literarisch stark angezweifelt. Die Amerikaner erwarten von Zeina, dass sie als Translatorin vollständig die Position der Amerikaner vertritt. Die Skepsis, die sich in dieser literarischen Darstellung offenbart, verstärkt das Rollenklischee vom Übersetzer als zerrissene Person und damit potenzieller Verräter *traduttore traditore*, dem einige Übersetzer in Konfliktgebieten tatsächlich nicht selten zum Opfer fallen. In *Dolmetscher in Konfliktzonen: Die Grenzen der Neutralität* lenkt E. Kahane die Aufmerksamkeit des Faches auf diesen brisanten Zusammenhang, fordert im Hinblick auf den grausamen Tod des afghanischen Translators Ahmal Nakschabnadi durch die Taliban mehr Solidarität für Translatoren in Konfliktzonen und verlangt, dass der Beruf des Translators und seine Stellung in der Welt neu überdacht werden müssen.[8]

Der zweite Roman „Der untreue Übersetzer" bietet ein komplexes und differenziertes Bild übersetzerischer Praxis in autoritären Regimen. Anhand der Ausführungen über den Übersetzungsprozess, die Aufgabe des Übersetzers sowie die geeignete Übersetzungsmethode werden berufsethische Fragen thematisiert. Dabei steht der Begriff der Treue im Mittelpunkt. Die Reflexionen über die in den

---

[8] Kahane, E. (2007): *Dolmetscher in Konfliktzonen: Die Grenzen der Neutralität.* http://www.aiic.net/ViewPage.cfm/page2692.htm (20.10.2013)

Augen der Hauptfigur beste Methode des Übersetzens, bei denen er auf das Verhältnis vom Übersetzer zum Autor und Leser eingeht und den maßvollen Eingriff des Übersetzers in das zu übersetzende Werk als die Voraussetzung dafür betrachtet, dass das Werk den Lesern nahegebracht und dadurch verständlich wird und dass die Sprache der Verständigung und nicht der Verwirrung dient, erinnern an die Ausführungen von F. Schleiermacher in seiner Abhandlung *Ueber die verschiedenen Methoden des Uebersetzens,* die die Diskussion um die Übersetzung lange dominierten:

> Aber nun der eigentliche Uebersetzer, der diese beiden ganz getrennten Personen, seinen Schriftsteller und seinen Leser, wirklich einander zuführen, und dem letzten, ohne ihn jedoch aus dem Kreise seiner Muttersprache heraus zu nöthigen, zu einem möglichst richtigen und vollständigen Verständniß und Genuß des ersten verhelfen will, was für Wege kann er hierzu einschlagen? Meines Erachtens giebt es deren nur zwei. Entweder der Uebersetzer läßt den Schriftsteller möglichst in Ruhe, und bewegt den Leser ihm entgegen; oder er läßt den Leser möglichst in Ruhe, und bewegt den Schriftsteller ihm entgegen. Beide sind so gänzlich voneinander verschieden, daß durchaus einer von beiden so streng als möglich muß verfolgt werden, aus jeder Vermischung aber ein höchst unzuverlässiges Resultat nothwendig hervorgeht, und zu besorgen ist daß Schriftsteller und Leser sich gänzlich verfehlen... (S. 47ff)

Doch Hameds übersetzerisches Vorgehen unterscheidet sich von den Übersetzungsmaximen, von denen er redet, denn sein Vorgehen überschreitet die Grenze der Treue und ist gekennzeichnet von übertriebener, unverantwortlicher Freiheit bei der Sinndeutung und Sinnwiedergabe. Daher kommt dieses Vorgehen, wie im Falle der Übersetzung der englischen Novelle, bei der er das Ende ändert, um das Original beschönigend zu manipulieren und im Sinne der Leserschaft und der Politik des Landes umzuformen, der adaptierenden einbürgernden Übertragung näher als der Übersetzung. Sein Vorgehen ruft die *belles infidèles,* die schönen Untreuen des 17. Jahrhunderts, in Erinnerung.

Die Analyse beider Werke zeigt ein literarisch differenziertvermitteltes Berufsbild in der arabischen Gegenwartsliteratur. Dilettantismus in „Die amerikanische Enkelin" steht im Gegensatz zu Professionalismus in „Der untreue Übersetzer". Gemeinsam ist beiden Romanen aber, dass sie kein schwarz-weißes Bild vom Translator entwerfen. Denn das Verhalten des Translators schwankt hier zwischen Opportunismus und Altruismus: Zeina möchte ja aus ihrer Mehrsprachigkeit materiellen Nutzen ziehen, und daher bewirbt sie sich um die Tätigkeit als

Dolmetscherin, obwohl sie selbst diese mit Skepsis betrachtet. Sie hofft, dadurch ihrer Mutter und ihrem süchtigen Bruder eine höhere Lebensqualität garantieren zu können. Auch Hameds Verhalten zeigt Widersprüche. Während er am Anfang als ehrlicher, selbstloser Mann erscheint, der die vermeintlich freundliche Gesinnung des Sicherheitsbeamten nach dem Gespräch in der Sicherheitszentrale nicht ausnutzen will und diesen daher nicht um Hilfe bei der Klärung seiner Geschichte mit dem Literaturkritiker bittet, lässt er sich infolge der erlebten Korruption der intellektuellen Elite und der autoritären Machtkontrolle des Regimes missbrauchen und instrumentalisieren. Er schließt eine Übereinkunft mit dem skrupellosen Schriftsteller und unterstützt Plagiate, was gegen die Berufsethik und Moral verstößt und strafbar ist. Hamed handelt eigennützig und erhofft sich davon einen intellektuellen Sieg und Rache an dem großen Literaturkritiker, der seine Karriere und seinen Ruf als Übersetzer ruiniert hat. Am Ende zeigt er Reue, gibt zu, Fehler begangen zu haben und will nun einen neuen Anfang suchen.

Gemeinsam sind beiden Romanen weiterhin die negative Darstellung der Berufsrealität und die Unzufriedenheit mit dem Beruf. Im Irak wird das Dolmetschen als ein zu Depression führender und fragwürdiger Beruf dargestellt, der mit einem tragischen Schicksal enden kann. Auch im zweiten Roman klagt der Übersetzer von Anfang an über sein Leid beim Übersetzen. Sein Konflikt hätte ihn beinahe einen Mord begehen lassen. Am Ende des Romans entscheidet sich der Übersetzer dafür, seinem Leid ein Ende zu bereiten. Er befreit sich von seinen Ketten und gibt seine Karriere als Übersetzer auf. Nun sucht er einen neuen Anfang als freier Schriftsteller. Endlich hat er sich von der „Tyrannei" des Originals befreit, gegen die er immer gekämpft hat.

Die literarische Fiktionalisierung translatorischer Thematik greift zwar in beiden Romanen auf das Stereotyp vom Übersetzer als zerrissene Person und potenzieller Verräter zurück, aber auf unterschiedliche Weise. Schon der Titel des Romans „Der untreue Übersetzer" spricht das Thema an. An der Figur des in drei Übersetzerpseudonyme gespaltenen Hamed, der Verrat am Kunstwerk begeht, werden Begriffe der Treue und des Verrats am Autor zu einer Frage der Loyalität zum bzw. des Hochverrats am Vaterland. Zeina ist auch mit sich selbst uneins und steht zerrissen zwischen den Irakern und Amerikanern, aber sie bleibt bei der Ausübung ihrer Tätigkeit loyal. Der Konflikt zwischen beiden Welten und Identitäten, zwischen denen sie pendelt, ihre Emotionalität und Befangenheit sowie ihre Liebe zu ihren irakischen Verwandten können aus ihr keine Verräterin machen. Zeina respektiert die Verschwiegenheitspflicht des Translators, derer sie sich bewusst ist, und gibt keine geheimen Informationen, an die sie durch ihre Arbeit kommt, an die einanderfeindlich gesinnten Lager weiter. Trotz der Gebundenheit an ihre Ursprungskultur bleibt sie bis zum Ende gegenüber ihren Arbeitgebern loyal.

Die literarische Darstellung beider Hauptfiguren ruft das uralte Bild des Dolmetschers auf dem berühmten altägyptischen Dolmetscherrelief von Haremhab aus dem Neuen Reich in Erinnerung, das den zwischen beiden Seiten stehenden Dolmetscher als klein und gebückt darstellt. Einer solchen Darstellung widerspricht in beiden behandelten Romanen die Gestaltung der Hauptfiguren. Diese wollen nicht klein, meinungs- und machtlos bei der Ausübung ihrer Rolle bleiben. Ihr Verhalten und ihr übersetzerisches Vorgehen kennzeichnen sich durch eine „Umkehr der Schwäche in Macht" (Andres 2008: 388) und eine Grenzüberschreitung der Rolle eines Nur-Übersetzers bzw. Nur-Dolmetschers. Denn ein ohnmächtiges Kommunikationsinstrument wollen Zeina und Hamed nicht bleiben, sie wollen eine Stimme haben. Zeina sieht ihre moralische Aufgabe darin, die machtlosen Iraker zu verteidigen und zu schützen, auch wenn das gegen die in der Berufsethik hochgehaltene Neutralität verstößt. Hameds Vorgehen beim Übersetzen offenbart eine Art Grenzüberschreitung der übersetzerischen Tätigkeit, die Abschaffung des Begriffs der Treue sowie Machtausübung gegenüber dem Autor und seinem Kunstwerk. Diese autoritäre Macht des Übersetzers könnte als eine Art Reaktion auf die autoritäre Macht interpretiert werden, die er im wirklichen Leben und in der Berufspraxis erlebt.

Anhand der Analyse beider Romane zeigt sich auch, dass das vermittelte Bild von der Translation und dem Translator zum Teil mit dem ersten und dritten Grundmuster von Andres im Einklang steht. Im Roman „Die amerikanische Enkelin" überschreitet die Translatorin die Grenze der Neutralität, nicht aus Eigennutz, sondern aus Emotionalität und Befangenheit. Ihr Wunsch, die Machtlosen vor den Mächtigen zu schützen, ist ein moralisches Verhalten und entspricht dem dritten Grundmuster, während der zweite Roman „Der untreue Übersetzer" eher dem ersten Grundmuster entspricht, da der Übersetzer aus Eigennutz, nämlich dem Wunsch, sich an dem Literaturkritiker zu rächen, unmoralisch handelt und seine Macht gegenüber den zu übersetzenden Werken durch Plagiate missbraucht.

Bibliographie

ANDRES, Dörte (2008): *Dolmetscher als literarische Figuren. Vom Identitätsverlust, Dilettanismus und Verrat.* – München: Meidenbauer.

CURRAN, Beverly (2007): „The Embedded Translator: a Coming Out Story". In: SALAMA-CARR, Myriam (Hg.): *Translating and Interpreting Conflict. Approaches to Translation Studies.* – Amsterdam/New York: Editions Rodopi.

DELABASTITA, Dirk & GRUTMANN, Rainer (2005) (Hgg.): *Fictionalising Translation and Multilingualism.* – Antwerpen: Linguistica Antverpiensia 4.

KAINDL, Klaus & KURZ, Ingrid (2005) (Hgg.): *Wortklauber, Sinnverdreher, Brückenbauer? DolmetscherInnen und ÜbersetzerInnen als literarische Geschöpfe.* – Berlin: LIT.

KAINDL, Klaus & KURZ, Ingrid (2008) (Hgg.): *Helfer, Verräter, Gaukler? Das Rollenbild von TranslatorInnen im Spiegel der Literatur.* – Berlin: LIT.

KAINDL, Klaus & KURZ, Ingrid (2010) (Hgg.): *Machtlos, selbstlos, meinungslos? Interdisziplinäre Analysen von ÜbersetzerInnen und DolmetscherInnen in belletristischen Werken.* – Berlin: LIT.

KAINDL, Klaus (2013): „Das Potential des Fictional Turn für die Translationsdidaktik". In: MAYER, Felix & NORD, Britta (Hgg.): *Aus Tradition in die Zukunft. Perspektiven der Translationswissenschaft. Festschrift für Christiane Nord.* – Berlin: Frank&Timme.

KAINDL, Klaus & SPITZL, Karlheinz (2014) (Hgg.): *Transfiction. Research into the realities of translation fiction.* – Amsterdam: John Benjamins Publishing.

PAGANO, Adriana S. (2002): „Translation as Testimony: On Official Histories and Subversive Pedagogies in Cortizar". In: TYMOCZKO, Maria & GENTZLER, Edwin (Hgg.): *Translation and Power.* – Amherst: University of Massachusetts Press.

SALAMA-CARR, Myriam (2007) (Hgg.): *Translating and Interpreting Conflict. Approaches to Translation Studies.* – Amsterdam/New York: Editions Rodopi.

SCHLEIERMACHER, Friedrich (1838): „Ueber die verschiedenen Methoden des Uebersetzens". In: STÖRIG, Hans J. (1973) (Hg.): *Das Problem des Übersetzens.* – Darmstadt: Wissenschaftliche Buchgesellschaft, 38–70.

STEINER, Tina (2009): *Translated People, Translated Texts. Language and Migration in Contemporary African Literature*. – Manchester: St. Jerome.

STRÜMPER-KROBB, Sabine (2009): *Zwischen den Welten. Die Sichtbarkeit des Übersetzers in der Literatur*. – Berlin: Weidler.

TAWFIK, Nahla (2012): „Der Translator als Wanderer zwischen Sprachen und Identitäten. Oder: Der Obergefreite Roth zwischen Wörterbuchtreue und Vaterlandsverrat". In: SALAMA, Dalia Aboul Fotouh, METWALLY, Nadia, EL-DIB, Nahed (Hgg.): *Kairoer Germanistische Studien* (Im Druck). – Kairo: Universitätsverlag.

Internetseiten

AL-ALI, Khadim: *A Portrait of the Translator as a Political Activist*. http://www.academia.edu/7113235/A_Portrait_of_the_Translator_as_a_Political_Activist (25.09.2014)

KAHANE, Eduardo (2007): *Dolmetscher in Konfliktzonen: Die Grenzen der Neutralität*. http://www.aiic.net/ViewPage.cfm/page2692.htm (15.09.2013)

Quellenverzeichnis

HADDAD, Fawwaz: *Almutargim Alchain*. (Der untreue Übersetzer). – Beirut: Riad El-Rayyes.

KACHACHI, Inaam (2010): *Alhafida Alamerikia*. (Die amerikanische Enkelin). – Beirut: Aljadid.

A systematic approach to manipulation in translation
– a case study of Ye Junjian's 1958 translation of H. C. Andersen's tales

Wenjie Li
Guangdong University of Foreign Studies
Wenjie830@gmail.com

Manipulation, a common phenomenon in translation activities, has been attracting scholarly attention since the 1970s. Scholars like André Lefevere, Anton Popovič, Theo Hermans, Gideon Toury, and Susan Bassnett hold a similar view on the manipulative property of translation activities and are known as scholars of the "manipulation school". After the "culture turn" in translation studies, looking into the manipulative shifts in a translated text and exploring the reasons, mainly the ideological, cultural and political, behind them, became a very attractive topic among translation circles. However, because of its multi-faceted nature, manipulation in translation remains an under-explored phenomenon. Most studies are restricted to the investigation of traces of manipulation in the target text. Very few of them are devoted to defining or categorizing manipulation in translation. Moreover, as other topics in translation studies start to arouse academic' interests, the enthusiasm for manipulation research seems to have waned in recent years.

However, as some former studies have shown, manipulation in translation does not solely concern textual shifts or amendments. It is always involved with human agents in a particular cultural, ideological and political context, which determines its nature as a form of social behaviour and further endows translation activity with social nature. Furthermore, the investigation of manipulation in translation can offer an angle to investigate the power relations between the human agents involved in translation activity. Therefore, from a sociological perspective, manipulation in translation deserves systematic and in-depth research. This paper will, on the basis of previous studies, try to propose a model for systematic research on manipulation in translation. Moreover, by referring to the manipulation that takes place in Ye Junjian's 1958 translation of H. C. Andersen's tales, which is part of a research project on the Chinese translation of Andersen's tales, this paper will explicate various forms of manipulation as they appear at difference stages of translation and their influence on the target text and its reception.

The state of research on manipulation in translation

Manipulation, a common phenomenon in translation activities, has been attracting academic attention since the 1970s. Scholars like André Lefevere, Anton Popovič, Theo Hermans, Gideon Toury, Susan Bassnett, Itamar Even-Zohar have noticed that manipulative strategies are often adopted in translation.[1] Some of them even claim that "from the point of view of the target literature all translation implies a degree of manipulation of the source text for a certain purpose" (Hermans 1985: 11). These experts, who hold a similar view on the manipulative property of translation activities, are known as scholars of the "manipulation school" in translation studies. Their studies often take target culture as the point of departure, paying special attention to institutional and ideological factors that have influenced the translation process, especially that of literary translation. Observing and analyzing how manipulation takes place in translation helps them to explicate the influences exercised by these institutional and ideological factors. After the so-called "cultural turn" in translation studies in the 1980s, the "manipulation school" which approaches translation as a cultural and historical phenomenon, gained more and more weight in translation studies. Studies done by Lawrence Venuti (1992), Javier Franco Aixelá (1995), Nitsa Ben-Ari (2002), Ieva Zauberga (2001, 2004), Farzaneh Farahzad (1999, 2003), to name just a few, show that examining the manipulative shifts in a translated text and explor-

---

[1] For a comprehensive account of the theories and ideas about the manipulation in translation, please refer to Hermans' *Translation in Systems: Descriptive and System-oriented Approaches Explained* published in 1999.

ing the reasons, mainly ideological, cultural and political, reason behind them, has become a very attractive topic among translation circles. However, as Aiga Dukāte (2009) points out, manipulation in translation remains an under-explored phenomenon. Because of the multi-faceted nature of this phenomenon, most scholars are more interested in using this concept in their studies rather than defining or categorizing manipulation in translation and restricting their studies mostly to the investigation of the manipulation of the target text. Therefore, although manipulation is one of the most touched topics in translation studies it remains a familiar phenomenon that lacks essential research.

Farahzad has conducted some essential research on manipulation and tried to categorize manipulation in translation. By resorting to Gestalt psychology, she classifies manipulation in translation into conscious and unconscious manipulation (1999). Unconscious manipulation, according to Farahzad, is "the human tendency to perceive the incomplete as complete", which "urges translators to fill in gaps in the source text by adding new parts to it or assuming new relations between parts, in order to come up with a complete picture of it", while conscious manipulation often results from conscious processes "because of various social, political and other factors" (1999: 153). Her way of categorization has later been adopted by Aiga Dukāte's research. Nonetheless, when she explains that unconscious manipulation is manifested through "additions and deletions of parts and assuming new relations between them" (1999: 153), it is apparent that she still focuses on manipulation that leads to shifts in the target text. In 2002, Ben-Ari defines didactic manipulation in her article "The Double Conversion of Ben-Hur: A Case of Manipulative Translation". This type of manipulation can take the form of "direct" or "indirect" manipulation of the translated text and represented by the conversion of "small-scale units", "small-scale omissions" and "large scale-omissions" (Ben-Ari 2002). Evidently, her perspective is still confined to the manipulation of the translated text. In 2004, when Dukāte was a PhD candidate (she was Aiga Kramina then), she published one of her first articles on manipulation in translation. In this article, she discusses the nature of manipulation in translation, explains the causes of manipulation in translation and examines the consequences of manipulative translation strategies. In 2009, Aiga Dukāte published a monograph on manipulation in translation and interpretation in which manipulation in translation is defined based on the definition set out in 1991 by Hermans[2]. Further, manipulation in translation is classified into following categories:

> There are two major types of manipulation: text-external manipulation and text-internal manipulation. Under each of the major two types of manipulation one distinguishes further three types of manipulation: manipulation as improvement, manipulation as handling and manipulation as distortion, which can be either conscious or unconscious. (Dukāte 2009: 89)

Although claiming a type of manipulation to be improvement or distortion of the source text is very subjective, especially when manipulation occurs in a literary translation, Dukāte's classification offers a systemic view of the theoretical thinking behind manipulation in translation. Moreover, she has brought text-external manipulation, a form of manipulation that has seldom attracted academic attention, into the scope of research. However, when Dukāte points out that one has to differentiate between manipulation as process and a product, as a general strategy and a particular strategy, conscious and unconscious manipulation, or text-internal and text-external manipulation, she is actually suggesting more categories of manipulation than that she has categorized earlier. Moreover, due to the limitations of space, Dukāte does not offer any model for the analysis of manipulation. Neither does she give enough space to manipulation in the pre-production and post-production phases in translation nor point out the significant influence that manipulation in these two stages could have on the target text and its reception in the target culture.

As other topics in translation studies start to arouse academic' interests, the upsurge in manipulation research seems decline in recently years. Dukāte's study has not aroused many responses among experts on translation studies and the systematic structure she has proposed has never been tested or improved on by any further study. However, as former studies have shown, manipulation in translation is always connected with socio-political factors and often represents the power relation between the human agents involved in translation. This paper will take a sociological perspective and propose a model for systematic research

---

[2] In "Translational Norms and Correct Translations" published in 1991, Hermans gives his definition of manipulation. According to him, manipulation "bring[s] the target text into line with a particular model and hence a particular correctness notion, and in so doing secure[s] social acceptance, even acclaim" (Hermans 1991: 111).

on manipulation in translation. Furthermore, by referring to instances of manipulation takes place in the Chinese translation of Andersen's tales, this paper will explicate various forms of manipulation that appear at different stages of translation and their influence on the target text and its reception. At the same time, the investigation into the manipulation takes place in Ye's 1958 translation will hopefully also disclose the influence exercised by various human agents on translation activity.

A systematic study of manipulation in translation

In her book, Dukāte defines manipulation in translation as:

The process and product of the translator's handling of a text that results in the adaptation of the text for the target audience, considering the cultural, ideological, linguistic and literary differences between the cultures in contact, which takes place within a particular cultural setting, and is carried out by a human agent, with the consequence of a possible influence of personal or psychological factors upon the end product. (Dukāte 2009: 84)

The term *manipulation in translation* used in this paper will basically be understood in accordance with Dukāte's definition, except that manipulation in this paper is considered a conscious action, which is slightly different from Dukāte's understanding. For her, manipulation in translation can be conscious or unconscious. However, according to the Oxford dictionary "to manipulate" is "to control or use something in a skilful way", which indicates that a manipulative activity must always involve certain purposes. Moreover, to spare the potential risk of being subjective, Dukāte's categorization of manipulation will be adopted critically, which means that this study will not classify manipulation from the perspective of improvement or distortion of source text. Instead, instances of manipulation in translation will be classified according to the various stages of translation they take place in, the different factors that can cause them and the different places they happen. The following part will explain the classification criteria.

I agree with Dukāte that manipulation in translation can take place in all three stages of translation, namely the "pre-production", "production" and "post-production" stages of translation (Dukāte 2009). Hence, there are three types of manipulation: First, pre-production manipulation, which in practice often includes manipulative actions like the selection of text to translate or the selection of translator; second, production manipulation, which is a form of manipulation occurs during the process of translation and often concerns the manipulative strategies applied to the translated text; third, post-production manipulation, which is often implemented through paratexts (reviews, criticisms, interviews, etc.) that appear after the translation process is completed and aim at affecting the reception and interpretation of the translated text.

If we classify manipulation according to the different types of factors that trigger manipulation in translation, it can be categorized into ideological manipulation, cultural manipulation and linguistic manipulation. Ideological manipulation indicates the type of manipulation caused by the political-ideological context of the target culture[3]. Cultural manipulation is a type caused by the effort to bridge the gap between the source culture and target culture. Linguistic manipulation often takes place when the translator tries to adapt his/her translated text to the linguistic norms of the target language.

Further, manipulation in translation can also be classified either as text-internal manipulation, namely "manipulation that takes place within the text", or as text-external manipulation, indicating "manipulation that takes place outside the text" (Dukāte 2009: 86).

In practice, a certain manipulative action could bear the properties of more than one type of manipulation mentioned above. For example, a manipulative action which appears in the post-production stage can be triggered by either an ideological factor or a cultural factor; ideologically-generated manipulation can take place both within the text and outside the text. Therefore, in translation one finds post-production ideological manipulation and post-production cultural manipulation, text-internal ideological manipulation and text-external ideological manipulation. In contrast, some manipulative action never integrates properties of certain categories of manipulation. For instance, text-internal manipulation never takes place in the post-production stage. Therefore, there is no post-

---

[3] As a matter of fact, political ideology composes only part of an ideological system. It is only for the sake of succinctness that "ideological manipulation" is used specifically to indicate the manipulation in translation triggered by political ideological factors in this paper.

production text-internal manipulation. The following table shows how manipulation in translation is sorted according to the criteria explained above.

Manipulation in translation							
Text-internal			Text-external				
Ideological	Cultural	Linguistic	Ideological		Cultural		
Production	Production	Production	Pre-production	Postproduction	Pre-production	Postproduction

Table 1 Types of manipulation in translation

In the next section, various types of manipulation in translation will be discussed by referring to examples from Ye Junjian's complete direct translation of Andersen's tales published in 1958. Moreover, the influence that manipulation in translations has on both the target text and the translated impression of Andersen's tales will also be covered. With this systematic model, this paper hopes to answer questions such as: Who are involved in manipulation? What manipulation strategies are often adopted? What has been manipulated? What are the influences of manipulation?

Case study

In what follows, Ye Junjian's direct translation of Andersen's tales published in 1958 (hereafter referred to as "1958 version") will be used as a case study to illustrate various types of manipulation that could appear in translation activity.

The 16 volumes of 1958 version were published by the New Literary & Art Publishing House in Shanghai in succession from 1957 to 1958. This complete translation is entitled "安徒生童话全集" (The Complete Fairy Tales of Andersen) and consists of 163 tales. It was the first complete direct translation of Andersen's tales in China. It was rendered from *H. C. Andersens Eventyr og Historier*. All four volumes of this collection of tales were published in succession from 1949 to 1952 by Flensteds Forlag, Odense and include illustrations by Vilhelm Pedersen, Lorenz Frølich and Herluf Jensenius. In contrast to the 9 volumes of selected translation published during 1953 and 1954, according to Ye himself, every tale in this version is translated directly from the Danish text and therefore this version is a brand-new translation (Ye 1998: 50). On the flyleaf of each volume is a short summary of the selected tales and a postscript about the year of publication, the Danish title, and the creative motivation of the respective tales as they were originally published in Denmark.

After comparing the Danish STs and Ye's Chinese translations, one can tell that although the Chinese literary norms during this period were quite politicized, one finds very little in the translated texts that echoes this political and ideological tendency. Generally speaking, Ye has made great efforts to keep his translations as close to the original Danish text as possible. Hence, the ideological manipulation during the production process is not overt. There are very few signs of textual manipulation caused by political-ideological factors. For example, Ye hardly tried to amend Andersen's tales that bear religious color or meaning in his translations, although religion was a taboo topic in communist China in the 1950s. He has retained and translated fully and faithfully those parts that praise the mercy and power of God, which is quite a risky choice. However, this does not mean that he is immune to the influence of the mainstream ideology of his time. Instead, he also holds a critical view on the religious belief expressed in Andersen's tales. It is only that he has chosen another way to 'disinfect' his translations and guide his readers, which will be discussed in the latter part of this paper. All in all, it is lucky for Chinese readers as well as for Andersen that Ye has not tried to manipulate the translated texts in accordance with prevailing political and ideological norms. The reason for this choice is rooted in Ye's thoughts on the criteria for good translation, which are inherited mainly from the translation theories initiated by Yan Fu and known as the three principles *Xin*, *Da*, *Ya* (faithfulness, intelligibility, and elegance).[4] In "关于文学翻译的一点体会" (A Re-

---

[4] Ye Junjian has never engaged in any theoretical research on translation. However, he expressed his thoughts on literary translation in two essays. One is "关于文学翻译的一点体会" (A Reflection on Literary Translation) published in 1989. It was re-titled "谈文学作品的翻译" (On Literary Translation) and published in "名家翻译经验谈" (Reflections on Translation by Famous Translators) in 1998 with minimal amendments. The other is "安徒生童话的翻译" (On the Translation of Andersen's Fairy Tales) published in 1999. In addition, in some of the forewords to his translation works we can also find his opinions on translation.

flection on Literary Translation), Ye claims that Yan Fu's criteria should still be the standards for literary translation in communist China. Faithfulness, for Ye, is the supreme principle of translation.

On the other hand, Ye understands that a literary work usually provoke various interpretations in different times and among different readerships. The uncertainty of the meaning of a literary work makes it almost impossible to produce a translation that is completely equivalent to its source text. Moreover, word for word translations cannot be successful in translation, especially when it comes to translating Western literary works, because of the differences between the two cultures and the linguistic gaps between Chinese and Western languages. Therefore, the criterion of *Xin*, according to Ye, actually requires that a translator tries his/her best to transfer the content and message contained in the original literary work to his/her translation as closely and completely as possible, but not necessarily all the linguistic features of the source text. The result of this interpretation of *Xin* is that although Ye has tried his best to transfer the stylistic features in Andersen's tales, one can still find traces of text-internal linguistic and cultural manipulation in Ye's translations. For example, Ye sometimes would add translator notes to his translations to explain cultural and religious terms or stylistic features in Andersen's tales. Sometimes, he would also try to correct Andersen's mistakes in the notes. In Andersen's *Nattergalen*, the courtier said "Tsing-pe!" when the emperor ordered his to find Nightingale. Ye translates this short answer into "钦佩' and gives a note to it, stating that "Tsing-pe" actually is a transliteration of "钦佩' (Pinyin: Qingpei). Evidently, Ye is trying to explain the stylistic feature in Andersen's tale with this note. Another instance of text-internal cultural manipulation in Ye's "夜莺' (The Nightingale) is the note he adds to "咖啡会'. In this note, Ye first explains that "Kafeeselskab" in the original text indicates a popular social gathering in Northern Europe. He continues to point out that in China people usually drink tea on similar occasions and that Andersen has made a mistake in his tale.[5] It is evident that Ye tries to guide his readers here. In addition to text-internal manipulation related to cultur-

---

[5] The original text in Ye's note is "请朋友吃咖啡谈天 (Kafeeselskab) 是北欧的一种社交习惯；中国一般的习惯是吃茶。作者在这儿弄错了。" (Vol. 3: 135), meaning "inviting friends for coffee and chatting (Kafeselskab) is a social custom in Nordic countries; the Chinese custom is normally tea-drinking. The author has made a mistake here".

al factors, text-internal linguistic manipulation also appears in Ye's translation because of the syntactic difference between the Danish and Chinese language. The comparison between two excerpts from Andersen's "Den grimme Ælling" and Ye's "丑小鸭" will help illustrate this:

Der var saa deiligt ude paa Landet; det var Sommer, Kornet stod guult, Havren grøn, Høet var reist i Stakke nede i de grønne Enge, og der gik Storken paa sine lange, røde Been og snakkede ægyptisk, for det Sprog havde han lært af sin Moder.[6]
Gloss: It was so beautiful out in the country; it was summer, the grain stood in gold color, the oats were greet, the hay was piled in stacks in the green meadows, and the stork went with his long red legs chattered in Egyptian, the language he had learned from his mother.
乡下真是非常美丽。这正是夏天！小麦是金黄的，燕麦是绿油油的。干草在绿色的牧场上堆成垛，鹳鸟用它又长又红的腿子在散着步，噜嗦地讲着埃及话。① 这是它从妈妈那儿学到的一种语言。
①因为据丹麦的民间传说，鹳鸟是从埃及飞来的。(Ye 1958, Vol. 4:6)
Gloss: It is really beautiful in the countryside. It is summer! The wheat is in golden yellow color, the oats were green. The hay was piled in stacks, the stork is walking with his long red legs, chatting in Egyptian. This is a language he has learned from his mother.

The original text is composed of long sentences with simple and loose syntactic structure, which is typical Andersenian style and is grammatically acceptable according to Danish syntax.[7] However, it is not possible to transplant this sentence structure into Chinese because a Chinese sentence is often organized to express one sense group, which means a sentence is complete and finished when a message has been expressed thoroughly. A new sentence will usually be introduced when one starts to express another message. Therefore, although Ye has done his best in keeping the sequence of all the sentence periods and transferring the S+V structure in each sentence period of Andersen's text, he

---

[6] The original texts of Andersen's tales in this paper are all retrieved from Arkiv for Dansk Litteratur online (www.adl.dk), which are based on *Eventyr vol. 1–7*, published by DSL/Hans Reitzel from 1963 to 1990 and edited by Erik Dal.

[7] According to the explanation offered by ordnet.dk, "sætning" (sentence) means "rækkefølge af ord som udgør en afgrænset helhed indeholdende subjekt og verbal, og som fremsætter et udsagn, et spørgsmål eller en opfordring" (sequence of words which form a distinct whole containing subject and verb and makes a statement, a question or an invitation), which stresses the formal completeness of a sentence. A sentence is complete when the form is complete and a compound sentence could be constructed by several sentences with several sense groups.

still has to divide the original text into several short sentences in the translated text.

Another type of manipulation in translation in Ye's translation is text-external manipulation. Given the different factors that have led to this manipulation and the different stages of translation at which it occurs, this type could be further divided into four sub-categories, namely text-external ideological manipulation in the pre-production stage, text-external ideological manipulation in the post-production stage, text-external cultural manipulation in the pre-production stage, and text-external cultural manipulation the in post-production stage. The following part of this paper will illustrate the strategies used for these four categories of manipulation, their manifestation in translation and their influence on the translated impression of Andersen's tales.

The pre-production stage in translation usually relates to the selection of a text to be translated. That is to say, the texts to be translated are never chosen randomly. There are always certain powers and influences that come into play in the selection process for different reasons. This also applies to Ye's case, especially in the occasion that his translation was done in period with dense political atmosphere. Those who are familiar with the political environment in China during the 1950s would know that after the establishment of the PRC, China became a member of the socialist camp and adopted the 'leaning to one side' policy from the 1950s. The Soviet Union, as the "older brother" and the leader of all communist countries, became the idol of Chinese people. Eventually, the Soviet literature replaced Western literature and occupied the central position of translated literature in China. According to statistics offered in Wolfgang Bauer's book (Bauer & Institut für Asienkunde 1964: 67), during the period between October 1949 and July 1960, 83.8% of all translated books were originally written in Russian, and only 16.2% in other languages; while from 1910 to 1935 only 361 out of 3888 translated books (9%) were Russian. However, Andersen's tales, regarded as fairy tales from a capitalist western country, were still favored by New Literary & Art Publishing House, a newly established state-owned publishing house, which seems quite extraordinary. In fact, Bauer's statistics show that although the number of books translated from Western languages fell sharply after 1949, in terms of overall readership, H. C. Andersen remained the most popular foreign writer in China during this period. According to Bauer's survey,

Andersen is on the top of the list of most popular authors from 1949 to 1960 in communist China. The number of editions of Chinese Andersen translations during this period was 64, and the total number of printed copies exceeded 1,173,500). (Bauer and Institut für Asienkunde 1964) The reason behind his popularity in communist China can be explained by the fact that Andersen occupied fourth place on the list of the most popular Western authors in Soviet Russia (from 1918 to 1957). As represented by the comment from Nikolai Nikolai Dobrolyubov, Soviet revolutionary critics often considered Andersen's works as "an example of the fusion of realism and fantasy, and in an extremely poetic manner" (Rossel 1996: 279). In fact, this interpretation was also an overwhelming and mainstream one among both Chinese translators and readers of this period. The favour of the "big brother" somehow guaranteed the political correctness of translating Andersen's tales. Moreover, as the son of a shoemaker, Andersen was seen as a 'writer of the people' who sympathized with the poor and wrote for them. This is also why his tales were still permitted to be translated and published when most western literary works had lost their popularity and legitimacy in China.

In addition, the review of Andersen's tales is another form of ideological manipulation. In 1955, on the occasion of the 150th anniversary of Andersen's birth, critics like Chen Bochui and Ye Junjian wrote a series of reviews to commemorate this great fairy tale writer. Andersen's talent of telling stories from children's point of view, the poetic beauty and the colloquial style in his tales are still highly praised in these reviews. In addition, Andersen's tales were also praised as great realistic works rooted in reality. However, Chinese critics were not comfortable with the religious undertones embedded in Andersen's tales. Both Chen and Ye stressed this in their articles published in 1955. They regarded these religious undertones as limitations and defects in Andersen's tales, ascribing them to the fact that Andersen lived in a capitalist and religious society and his view of the world was inevitably influenced by his time. Hence, they all stressed that Andersen's tales should not be received uncritically. These views had not only secured the legitimacy of translating Andersen's tales but also helped mould the image of him and his tales among Chinese readers. From the reviews published later, we learn that these views on Andersen's tales were widely accepted up until the late 1970s. Therefore, text-external ideological manipulation in the pre-production stage of translation not only determines whether a source text will be translated in the first place, but can also influence the interpretation of the source text as well as the translated text.

Text-external ideological manipulation also occurs in the post-production stage of Ye's translation. Compared with text-internal manipulation, this type of manipulation does not seek to influence the translated text directly but aims at manipulating the interpretation and reception of the translated text. As mentioned above, in Ye's translation of Andersen's tales, ideological manipulation does not occur evidently during the production stage altering the target texts. However, that is not to say that the 1958 version is entirely immune from political influence. In fact, in the postscripts of the 1958 version, Ye has tried to influence readers with political and ideological interpretations, a common pattern of literary criticism after the Anti-Rightist Movement in 1957.

There are already hints of ideological interpretation, between the lines of the postscripts following the translated texts of every volume, which are in conformity with the socio-political atmosphere in China at the time. For example, in the postscript of volume 11, Ye writes in the last paragraph that:

From these tales... We can also trace the development of his democratic ideas: he eulogizes people who were born low and poor but have contributed to human wellbeing (for example in the "Two Brothers" and "The Old Church Bell"), and to rustic and simple-hearted countrymen (for example in "What the Old Man Does is Always Right")... . In the Ice Maiden, Andersen starts to express his suspicions about God because God fails to resolve people's problems in real life – through this tale his disillusionment is subtly expressed. (Ye 1958: 185–186)[8]

The atheistic interpretation of these tales from the perspective of historical materialism is expressed quite explicitly in this paragraph. Moreover, this ideological manipulation is also represented by the translator's preface to "安徒生童话选集" (Selected Fairy Tales of Andersen), which is a collection of tales published shortly after the publication of the last volume of Ye Junjian's 1958 version. In this preface, Ye introduces Andersen as a writer born into a proletar-

---

[8] The original text is in Chinese. The quotation here is my translation. All the quotations from Chinese critics and translators used in this paper are my translations if not otherwise stated.

ian family and has native sympathy with poor people. Moreover, Ye reminds his readers to resist the negative influence that blind faith in God could have. The following excerpt from this preface will illustrate this manipulative strategy more explicitly:

> Through these characters (in his tales), he has exposed many unfair phenomena in an unfair society: the ruling class leads an extravagant and luxurious life while the working people lead a diligent but impoverished life. For the former, he has depicted and satirised their stupidity; for the latter he has described enthusiastically their sincerity and frankness. (Ye 1958 in Wang 2005: 88)

Furthermore, Ye also instructs his readers in this preface how to interpret specific tales. He tells them that the clergyman in "Great Claus and Little Claus" can be seen as a corrupt hypocrite who tries to seduce the peasant's wife. Ye believes that through "Great Claus and Little Claus" Andersen shows his readers "what effect money could have in a class society": "For money the two neighbours with the same first name become deadly enemies and adopt every means to entrap each other." (Ye 1958 in Wang 2005: 84). Ye also states that Andersen has integrated reality into his tales exposing the essence of a class society. Evidently, such interpretation performs the function of reading guidance and will affect readers' reception of translation.

Therefore, in Ye's case, we can see that ideological factors do not always influence translation practice by directly manipulating the source text. They can also be apparent in paratexts like prefaces, postscripts, comments, notes, etc., which relate to the translated text. Through these paratexts the translator becomes 'visible', trying to manipulate his readers by offering 'the standard' interpretation of Andersen's tales. In contrast to textual manipulation, Ye's approach to manipulation mostly avoids altering the translated texts themselves, but nevertheless casts significant influence on the readership.

The analysis of text-external ideological manipulation in pre- and post-production stage of translation shows that the socio-political environment of the 1950s requires the majority of critics and translators, as part of the readership, to focus on and magnify some features of Andersen's tales which accorded with the controlling ideology at the time, while ignoring other features that were in conflict with socio-political norms. The translated impression of Andersen was shaped jointly by mainstream interpretations in this particular era as well as by selected facts about him and his tales. In brief, socio-political influence manipulated the interpretations of Andersen and his tales, and further manipulated Andersen's image in China.

Besides ideological manipulation, cultural factors have also shed their influence on Ye's translation in both pre-production and post-production stages. Ye's motivation for retranslating all the tales directly and solely from the Danish texts can give us clues about the cultural factors that have manipulated his direct translation of Andersen's tales. In an article published in 1999, Ye states that he planned to "transplant all of Andersen's tales to China to enrich the literature available to Chinese children and provide reference points for Chinese authors" (Ye 1999: 50). His motivation reminds us that until as late as the 1950s original Chinese literature for children had never been able to marginalize translated children's literature. Andersen's tales were considered to be a form of compensation for the unfruitful original children's literature in China. The unfruitful native children's literature was a cultural factor that triggered the retranslation of Andersen's tales.

Additionally, the criticisms on Andersen's tales during this period also impacted Ye's translation. In an article published in 1957, Chen Bochui, a famous critic and writer of children's literature gives his comments on Andersen's literary achievement:

He (Andersen) wrote poetry, plays, as well as novels. He was worse than merely unsuccessful in these fields – he was a total failure. However, when he selected themes from Scandinavian, and especially from Danish folk tales, to create fairy tales, (…), he won great success. (Chen 1957: 25)

Chen's opinions are evidently inherited from the reviews on Andersen's tales during the "May-fourth Movement", when most Chinese critics agreed that Andersen's tales represent his highest literary achievement. But Chen takes a step further in asserting that Andersen's other literary creations are failures. In fact, later in 1958 and 1978[9] Ye expressed a similar opinion on Andersen's liter-

---

[9] In the translator's preface of "安徒生童话选" (A Selection of Fairy Tales of Andersen) published in 1958, Ye declares that "his (Andersen's) major works are fairy tales, and his talent is fully exerted and developed only through this genre" (Wang, 2005: 84). In the

ary career, confirming that Andersen's tales have always been valued more than his other literary creations in China. Anyway, criticisms like this prevailed among critics and translators in the 1950s and to a certain extent prevented Ye from including Andersen's other writings in his 1958 translation. As Ye's 1958 version becomes popular among Chinese readers, Andersen's image as a master of fairy tales is enhanced, while his other identities as novelist, poet, etc. remain under-recognized in China.

The cultural manipulation of Andersen's tales is also evident if considering the selection of Ye's translations into the Chinese textbook. According to Shen Dan (2005), tales like "卖柴的小女孩儿" (The Little Match-selling Girl) were started to be selected into Chinese textbook since the early 1960s. With the promotion of the education system, Andersen's tales, together with Ye Junjian's translations, achieved canonized status in the Chinese literary system. Thus, text-external cultural manipulation in the post-production stage has also affected the reception of the translated text as well as the source text in the target culture.

Conclusion

From Ye Junjian's case, it is apparent that manipulation in translation takes place at all stages of translation. In addition, manipulation in translation does not solely concern textual shifts or amendments. Criticism of a translation itself and its source text, the preface and postscript attached to a translated text, promotion or banishment by governmental institutions, and translation instructions prescribed by publishing houses could all represent text-external strategies of manipulation. These manipulative strategies are usually conducted with certain purposes in mind, and often jointly model the image of a source text and its author in the recipient culture. Moreover, Ye's case also reveals that manipulative strategies are always carried out by the human agents involved in translation activity. These agents include the author, translator, patronage, and readership in a

---

1978 version, which is actually a reprint of Ye's 1958 translation, Ye expresses the similar opinion and states that "(…) all the efforts he made on literary and artistic creation, include his failures, are actually the preparation for this 'immortal work'" (Ye 1978: VI–VII).

particular cultural, ideological and political context, making manipulation in translation a form of social behavior, which further emphasizes the social nature of translation activities. Furthermore, Ye's case also shows that if we analyse translation from a sociological perspective, an in-depth and systematic approach to researching manipulation in translation can offer an angle to investigate the power relations between the human agents involved in translation activity.

References

AIXELÁ, Javier Franco. (1995): "Specific Cultural Items and Their Translation". In: JANSEN, Peter (ed.): *Translation and the Manipulation of Discourse. Selected Papers of the CERA Research Seminars in Translation Studies 1992– 1993*. CETRA-The Leuven Research Center for Translation, Communication and Cultures, 109–125.

BAUER, W. and Institut für Asienkunde (Hamburg, Germany) (1964): *Western Literature and Translation Work in Communist China.* – Frankfurt am Main: A. Metzne.

BEN-ARI, Nitsa (2002): "The Double Conversion of Ben-Hur: A Case of Manipulative Translation", *Target* 14 (2), 263–302.

CHEN, Bochui (1955, April 02): "向安徒生学习什么"[What should we learn from Andersen]. *"人民日报' [People's Daily]*.

CHEN, Bochui (1955, May 05): "安徒生童话的艺术——纪念安徒生诞生一百五十周年' [The art of Andersen's fairy tales – in memory of Andersen's 150th birthday]. *"大公报' [Ta Kung Pao]*.

CHEN, Bochui (1957): "试淡童话' [A discussion of fairy tales]. In: CHEN, Bochui (ed.): *"儿童文学简论' [A Brief Discussion of Children's Literature]*. – Wuhan: Changjiang Literature and Art Publishing House, 22–37.

DUKĀTE, Aiga (2009): *Translation, Manipulation, and Interpreting.* – Frankfurt am Main: Peter Lang.

FARAHZAD, Farazaneh and ALLAMEH, Tabatabal: (1999). *A Gestalt Approach to Manipulation.* – Copenhagen: Museum Tusculanum Press University of Copenhagen.

HERMANS, Theo (1991): "Translational Norms and Correct Translations". In: VAN LEUVEN-ZWART, K. & NAAIJKENS, T. (eds.). *Translation Studies: The State of the Art* – Amsterdam/Atlanta: John Benjamins Publishing, 155–170.

HERMANS, Theo (1999): *Translation in Systems: Descriptive and System-oriented Approaches Explained.* – Manchester: St. Jerome Publishing.

ROSSEL, Sven Hakon (ed.) (1996): *Hans Christian Andersen: Danish Writer and Citizen of the World.* – Amsterdam/Atlanta: Rodopi

SHEN, Da'an (2005): "今天我们怎样读'卖火柴的小女孩'" [How to Interpret "The Little Match-selling Girl" Today]. "基础教育" *[Fundamental Education]* (7,8), 51–52.

VENUTI, Lawrence (1992): "Introduction". In: Venuti, Lawrence (ed.): *Rethinking Translation: Discourse, Subjectivity, Ideology.* – London/New York: Routledge, 1–17.

YE, Junjian (1955): "安徒生和他的作品" [Andersen and his works]. "人民文学" *[People's Literature]* 5, 107–110.

YE, Junjian (1958): "译者前言" [The translator's preface]. In: "安徒生童话选集" *[A Selection of Andersen's Fairy Tales] (16 Vol.).* – Shanghai: New Literary & Art Publishing House.

YE, Junjian (1978): "译者前言" [The translator's preface]. In: "安徒生童话全集" *[The Complete Andersen's Fairy Tales].* – Shanghai: Shanghai Translation Publishing House.

YE, Junjian (1989): "关于文学翻译的一点体会" [A reflection on literary translation]. In: WANG, Shoulan (ed.): "当代文学翻译百家谈" *[One Hundred Contemporary Translators on Literary Translation].* – Beijing: Beijing University Press, 112–126.

YE, Junjian (1999): "安徒生童话的翻译" [On the translation of Andersen's fairy tales]. In: ZHOU, Jing (ed.): "东方赤子大家丛书 叶君健卷" *[The Oriental Great Masters: A Volume for Ye Junjian].* – Beijing: Sino-culture Press, 48–52.

ZAUBERGA, Ieva. (2001): "Ideological Dimension in Translation". In: VEISBERGS, Andrejs (ed.): *Contrastive and Applied Linguistics 640.* – Riga: University of Latvia, 113–122.

ZAUBERGA, Ieva. (2004): *Theoretical Tools for Professional Translators.* – Riga: N.I.M. S.

Der Krieg mit den Mol(o)chen: Politik und Ideologie in der Rezeption eines tschechischen Romans in Portugal

Jaroslav Špirk, Ph.D.[1]
Institut für Translatologie, Philosophische Fakultät der Karlsuniversität, Prag
Jaroslav.Spirk@seznam.cz

This paper deals with the second-hand Portuguese translations of Karel Čapek's War with the Newts *(1936), an early masterpiece of science fiction with strong political undertones: a warning against fascism and Nazism. All of the three target texts (1965, 1979 and 2009) are indirect translations, each with a different mediating text as its source. The paper discusses the political, historical and cultural circumstances under which the three translations were made and subsequently analyses the paratexts as the most striking loci of the books' communication with the extra-textual world. For reasons of space, the translations themselves are discussed only briefly by way of supporting the main thesis of the paper.*

Der Tscheche, der Science Fiction schreibt: aber nicht nur

Karel Čapek (1890–1938) war einer der vielfältigsten tschechischen Künstler der ersten Hälfte des 20. Jahrhunderts. Er verdiente seinen Lebensunterhalt zuvorderst als Journalist, war aber gleichzeitig Fotograf, Übersetzer, Dramatiker und einer der wichtigsten tschechischen Schriftsteller überhaupt. Seine Prosa, Dramen, Reiseberichte sowie Kinderbücher gehören zu dem Feinsten, was die tschechische Literatur zu bieten hat. Auch wenn er seine Werke zwischen 1910 und 1938 schuf, wird er bis heute gelesen – nicht (nur) als Klassiker, sondern als

---

[1] An der Forschung für diesen Artikel beteiligte sich auch meine Ehefrau, Edita Spirkova, der dafür mein aufrichtiger Dank gebührt.

ein Intellektueller, der uns, quer durch die sozialen Schichten, noch im 21. Jahrhundert mit beklemmender Aktualität, beißender Satire und menschenfreundlichem Humor anspricht, und dessen Sprache nicht veraltet ist. Zwischen 1932 und 1938 wurde er mehrmals für den Nobelpreis für Literatur vorgeschlagen.[2]

Im Ausland ist Čapek reduktiv vor allem als Science-Fiction-Autor bekannt und fast alle Quellen geben ebenfalls an, dass er in seinem Theaterstück *R.U.R.* das inzwischen zum Internationalismus gewordene Wort Roboter geschaffen habe. Das, jedoch, ist umstritten: die Erfindung des Wortes wird eigentlich seinem Bruder Josef zuerkannt.[3] Selbst die *Tentative List of Representative Works of World Literature* der UNESCO (1972)[4] erwähnt nur *R.U.R.* und *Der Krieg mit den Molchen* als die einzigen Werke Čapeks, die zur Weltliteratur zählen.

Dabei sind bspw. Čapeks Romantrilogie *Hordubal, Der Meteor, Ein gewöhnliches Leben* (tsch. 1933–34), sein Drama *Die Mutter* (1938), sein Reisebericht *Seltsames England* (1924), sein als Buch erschienenes Interview mit dem ersten tschechoslowakischen Präsidenten *Gespräche mit Masaryk* (1928–35) oder seine *Märchen* (1932) glanzvolle Beispiele für die erstaunliche Breite seines künstlerischen Talents.

Sogar als Übersetzer hat er sich einen Namen gemacht. In seiner 1920 erschienenen Übersetzung moderner französischer Poesie (von Baudelaire bis Apollinaire) beeinflusste er mit seinem Stil mehrere einheimische Dichter (z.B. Vítězslav Nezval).

Das Buch wird übersetzt: wiederholt

Der Krieg mit den Molchen (tsch. *Válka s Mloky*), veröffentlicht zum ersten Mal in Fortsetzungen in der Prager Zeitung *Lidové noviny* von 1935 bis 1936, ist das wohl am häufigsten übersetzte Buch Čapeks.[5] Es wurde u.a. ins Katalanische,

---

[2] Vgl. bspw. hier http://kramerius.mzk.cz/search/i.jsp?pid=uuid:9a7cee03-559c-438c-8e2f-19f4f56169c0 (31.08.2014).
[3] Vgl. http://blog.abchistory.cz/cl97-karel-capek-o-slove-robot.htm (31.08.2014).
[4] Siehe http://unesdoc.unesco.org/images/0000/000012/001229EB.pdf (31.08.2014).
[5] Für 2015 ist sogar eine Verfilmung geplant (Regie: Agnieszka Holland, Tomáš Krejčí), siehe http://www.csfd.cz/film/261585-valka-s-mloky/videa/ (31.08.2014).

Ukrainische, Dänische, Norwegische (Bokmål), Isländische, Hebräische, Usbekische, Japanische und Esperanto übersetzt.

Im Gegensatz zu kanonischen Werken großer Literaturen (etwa *Hamlet* oder *Faust*) ist es eher selten der Fall, dass es von einem Buch einer kleineren bzw. mittelgroßen Literatur wie der tschechischen mehrere Übersetzungen in den großen Sprachen gibt. Doch vom *Krieg mit den Molchen* existieren zwei Übersetzungen ins Deutsche (1937 von Julius Mader, 1964 von Eliška Glaserová, 1985 gründlich überarbeitet und z.T. neu übersetzt von Mirek Ort); zwei Übersetzungen ins Englische (1937 von Marie und Robert Weatherall, 1985 von Ewald Osers); mehrere Übersetzungen ins Spanische (1944 von Maurício Amster in Santiago de Chile, 1945 von Carmen Díez de Oñate und Mildred Forrester, 1965 von Anna Falbrová, 2010 von Helena Voldan in Buenos Aires), wenn auch nur eine im Französischen (1961 von Claudia Ancelot).

Der Krieg mit den Molchen wird weltweit und wiederholt rezipiert, wobei einer der vielen Gründe dafür zu sein scheint, dass es sich um keine simple Science-Fiction-Story handelt, sondern um eine Dystopie, die zugleich als prophezeiende Allegorie für den Faschismus und Nazismus gilt, die beide bereits 1935 ihre dunklen Schatten vorauswarfen. Sowohl das Werk als auch seine Rezeption sind daher zutiefst politisch.

Das Buch gelangt nach Portugal: auf Umwegen

In Portugal ist *Der Krieg mit den Molchen* das am häufigsten übersetzte Buch der tschechischen Literatur. Kein anderes Buch eines tschechischen Autors wurde dreimal in die portugiesische Sprache übersetzt (vgl. Špirk 2014). Das Verblüffende dabei ist, dass keine der portugiesischen Übersetzungen direkt aus dem Original übertragen wurde und dass auch noch jeder ein anderer Ausgangstext als Vorlage diente. Als da wären:

- *A GUERRA DAS SALAMANDRAS*, veröffentlicht 1965 vom Verlag Livros do Brasil; aus der ersten englischen Übersetzung von M. und R. Weatherall (1937) ins Portugiesische übertragen von Lima de Freitas;
- *A guerra das salamandras*, veröffentlicht 1979 vom Verlag Caminho, nachgedruckt 1985; aus der (einzigen) französischen Übersetzung von

Claudia Ancelot (1961) ins Portugiesische übertragen von Mário de Sousa;
- *A Guerra das Salamandras*, veröffentlicht 2009 vom Verlag Publicações Europa-América, aus der zweiten englischen Übersetzung von Ewald Osers (1985) ins Portugiesische übertragen von Isabel Neves.

Wir haben hier ein hochinteressantes Phänomen vor Augen: ein Buch, das für wichtig genug gehalten wird, dass es immer wieder übersetzt bzw. nachgedruckt wird, wird nie direkt aus dem Original übersetzt. Und das, obwohl dieses Werk offensichtlich als ein kanonisches betrachtet wird – der Verlag Publicações Europa-América publiziert das Buch in der Buchreihe *Grandes Clássicos do Século XX* (Große Klassiker des 20. Jahrhunderts).

Damit hängt natürlich zusammen, dass es in Portugal kein Institut für die tschechische Sprache gibt, dass man Tschechisch nirgendwo in Portugal studieren kann, dass es keine in Portugal veröffentlichten oder zur Verfügung stehenden tschechisch-portugiesischen Wörterbücher gibt, dass es, kurzum, keine Portugiesen gibt, die aus dem Tschechischen übersetzen.

Allerdings heißt das nicht, dass in Portugal niemand aus dem Tschechischen ins Portugiesische übersetzen könnte. Unter den in Portugal lebenden Tschechen gibt es zwei Übersetzerinnen, die jeweils Václav Havel (Anna de Almeidová) und Bohumil Hrabal (Ludmila Dismánová) der portugiesischen Leserschaft nähergebracht haben. Almeidová lebt in Lissabon, Dismánová in Porto, beide sind als literarische Übersetzerinnen und als prominente Vermittlerinnen zwischen der tschechischen und der portugiesischen Kultur bekannt.

2009 kann also ein portugiesischer Verlag nicht behaupten, eine direkte Übersetzung aus dem Tschechischen wäre nicht möglich. Es gab offensichtlich einen anderen Grund – aller Wahrscheinlichkeit nach den Kostenpunkt: eine Übersetzung aus einer großen Sprache ist gewöhnlich billiger als eine aus einer kleine(re)n. Die Auswahl an ÜbersetzerInnen ist größer und der Skaleneffekt drückt die Preise.

Anders verhielt es sich bei den beiden Übersetzungen aus dem 20. Jahrhundert: 1965 lebte nur ein (kulturell aktiver) Tscheche in Portugal, Jorge (František) Listopad (geboren 1921 in Prag), seinen eigenen Worten nach tschechischer Dichter und portugiesischer Dramatiker, der Poesie ausschließlich auf

Tschechisch und seine Dramen lediglich auf Portugiesisch verfasst. Über das Übersetzen sagte er 2004 in einem Interview für den Tschechischen Rundfunk (das seltsamerweise nur auf Französisch zu finden ist):

J'ai essayé de faire des traductions, mais je n'aime pas traduire. Quand je traduis, j'écris une autre chose. Je crois que je ne suis pas doué. En plus, j'essaie de découvrir de nouvelles choses, et la traduction c'est une espèce de perfection technique qui ne m'intéresse pas tellement.[6]

Listopad selbst übersetzte auch nur ein einziges literarisches Werk, sein eigenes Essay *Tristan oder Der Verrat des Intellektuellen* (zum ersten Mal veröffentlicht 1954 in Wien).

Das Buch lebt sich in Portugal ein: insgeheim

Als der Verleger und Gründer (1944) von *Livros do Brasil*, António Augusto de Souza-Pinto, 1965 beschloss, Čapeks *Krieg mit den Molchen* ins Portugiesische übersetzen zu lassen, war Salazar noch Portugals Premierminister und der *Estado Novo* in vollem Gange. Ein Buch von jenseits des Eisernen Vorhangs zu veröffentlichen war damals eine riskante Angelegenheit. Im Gegensatz zur Presse, bei welcher die Vorzensur angewandt wurde, galt bei Büchern die Nachzensur. Es lag also in der Verantwortung des Verlegers, bei seinem Publikationsplan vorwegzunehmen, was vom Regime als schädlich betrachtet werden, genauer: den Zensoren missfallen könnte. Im schlimmsten Falle riskierte er, dass seine Firma für bankrott erklärt und geschlossen wird.

Wenn man in einem unlängst faschistischen, nun korporativistischen Regime ein Buch publizieren wollte, das ein offensichtlicher Affront gegen den Faschismus darstellte, musste man sehr vorsichtig sein, um nicht aufzufallen. Das sieht man in erster Linie auf dem Buchumschlag, dem wichtigsten Paratext von allen. Der Übersetzer Lima de Freitas (1927–1998), der ebenfalls Maler war, hat auch das Bild für den Buchumschlag angefertigt.[7] Sonst steht darauf aber nur:

---

[6] Siehe http://www.radio.cz/fr/rubrique/literature/frantisek-listopad-lecrivain-entre-la-tchequie-et-le-portugal (31.08.2014).

[7] Siehe http://coleccaoargonauta.blogspot.cz/2011/09/n-102-guerra-das-salamandras.html (31.08.2014).

Uma obra-prima de antecipação
do clássico checo
Karel Capek
A GUERRA DAS SALAMANDRAS

Colecção Argonauta

„Ein prophetisches Meisterwerk des tschechischen Klassikers, Karel Capek, *Der Krieg mit den Molchen*, Buchreihe Argonaut" [Band Nr. 102]. Der „tschechische Klassiker" ist entsprechend klein, um nicht allzu viel Aufmerksamkeit auf sich zu lenken. Auf der Rückseite steht schon die Werbung für das nächste Buch.

Die Buchreihe selbst lenkt von dem politischen Potenzial, das dem Roman innewohnt, ab: es ist eine Science-Fiction-Reihe, welche in diesem Genre in Portugal zwar Pionierarbeit leistete und allgemein beträchtlichen Einfluss gewann (das erste Buch erschien 1953; der 553. Band im Jahre 2004), aber der politische Aspekt blieb verkappt. Čapek befindet sich in Gesellschaft von anderen Science-Fiction-Autoren wie Clifford D. Simak, Ray Bradbury, Issac Asimov, Arthur C. Clarke usw.

Ein weiteres Werk Čapeks, sein berühmtes Theaterstück *R.U.R.*, erschien sogar bereits im 100. Gedenkband dieser Reihe (1965), zusammen mit Erzählungen von Jules Verne, H. G. Wells, Daniel Keys, Arthur C. Clarke, Ray Bradbury (ausgewählt und übersetzt auch von Lima de Freitas). Und der Vollständigkeit halber muss noch ergänzt werden, dass Livros do Brasil in der Buchreihe *Miniaturas* (Band Nr. 140) einen anderen Science-Fiction-Roman Čapeks veröffentlichte: *Das Absolutum oder die Gottesfabrik* (1962 als *A fábrica de absoluto*, ins Portugiesische aus der französischen Übersetzung übertragen von M. Gomes dos Santos).

Čapek war also kein Neuling im Verlag *Livros do Brasil* und die Buchreihe sicherte einen gewissen Schutz vor der Zensur, denn Science Fiction wurde als eine Art Märchen für Erwachsene, als literarischer Schund für das (einfache) Volk betrachtet – nicht wirklich gefährlich für das Regime.

Das Buch landete trotzdem einige Monate später, am 1. Februar 1966, bei der Zensurbehörde. Der entsprechende Bericht Nr. 7689 befindet sich zwar nicht mehr im Torre do Tombo, dem portugiesischen Nationalarchiv in Lissabon, aber diese Information können wir dem nächsten Zensurbericht, der sich mit Čapeks *Krieg mit den Molchen* befasst, entnehmen, dem Bericht Nr. 8059 vom 2. Mai 1967, in dem steht:

Por ordem superior fica cancelado o despacho exarado em 1-2-1966 no Relatório de Leitura nº 7689 referente ao livro acima referido.[8]

Dies lässt vermuten, dass der erste, verschollene Bericht ein Verbot für den Roman Čapeks aussprach, denn der neue Bericht, unterschrieben vom Direktor der Zensurbehörde selbst, besagt „autorisado".

Wir wissen leider nichts Konkreteres über den Zensurprozess. Bei „proveniência", d.h. woher das Buch in die Zensurbehörde kam, steht leider keine Angabe. Angesichts der Stellungnahme der Zensoren zu dem Buch (zuerst verboten, dann genehmigt), ist es auch unwahrscheinlich, dass der Verleger selbst, was bisweilen geschah, das Buch der Zensurbehörde zukommen ließ. Kurzum: der unauffällige Buchumschlag, der nicht nur für die Zensoren, sondern auch für potentielle Leser wenig ansprechend wirkte, reichte nicht aus, um dem Spinngewebe der Zensur zu entkommen.

Das Buch erscheint in neuem Gewand: zweimal

Als der ein Jahr nach der Nelkenrevolution gegründete Buchverlag Editorial Caminho 1979 beschloss, Čapeks *Krieg mit den Molchen* zu veröffentlichen, wollte er ein ähnliches Publikum ansprechen. Schließlich begann er weniger Jahre später (zwischen 1982 und 1999) den *Prémio Editorial Caminho de Ficção Científica* (Preis des Verlags Caminho für Science Fiction) zu verleihen. Eine neue Übersetzung wurde wahrscheinlich aus zwei Gründen angefertigt: erstens wegen der Urheberrechte von Lima de Freitas und Livros do Brasil, zweitens weil die erste portugiesische Übersetzung auf der relativ alten englischen Übersetzung von 1937 basierte, während die neuere französische von 1961 aktueller war.

---

[8] Kraft Befehls von höherer Stelle wird der am 1.2.1966 eingetragene Bericht Nr. 7689, der auf das obengenannte Buch Bezug nimmt, annulliert. (Übersetzt von J.Š.)

Mário de Sousa, übersetzte mehrere mittel- und osteuropäische Autoren, u.a. Arkadi Strugazki, Ferenc Karinthy, Alexander Fadejew, obwohl die portugiesische Nationalbibliothek nicht anführt, aus welcher Sprache.[9] Klar ist jedoch, dass er seine Übersetzungen Ende der siebziger, Anfang der achtziger Jahre anfertigte, was genau mit dem Zeitraum korreliert, in dem Portugal seine eigene politische Richtung suchte und daher eine Nachfrage nach den Werken von jenseits des Eisernen Vorhangs bestand. Die Motivation des Übersetzers scheint daher teils politisch, teils profitorientiert gewesen zu sein.

Dem Verlag hingegen ging es, neben der selbstverständlichen Motivation zum Gewinn, zumindest *auch* um das Genre. 1979 erschien das Buch noch in der kleinen Buchreihe *Mamute*, die Neuauflage von 1985 war dann schon der 13. Band der Buchreihe *Ficção Científica* (Science Fiction).

Auf dem Buchumschlag sieht man den Wandel der Zeit.[10] Auf der hinteren Seite des Buchumschlags von 1979 stehen u. a. folgende Worte:

Karel Čapek (1890–1938), autor, entre outros, dos romances **A Fábrica de Absoluto** e **Krakatite**, e das peças de teatro **R.U.R.** e **A Vida dos Insectos**, é um dos escritores checos mas conhecidos do mundo inteiro... Čapek pode com justiça ser considerado um dos fundadores da ficção científica moderna – e não apenas pelo facto de ter sido o criador da palavra Robot. Mas, por trás do assunto que trata, encontra-se sempre a preocupação pelo destino da humanidade nos conturbados tempos em que viveu...[11]

Dies ist eine ganz klare Werbung, wie wir sie auch heute kennen: kein Ausweichen vor der politischen Dimension des Werkes, kein Verstecken vor der Zensur, sondern eine ganz klare Lobpreisung der Qualität des Autors und des Werks, die den Leser dazu bewegen will: „Kaufen Sie dieses Buch!"

---

[9] Siehe http://porbase.bnportugal.pt (31.08.2014).

[10] Siehe http://luso-fc.blogspot.cz/2012/08/n-2-guerra-das-salamandras-valka-s-mloky.html (31.08.2014).

[11] Karel Čapek (1890–1938), Autor u.a. von Romanen wie *Das Absolutum oder die Gottesfabrik* und *Krakatit*, und von Theaterstücken wie *R.U.R.* und *Aus dem Leben der Insekten*, ist einer der bekanntesten tschechischen Schriftsteller in der ganzen Welt... Čapek kann zu Recht als einer der Gründerväter der modernen Science Fiction angesehen werden – und nicht nur weil er der Schöpfer des Wortes *Roboter* ist, sondern weil man – hinter dem von ihm behandelten Thema – immer auch die Sorge um das Schicksal der Menschheit in den bewegten Zeiten, in denen er lebte, findet... (übersetzt von J.Š.).

Ein weiterer auktorialer Paratext ist ab jetzt Teil der portugiesischen Rezeption dieses Werks – das Wort des Autors zu der Entstehung seines Werks. Ein wichtiger Text, in dem Čapek gesteht, dass der Roman erstrangig von Menschen, nicht von Molchen handelt, und dass es keine Utopie sei, sondern „das Heute" (d.h. um 1935):

> Ich kann mir nicht helfen, aber eine Literatur, die sich nicht um die Wirklichkeit kümmert und darum, was mit der Welt tatsächlich geschieht, ein Schrifttum, das darauf nicht so stark reagieren will, wie es nur dem Wort und dem Gedanken gegeben ist, eine solche Literatur ist nicht mein Fall.[12]

Dieser, von Čapek selbst nach der Erstveröffentlichung des Originals geschriebene Text ist aber nicht immer Teil der Ausgaben von *Der Krieg mit den Molchen* – nicht einmal auf Tschechisch. Hier kommt nämlich ein weiterer politischer Aspekt hinzu: Čapek selbst war kein Kommunist und dies äußerte er unmissverständlich bereits am 4. Dezember 1924 in der Zeitschrift *Přítomnost* (Gegenwart).[13] Sein Hauptargument gegen den Kommunismus ist seither zum geflügelten Wort geworden: „Ich bin kein Kommunist, weil mein Herz auf der Seite der Armen steht."

So konnte dieser wohl größte tschechische Schriftsteller der ersten Hälfte des 20. Jahrhunderts in der zweiten Hälfte desselben in seinem eigenen, von der Kommunistischen Partei regierten Heimatland nicht unkommentiert erscheinen. Die für diese Forschung zur Verfügung stehenden tschechischen Ausgaben von 1954 und 1972 enthalten eben nur in einem Falle (1954) diese Bekennung des Autors zur Entstehung des Romans, dafür verfügen beide über ein Vorwort (1954) bzw. Nachwort (1972) von einem „ideologisch unproblematischen" Literaturkritiker (František Buriánek), der für dieses Werk den „richtigen" Kontext herstellte. Man vergleiche etwa folgende „intrakulturelle ideologische Aktualisierung":

---

[12] „Nemohu si pomoci, ale literatura, která se nestará o skutečnost a o to, co se opravdu děje se světem, písemnictví, které na to nechce reagovat tak silně, jak jen je dáno slovu a myšlence, taková literatura není můj případ." (Čapek 1954: 287).

[13] Siehe http://www.pritomnost.cz/cz/component/content/article/15-spolecnost/394-proc-nejsem-komunistou (31.08.2014).

Genauso wie R.U.R. halten die Romane Absolutum oder die Gottesfabrik und Krakatit der kapitalistischen Ordnung, die einer Katastrophe zutreibt, den wahren Spiegel vor, obgleich auch da dieser Spiegel abgeschrägt ist und die Hauptfrage der Klassengesellschaft nicht erfasst oder verzerrt wird: den Kampf des arbeitenden Volkes für eine bessere, gerechtere Ordnung, welche die technischen Erfindungen in den Dienst der Menschheit stellen würde.[14]

Die Rezeption Čapeks in seinem Heimatland ist an sich hochinteressant, doch das wäre ein Thema für einen anderen Artikel. Für die portugiesische Rezeption ist es wichtig, dass die französische Übersetzung diesen Paratext beinhaltet, im Gegensatz zu den beiden englischen – und das spiegeln die portugiesischen Übersetzungen jeweils wider. Als 2009 die neueste portugiesische Übersetzung veröffentlicht wurde, erschien sie wieder ohne diesen Autorentext.

Im Jahr 1985, da die zweite Auflage der Übersetzung von Mário de Sousa herausgegeben wurde, steht zum ersten (und bislang letzten) Mal auf der vorderen Seite des Buchumschlags ein Auszug aus dem ersten Kapitel des Buchs:

O capitão Van Toch continuou o interrogatório. Sim, havia diabos lá em baixo! Milhares e milhares. Tinham o tamanho de crianças de dez anos, capitão, e andam de pé lá no fundo. Sim, de pé.[15]

Auf der hinteren Seite des Buchumschlags wird aber 1985 bei diesem in Portugal mittlerweile „altgewordenen Klassiker" Neues behauptet:

...O êxito já verificado destes livros em Portugal, particularmente «A Guerra das Salamandras», torna imperioso que o público volte a dispor deste romance singular e hilariante, que há muito se encontrava esgotado na anterior edição da Editorial Caminho. Convém sublinhar, aliás, que foi na nossa edição que o público português pôde ler pela primeira vez uma edição «integral» de «A Guerra das Salamandras».[16]

---

[14] „Stejně jako R.U.R. nastavují i romány Továrna na absolutno a Krakatit pravdivé zrcadlo kapitalistickému řádu, který se žene do katastrofy, třebaže i zde je toto zrcadlo postaveno zkoseně a nezachycuje nebo skresluje hlavní otázku třídní společnosti: boj pracujícího lidu o lepší, spravedlivější řád, který by obrátil vynálezy techniky k prospěchu lidstva." František Buriánek in Čapek (1954: 8).

[15] „Kapitän J. van Toch setzte das Kreuzverhör fort... Ja, es sind Teufel dort... Tausende und aber Tausende. Sie sind etwa so groß wie ein zehnjähriges Kind, Herr, und... auf dem Boden gehen sie auf zwei Beinen. Auf zwei Beinen..." (Čapek 1954/1937: 18).

[16] Der bereits erwiesene Erfolg dieser Bücher in Portugal, vor allem von *Der Krieg mit den Molchen*, macht es erforderlich, dass dieser einzigartige und erheiternde Roman, der in

Neben der erneut hervorgehobenen Bedeutung des Autors und des Werks, das nun Teil des Weltkulturerbes ist (*património universal*), wird betont, dass die Erstauflage bei Caminho von 1979 längst ausverkauft ist (*esgotado*), und vor allem behauptet, dass die portugiesische Leserschaft in den Ausgaben dieses Verlags zum ersten Mal den ganzen Text (*edição integral*) in den Händen hält. Der aufmerksame Leser von Paratexten erfährt, dass es von einem anderen Verlag eine frühere portugiesische Übersetzung dieses Romans gibt, die aber angeblich nicht vollständig sei.

Abgesehen von den unterschiedlichen Ausgangstexten für die portugiesischen Übersetzungen von Lima de Freitas und Mário de Sousa ergab unsere Forschung folgende zwei Unterschiede zwischen den Ausgaben von Čapeks Roman bei Livros do Brasil und bei Caminho: Zum einen enthält die neuere Version (von de Sousa) die obengenannte Äußerung des Autors zur Entstehung des Romans (*Karel Capek: a propósito da génese deste romance*, übersetzt aus dem Französischen: *Comment m'est venue l'idée de « La guerre des salamandres »* par Karel Čapek).

Zum anderen fehlt im Inhaltsverzeichnis der ersten Version (von de Lima) die Information darüber, dass das letzte Kapitel des ersten Buchs (der Roman besteht aus drei Büchern in einem Band) das Nachwort „Über das Geschlechtsleben der Molche" (*Apêndice: A vida sexual das salamandras*) enthält. Dieses Nachwort wurde aber übersetzt und ist Bestandteil der Ausgabe von Livros do Brasil. Im Jahre 1965 unter dem *Estado Novo* war dies nur unwahrscheinlich ein Übersehen. Vielmehr war es Teil der Verlagspolitik von Livros do Brasil: angesichts des heiklen Themas wollte der Verleger die Aufmerksamkeit von naseweisen Zensoren nicht zu sehr auf das Buch lenken.

Strenggenommen kann man also nicht behaupten, dass die neuere Version von Caminho die erste „vollständige Ausgabe" des *Kriegs mit den Molchen* in portugiesischer Sprache ist. Bewusst oder nicht, die Behauptung war Teil der Verlagspolitik, welche in diesem Falle Werbezwecke verfolgte.

---

der früheren Ausgabe des Verlags Caminho seit langem ausverkauft ist, den Lesern wieder zur Verfügung steht. An dieser Stelle ist es übrigens angebracht zu betonen, dass die portugiesischen Leser in unserer Ausgabe das erste Mal den vollständigen Text von *Der Krieg mit den Molchen* lesen können. (übersetzt von J.Š.)

Das Buch betritt das neue Jahrtausend: kaum verändert

Auf dem Buchumschlag der Ausgabe vom Verlag Publicações Europa-América von 2009 finden wir wenig Neues:

> Esta é uma das grandes sátiras antiutópicas do século XX e é uma inspiração para muitos autores, de Orwell a Vonnegut... Ao longo da obra assistimos à satirização da ciência, do capitalismo, do fascismo, do jornalismo, do militarismo, e até de Hollywood...
> KAREL CAPEK (1890–1938) é considerado o maior autor checo da primeira metade do século XX... As suas peças de teatro estrearam na Broadway pouco tempo depois da sua estreia em Praga e os seus livros foram traduzidos em várias línguas.[17]

Die indirekte Rezeption, diesmal mittels der englischsprachigen Poly-Kultur, ist hier nicht zu übersehen. Irgendwie sollte es für den portugiesischen Leser von Belang sein, dass die Theaterstücke von einem tschechischen Schriftsteller vor etlichen Jahrzehnten auf dem amerikanischen Broadway aufgeführt wurden. Vermutlich soll das den Portugiesen beeindrucken, dass der kleine Tscheche es auch in der großen Welt in Amerika geschafft hat. Darin spiegelt sich der ganze Minderwertigkeitskomplex kleinerer Nationen wider.

Der Urtext und sein Wandel

Neben den Paratexten, welche die bedeutendsten Lozi für die Kommunikation eines Buches mit der Außenwelt darstellen, finden wir auch im eigentlichen Text des Romans ein paar (wenige) Stellen, die für die portugiesische Zensur von Interesse sein konnten. Um den Rahmen dieses Artikels nicht zu sprengen, beschränken wir uns auf drei Auszüge, welche die Religion (Katholizismus), die Moral (Anspielungen auf Sexualität) und die Politik (Antisemitismus) betreffen.

---

[17] Dies ist eine der großen antiutopischen Satiren des 20. Jahrhunderts und eine Inspiration für viele Autoren, von Orwell bis Vonnegut... Im Laufe des Romans wohnen wir einer Satirisierung der Wissenschaft, des Kapitalismus, des Faschismus, des Journalismus, des Militarismus und sogar von Hollywood bei... KAREL CAPEK (1890–1938) wird für den größten tschechischen Autor der ersten Hälfte des 20. Jahrhunderts gehalten... Seine Theaterstücke wurden kurz nach ihrer Aufführung in Prag auf dem Broadway aufgeführt und seine Bücher wurden in verschiedene Sprachen übersetzt. (übersetzt von J.Š.)

Bei allen drei unterscheidet sich das tschechische Original vom portugiesischen Zieltext und der wissenschaftlichen Genauigkeit halber interessiert uns auch die Frage, ob es zu der Ausdrucksverschiebung (Popovič 1975) bereits in der ersten (vermittelnden) Übersetzung, d.h. in der Vorlage für die portugiesische Übersetzung, oder erst im portugiesischen Zieltext kam – obschon diese Frage keine Relevanz für den Rezipienten in der Zielkultur hat.

Um der Übersichtlichkeit und Verständlichkeit willen werden zunächst das tschechische Original und die zwei deutschen Übersetzungen nebeneinandergestellt und danach kommen die drei portugiesischen Übersetzungen mit ihren jeweiligen Vorlagen.

Beispiel 1 – die Religion

Karel Čapek (1936)	Julius Mader (1937)	Eliška Glaserová (1964)
„Možná; ale irská mše je lepší. U nás jsou, člověče, **čertovští flanďáci**, kteří dovedou zrovna čarovat. Docela jako **fakíři** nebo **pohani**."	„Vielleicht; aber eine irische Messe ist besser. Bei uns, Mensch, gibt es **Teufelspfaffen**, die zaubern können. Ganz wie **Fakire** oder **Heiden**."	„Kann schon sein. Aber eine irische Messe ist besser. Bei uns, da gibt's **Teufelskerle**, Mensch, die können einfach zaubern. Genau wie **Fakire** oder **Heiden**."

Das tschechische Wort *flanďák* ist eine pejorative Bezeichnung für einen Kleriker, etwa wie „Pfaffe"; *čertovští flanďáci* sind wortwörtlich „teuflische Pfaffen" oder eben „Teufelspfaffen". Glaserová trifft die Nuance nicht ganz; Čapek am nächsten steht Mader.

M. & R. Weatherall (1937)	Lima de Freitas (1965)
"It could be; but an Irish mass is the real thing. In my home, man, **the Jesuits are devils**; they can nearly do wonders. Just like **witch doctors** or heathens."	– Talvez; mas uma missa irlandesa, isso, sim, é que tem valor. Na minha terra, homem, **os Jesuítas são levados dos demónios**; quase que fazem milagres. Como os **curandeiros** ou os pagãos.

M. und R. Weatherall konkretisieren, ja lokalisieren – und verschieben daher den Ausdruck in ganz andere Gefilde, indem sie den Orden der Jesuiten miteinbringen, von dem Čapek an keiner Stelle seines Romans spricht. Fakire, die einem britischen Publikum mit seinen Kolonien u.a. auch in Indien sicherlich bekannt waren, werden zu Medizinmännern. Lima de Freitas hält sich an seinen Ausgangstext, wobei er von Quacksalbern spricht und seine Jesuiten explizit vom Teufel verleitet sind (angestiftet werden).

Claudia Ancelot (1961)	Mário de Sousa (1979)
– Peut-être bien, mais une messe irlandaise, c'est mieux. Chez nous, il y a des **ratichons du diable**, de vrais magiciens. Comme des **fakirs** ou des **païens**.	– Talvez seja bom, mas uma missa irlandesa é melhor. Na minha terra há uns **padrecas do diabo**, autênticos mágicos. Como os faquires e os **hereges**.

Ancelot übersetzt einwandfrei äquivalent; Sousa führt Häretiker ins Feld, die weder dem Original noch der französischen Vorlage entsprechen. Heiden und Ketzer sind nicht dasselbe.

Ewald Osers (1985)	Isabel Neves (2009)
'Could be. But an Irish Mass is better. Back home, man, we have **devil priests** who are downright wizards. Just like **fakirs** or **witch doctors**.'	– É capaz. Mas uma Missa Irlandesa é melhor. Lá na minha terra, homem, temos **padres de demónios** que são uns verdadeiros génios. Como os faquires e os **feiticeiros**.

Osers neutralisiert den abwertenden Ausdruck und führt wieder die Medizinmänner ein. Neves übersetzt, treu der englischen Version, d.h. farblos als Teufelspriester und Hexer.

Wie verzerren die portugiesischen Übersetzungen die Rezeption des portugiesischen Lesers im Vergleich zum Leser des tschechischen Originals? Um diese Frage zu beantworten, sei es dahingestellt, ob die Abweichung von Čapeks Sachverhalt im vermittelnden Text oder erst im portugiesischen Zieltext entstand. Der relevante Gesichtspunkt bei der Untersuchung dieser indirekten Übersetzungen ist und bleibt der Sachverhalt im Zieltext (vgl. Toury 1995) und seine Wirkung auf den Rezipienten in der Zielkultur.

Der Ire in Čapeks Roman vergleicht seine irischen katholischen Priester mit Fakiren und Heiden; ihm nach seien sie des Teufels Pfaffen. Damit äußert er eine harsche Kritik des (irischen) Katholizismus, indem seine offiziellen Vertreter kaum zu unterscheiden seien von anderen Scharlatanen. Sie werden also nicht als ehrwürdige Männer, sondern als Personen bezeichnet, die ein Theater inszenieren, das Volk für dumm halten und seine Dummheit ausnutzen.

Lima de Freitas' Jesuiten sind vollkommen unangebracht hier. Ein gebildeter Portugiese denkt sogleich an Simão Rodrigues de Azevedo (1510–79), den Kommilitonen von Ignatius von Loyola und ersten Provinzial in Portugal, und an die von ihm verursachten Skandale in Coimbra, an Franz Xaver, den Mitbegründer der Gesellschaft Jesu und Wegbereiter der aus Portugal gesandten christlichen Mission in Asien, an die portugiesischen Könige Dom João III, der die Jesuiten nach Portugal einlud, und Dom Sebastião, der von den Jesuiten erzogen wurde, und an die Geschichte der Jesuiten in Portugal allgemein. Eine ganze Kette unerwünschter Konnotationen schleicht sich ein, die bei der Rezeption von Čapeks Roman völlig fehl am Platz sind.

Mário de Sousas Häretiker rufen Assoziationen mit der Inquisition wach, die in Portugal 1536 begann, mit der ersten Einführung der Zensur in Portugal (die u.a. auch die Werke des tschechischen Reformators Jan Hus, dt. auch Johannes Huss, verbrennen ließ), mit der Stadt Évora, wo die „Heilige Inquisition" ihr Hauptquartier in Portugal fand und ihre Urteile fällte, usw. Alles Konnotationen, die den Leser in die Irre führen und Čapeks Aussage verschleiern.

Nur Isabel Neves' Version kann man, mit Vorbehalt, gelten lassen. Wie Čapek wählt auch sie Wörter die historisch/politisch/kulturell fern genug sind, um keine „falschen" Assoziationen hervorzurufen. Ihre Lösung ist (fast) genauso „assoziationsneutral" in diesem Kontext wie Čapeks Aussage: Teufelspriester anstatt von Teufelpfaffen stellt eine bloß stilistische Ausdrucksverschiebung dar, und Hexer anstatt von Heiden ist zwar nicht ideal, aber immerhin besser als Jesuiten und Häretiker.

Beispiel 2 – die Moral

Karel Čapek (1936)	Julius Mader (1937)	Eliška Glaserová (1964)
Mladomloci byli patrně pro pokrok bez výhrad a omezení…, nevyjímajíc ani kopanou, **flirt, fašismus a sexuální inverze**.	Die Jungmolche waren offenbar für den Fortschritt ohne Vorbehalte und Einschränkungen…, Fußball, **Flirt, Faschismus und sexuelle Inversion** nicht ausgenommen.	Die Jungmolche waren offenbar für Fortschritt ohne Vorbehalt und Einschränkung…, Fußball, **Flirt, Faschismus und sexuelle Inversion** nicht ausgenommen.

Altmolche und Jungmolche ist eine der wenigen Anspielungen Čapeks in diesem Roman auf die tschechische politische Szene – zuerst Ende des 19. Jahrhunderts noch unter Österreich-Ungarn, ab 1918 dann unter der ersten Tschechoslowakischen Republik. Als Jungtschechen wurden Mitglieder der Freisinnigen Nationalpartei bezeichnet, die sich 1874 von der Nationalpartei abspaltete, deren Mitglieder wiederum von da an als Alttschechen bekannt wurden. Ihrem Namen getreu waren die Jungtschechen fortschrittsorientierter als die konservativen Alttschechen. Das wird in keiner Übersetzung mit einer Anmerkung des Übersetzers erklärt, aber man könnte argumentieren, dass es keine Relevanz für die Geschichte hat und aus der Etymologie der Neuschöpfung hervorgeht. Mader und Glaserová übersetzen beide äquivalent.

M. & R. Weatherall (1937)	Lima de Freitas (1965)
The Young Newts apparently stood for progress without any reservations or restrictions..., not omitting even football, ø, fascism, and **sexual perversions**.	Aparentemente, os Tritões Novos eram pelo progresso sem quaisquer reservas ou restrições..., sem omitir sequer o futebol, ø, o fascismo e as **perversões sexuais**.

In der Übersetzung von M. und R. Weatherall kommt es erstens zu einer kaum zu erklärenden Auslassung – ausgerechnet bei einem Anglizismus (flirt) – und dazu noch zu einer Verschiebung, bei der ein abstrakterer, nicht automatisierter Ausdruck, sexuelle Inversion, den Čapek bewusst wählt, mit einem konkreteren, üblicheren Ausdruck ersetzt wird: sexuelle Perversion.

Claudia Ancelot (1961)	Mário de Sousa (1979)
Les Jeunes Salamandres semblaient être en faveur d'un progrès sans restrictions ni limites... ; y compris le football, le flirt, le fascisme et **l'homosexualité**.	As Jovens Salamandras pareciam ser a favor de um progresso sem restrições nem limites...; incluindo o futebol, o *flirt*, o fascismo e a **homossexualidade**.

Claudia Ancelot konkretisiert schamlos, aber – sofern wir es beurteilen können – richtig. Mário de Sousa bleibt im Schlepptau seiner Vorlage.

Ewald Osers (1985)	Isabel Neves (2009)
The Young Newts were evidently in favour of progress without reservations or restrictions...; not excepting football, **flirtation**, fascism and **sexual perversions**.	As Jovens Salamandras eram evidentemente a favor do progresso sem reservas nem restrições..., sem excluir o futebol, **os namoricos**, o fascismo e as **perversões sexuais**.

Ewald Osers entscheidet sich einmal für das Deverbativum flirtation, das als eine Tätigkeit durchaus gut passt, aber auch ihm kommen sexuelle Perversionen als erstes in den Sinn. Isabel Neves domestiziert das Fremdwort und ändert dadurch leicht die Konnotationen, den Perversionen Osers' bleibt sie treu.

Dies zeigt zweierlei: erstens legen die portugiesischen Übersetzer einen sehr hohen Grad an Treue (fast Wortwörtlichkeit) an den Tag. Ob das bedeutet, dass das portugiesische Polysystem eine treue Übersetzung vorzieht, bleibt offen. Klar ist, dass der Übersetzer aus zweiter Hand den Fehler des ersten Vermittlers nicht korrigieren kann. Aber allgemein fällt hier die Tendenz der indirekten

Übersetzer auf, die um diesen Umstand wissend und vielleicht dadurch bekräftigt dazu neigen, ihrer Vorlage so genau wie möglich zu folgen.

Lima de Freitas' Version verweigert dem portugiesischen Leser einen netten Witz von Čapek: dass die Altmolche selbst dem harmlosen Flirten abgeneigt waren. Sowohl Lima de Freitas als auch Isabel Neves machen in ihrem Text aus einer Inversion eine Perversion, was wieder zu den falschen Konnotationen Anlass geben kann. Man könnte sogar fragen, ob Homosexualität – im Gegensatz etwa zu Pädophilie oder Päderastie – tatsächlich (noch) als Perversion und nicht inzwischen (höchstens) als eine Inversion der Orientierung der Mehrheit angesehen wird. Auch wenn diese Diskussion im Portugal von 1965 kaum jemand geführt hätte, ist es für den heutigen Leser (was mit Neves' neuer Übersetzung noch aktueller wird) eine mittlerweile sozial und kulturell nicht unwichtige Frage (der Toleranz).

Mário de Sousas Homosexualität kann man hier mehr oder minder akzeptieren. Es ist zwar eine Konkretisierung, die dem Leser jede Einbildungskraft abspricht, aber eins bleibt erhalten: Čapek erscheint hier nicht als ein alter, bitterer Griesgram (ein Alttscheche), sondern als ein progressiver, toleranter Mensch, der auch unserer heutigen Denkweise nähersteht.

Beispiel 3 – die Politik

Karel Čapek (1936)	Julius Mader (1937)	Eliška Glaserová (1964)
MOLCHE, WIRFT JUDEN HERAUS! (Německý leták)	**Molche, jagt die Juden hinaus!** (Deutsches Flugblatt)	Molche, werft die Juden hinaus! (Deutsches Flugblatt)

Beim letzten Textausschnitt geht es einmal um das im Original unkorrekte Deutsch und zweitens um nonverbale Elemente, die politische Assoziationen hervorrufen. Im Tschechischen steht die Losung einfach nur in Großbuchstaben. In Maders Vorkriegsversion steht das Flugblatt in einer Form der Fraktur, in Glaserovás Nachkriegsversion wurde Rundgotisch (Rotunde) benutzt. Im Dritten Reich gab es bekanntlich den Antiqua-Fraktur-Streit, der 1941 mit dem Normalschrifterlass beendet wurde. Das erklärt die Schriftwahl in beiden deutschen Versionen. Keine ist daher mit den Nazis verbunden; beide sollen einfach „eine Art" alte deutsche Schrift darstellen.

M. & R. Weatherall (1937)	Lima de Freitas (1965)
Molches, wirft Juden heraus! (Newts, throw out the Jews!) (A German pamphlet.)	∅

Die Weatheralls, des Deutschen offensichtlich nicht mächtig, verballhornen die Losung, indem sie an den Plural „Molche" noch das englische Plural-s anhängen, den falschen Imperativ aber beibehalten. Für den englischen Leser übersetzen sie die Parole noch sicherheitshalber. Lima de Freitas begeht eine flagrante Auslassung.

Claudia Ancelot (1961)	Mário de Sousa (1979)
Molche wirft Juden heraus (Tract allemand)	MOLCHE WIRFT JUDEN HERAUS (Panfleto alemão)

Claudia Ancelot behält buchstabengetreu Čapeks Version, kommt aber ohne jedwede Interpunktion aus und benutzt die Minuskel. Mário de Sousa transkribiert – zwar ebenfalls ohne Interpunktion, dafür aber in Majuskeln, als ob er einer Eingebung folgte.

Ewald Osers (1985)	Isabel Neves (2009)
Newts, throw out the Jews! (A German leaflet)	Salamandras, expulsai os Judeus! (Um folheto alemão)

Um den zeitlich wie räumlich unterschiedlichen Bezug zur deutschen Kultur und Sprache wissend übersetzt Osers die Parole ins Englische, ohne die „local colour" beizubehalten. Isabel Neves folgt, wie erwartet, seinem Beispiel.

Das dritte Beispiel ist nur scheinbar banal. Erstens ist es nur unwahrscheinlich, dass Lima de Freitas' Auslassung durch ein Übersehen entstanden wäre. Vielmehr war sich de Freitas sehr wohl dessen bewusst, dass das Dritte Reich bis 1943 ein Verbündeter Salazars gewesen war – Salazar lebte 1965 noch und regierte weitere 3 Jahre unangefochten über sein Land – und dass vielleicht ein so offensichtlicher Affront gegen die Deutschen nicht taktisch wäre. Vielleicht dachte er auch, dass diese Parole sich überlebt hatte und das Deutschland von 1965 (die BRD oder die DDR?) nicht so direkt angegriffen werden sollte. Wie dem auch sei, ist die Auslassung kaum zufällig.

Isabel Neves' „Lusitanisierung" ist ebenfalls eine Ausdrucksverarmung (Popovič 1975). In der portugiesischen Übersetzung geht die ganze Form verloren – und dadurch wird auch der Inhalt ärmer. Die Erwähnung der Juden ist zwar geblieben und der Antisemitismus der Nazis ist wohl immer noch bekannt genug, aber anstatt eines merk-würdigen Ausdrucks blieb nur ein zu erwartender, unkreativer Ausruf. Und genau das läuft Čapeks Poetik zuwider. Seine Werke sprühen geradezu vor Ideen, Kreativität und Unerwartetem. Was uns Neves hier vor Augen führt, ist genau das, was Levý den Übersetzerstil nennt (2011: 85, 07, 109, 118).

Nur Mário de Sousas Version entspricht der von Čapek. Für den portugiesischen Leser ist es genauso unwichtig wie für den tschechischen und französischen, dass das Deutsch nicht fehlerfrei ist.

Schluss

Die oben analysierten Textausschnitte in ihren unterschiedlichen sprachlichen und nonverbalen Varianten erfüllen drei Funktionen.

An erster Stelle beweisen sie, relativ eindeutig, welche Ausgangstexte die portugiesischen Übersetzer benutzt haben. Das ist neu, denn in den portugiesischen Ausgaben steht nur: „tradução de Lima de Freitas" (1965); „traduzido do francês por Mário de Sousa" (1979, 1985) und „tradução de Isabel Neves" (2009). Im 21. Jahrhundert ist es in Portugal immer noch nicht gang und gäbe, eine indirekte Übersetzung bei ihrem Namen zu nennen und die vermittelnde Sprache/Ausgabe/Übersetzung anzugeben. Ist das etwa auch eine Instanz der Verlagspolitik? Oder mittlerweile eine vom autoritären Regime Salazars vererbte „kulturelle Tradition" des portugiesischen Polysystems?

Gleichzeitig sieht man hier sehr deutlich die Nachteile einer Übersetzung aus zweiter Hand. So treu sich der zweite Übersetzer an den ersten auch hält, wird er in jedem Fall, bei bestem Willen, seinem Publikum ein anderes Werk liefern, als wenn er direkt aus dem Original übersetzen würde. Wie beim Spiel „stille Post" entfernt man sich unwillkürlich immer weiter von der ursprünglichen Aussage des Autors.

Und nicht zuletzt: eine neuere Übersetzung ist einer älteren nicht immer überlegen. Vielmehr zeigt sich, dass nicht nur gute Werke nicht (so schnell) alt werden, sondern dass auch gute Übersetzungen dem Zahn der Zeit trotzen können.

Der breitere, gesellschaftliche Kontext, den wir vor allem in den Paratexten sahen, ermöglicht dann eine tentative Verallgemeinerung: die Übersetzung kann sich aktiv am ideologischen Kampf beteiligen: entweder geht sie der Ideologie an die Hand und stärkt so ihre Position oder sie kämpft im Krieg mit den Molochen der Ideologie und Zensur. Čapeks *Krieg mit den Molchen* zeigt dieses Potential der Übersetzung sehr deutlich.

Literatur- und Quellenverzeichnis

ČAPEK, Karel (1954/1936): *Válka s Mloky*. – Praha: SNKLHU.

— (1954/1937): *Der Krieg mit den Molchen*. – Berlin: Aufbau. Aus dem Tschechischen übertragen von Julius Mader.

— (1965): *A guerra das salamandras*. – Lisboa: Livros do Brasil. Tradução de Lima de Freitas.

— (1969/1961): *La Guerre des Salamandres*. – Verviers: Gérard et Co. Traduit du tchèque par Claudia Ancelot.

— (1972/1936): *Válka s Mloky*. – Praha: Československý spisovatel.

— (1985/1979): *A guerra das salamandras* [War with the Newts]. – Lisboa: Caminho. Traduzido do francês por Mário de Sousa.

— (1999/1985): *War with the Newts*. – North Haven, CT: Catbird Press/UNESCO. A New Translation from the Czech by Ewald Osers.

— (2009): *A Guerra das Salamandras*. – Mem Martins: Europa-América. Tradução de Isabel Neves.

— (2009/1964): *Der Krieg mit den Molchen*. – Berlin: Aufbau. Aus dem Tschechischen von Eliška Glaserová.

— (2010/1936): *Válka s Mloky*. – Praha: Fragment.

— (2010/1937): *War with the Newts*. – London: Penguin Books. Translated by M. and R. Weatherall (with the assistance of W. Francis and G. Johnston).

DAVIES, Norman (1996): *Europe: A History*. – Oxford: OUP.

DUARTE, João Ferreira, ROSA, Alexandra Assis & SERUYA, Teresa Seruya (eds.) (2006): *Translation Studies at the Interface of Disciplines*. – Amsterdam/Philadelphia: John Benjamins Publishing.

KLÍMA, Jan (2007): *Dějiny Portugalska*. – Praha: Lidové noviny.

KUNDRÁTOVÁ, Linda (2003): "Os contactos da oposição portuguesa antisalazarista com a Checoslováquia entre 1933–1974. Contribuição para o estudo das relações luso-checas."
http://www.premioiberoamericano.cz/documentos/9naedicion/3erPremioIX_LindaKudratova.pdf (31.08.2014).

LEVÝ, Jiří (2011): *The Art of Translation*. – Amsterdam/Philadelphia: John Benjamins Publishing.

MUNDAY, Jeremy (2007): "Translation and Ideology: A Textual Approach", *The Translator. Special Issue. Translation and Ideology: Encounters and Clashes*, 13 (2), 195–217.

NERGAARD, Siri (2007): "Translation and power: recent theoretical updates". In: BUZZONI, Marina & BAMPI, Massimiliano (eds.) *The Garden of Crossing Paths: The Manipulation and Rewriting of Medieval Texts*. – Venezia: Libreria Editrice Cafoscarina, 33–43.

PÉREZ, María Calzada (ed.) (2003): *Apropos of Ideology: Translation Studies on Ideology – Ideologies in Translation Studies*. – Manchester, Northampton: St. Jerome.

POPOVIČ, Anton (1975): *Teória umeleckého prekladu: Aspekty textu a literárnej metakomunikácie*. – Bratislava: Tatran.

ŠPIRK, Jaroslav (2014): *Censorship, Indirect Translations and Non-translation: The (Fateful) Adventures of Czech Literature in 20th-century Portugal*. – Newcastle upon Tyne: Cambridge Scholars Publishing.

STOLZE, Radegundis (2008): *Übersetzungstheorien: eine Einführung*. – Tübingen: Gunter Narr. 5. Auflage.

TOURY, Gideon (1995): *Descriptive Translation Studies and Beyond*. – Amsterdam/Philadelphia: John Benjamins Publishing.

Censorship of translated literature under Franco's dictatorship: Self-censorship of Czech literature

Petra Vavroušová
Institute of Translation Studies, Faculty of Arts, Charles University of Prague
petra.vavrousova@seznam.cz

This chapter describes the reception of translated Czech literature based on a German source text in Spain in the years 1939 to 1983. The chapter draws on censors' reports provided by the General Administration Archives in Alcalá de Henares (Madrid). It seeks to arrive at an answer to the following research question: What was the reaction of the Spanish censorship to the Czech literature? The genesis of translations is explained using the following methodological tool – critical discourse analysis based on controversial metatexts (Popovič 1975) or paratexts (Genette 1997), in other words, on censors' reports of following books: Hašek's novel The Good Soldier Švejk and other Czech novels by Ota Filip, Pavel Kohout, Bohumil Hrabal, Jan Procházka and Ota Hofman. The research contributes to the clarification of the Czech-Spanish literary relationship, including the important mediating role of the German language.

Introduction

The present chapter deals with the reception of the Czech literature in the Spanish speaking part of the Iberian Peninsula that was – throughout the twentieth century – translated indirectly from the German source text into Spanish, in special reference to the period from 1939 to 1983, during which all types of literary production were subject to official censorship. In the General Administration Archives (*Archivo General de Administración* or AGA) in Alcalá de Henares (Madrid), there are deposited thirty three censors' reports that analyse the Czech prose[1]. For the purposes of this research only seventeen[2] censorship files are relevant because these analyse the translation of Czech novels based on a German source text.

Methodology and material

In fact, the research aims to answer the following question: What was the reaction of the censorship to Czech novels published under the Franco's dictatorship, especially to Hašek's *Švejk*? The selected corpus to be examined in terms of censorship consists of nine books: one by Jaroslav Hašek (analysed in detail as a case study), one by Pavel Kohout, two by Ota Filip; then three by Jan Procházka and two by Ota Hofman, which are books for children.

The case study draws on the Czech novel *Osudy dobrého vojáka Švejka za světové války* (1920–23) [*The Fateful Adventures of the Good Soldier Švejk During the World War*] by Jaroslav Hašek chosen from the following reasons: (1) This unfinished satirical novel ranks among the principal works of Czech (and even world) literature, it has been translated into many languages and the character of Švejk has become a literary archetype and it is considered the epitome of a Czech man. (2) It was only in 1980 that *Švejk* was published for the first time in Spain[3]. The translation was made in the late sixties; however it was not approved by the censors and thus could only be published after the fall of Franco's regime. This translation by Alfonsina Janés bearing the title *Las aventuras del valeroso soldado Schwejk* was and still is published by the *Destino* publish-

---

[1] The reception of Czech novels translated directly into Spanish in the twentieth century is analysed in the doctoral dissertation by Miguel Cuenca entitled *Influence of the Spanish Polysystem on Czech-Spanish Translation during the Second Half of the 20th century* (2013) which deals with the influence of censorship on the translation of Čapek's novel *War with the Newts*.

[2] On the other hand this number shows that at that time literary production from literatures of lesser diffusion used to be translated indirectly because there was a lack of translators who would master the original language.

[3] The first Spanish translation (into Argentinian Spanish), by Ricardo de Benedetti, was published in 1946 under the title *El buen soldado Schweik* in Buenos Aires by the *Siglo Veinte* publishing house.

ing house. It is a second-hand translation based on a 1926–1927 German source text by Grete Reiner.[4] (3) The novel is set during World War I in Austria-Hungary and it also deals with broader anti-war issues, e. g. a series of absurdly comic episodes, it explores both the pointlessness and futility of conflict in general and of the military discipline in particular. In addition to satirising the Habsburg authority, Hašek repeatedly points to the corruption and hypocrisy attributed to priests of the Catholic Church. All of these aspects were alarming for the Francoist censorship.

I shall primarily focus on the censors' reports from the AGA, the analysis of which shall provide a background for the life of Hašek's novel in the Spanish literary polysystem. Last but not least, I shall comment on interviews with the translator and the publisher which I conducted in Barcelona in 2012. Their testimonies supplement the overall image of the reception of the Czech novel in the Spanish environment. The selected excerpts represent controversial sections subject to the censorship examination: references to morals, regime, censorship, antimilitarism, anticlericalism (cf. Neuschäfer 1994: 49–50, Špirk 2011: 271).

A literary work (a book) consists of two parts: the text of the work itself (the primary text) and paratext(s), one or more second-degree texts (Genette 1997). Paratexts play an active role in readers' reception of the primary text in question. The latter is the focus of a number of specifically written texts by other authors, be it in the book itself or outside it; the purpose of such texts is to inform the potential recipient of the work, evaluate and reflect on it, promote it, make the reader buy the book and affect its future reception, or as the case may be, prompt a publisher to publish the book. Paratexts consist of two elements, which Genette (1987: 11) describes as follows: "paratext = peritext + epitext". Peritexts surround the text and appear in its immediate environment as they complement the material form of the book and logically form part of it (author's name, title, texts on jacket flaps, dedication, foreword, contents, notes, chapter names, epilogue etc.). From a translation scholar's point of view, it is surprising that Genette does not take into account the author's name, the language of the source text etc. (cf. Pym 1998: 62). Epitexts do not form part of the text, they

---

[4] In 2008, a new translation by Monika Zgustová was published under the title *Las aventuras del buen soldado Švejk* by the *Galaxia Gutenberg* publishing house.

exist on their own and appear in the surrounding of the book (they are either public or private, they may be comments or statements on the book, interviews, reviews, diary entries, letters etc.). Popovič differentiates between primary and secondary literary communication and introduces the term "metacommunication" for the latter (1975, 1983). Popovič (1975: 286) defines a prototext as an original text which serves as a basis for secondary manipulation with the text. According to Popovič (1983: 129) metatexts may be divided into affirmative (approving, positive, non-polemic follow-up metatexts) and controversial (non-affirmative, critical, polemic follow-up metatexts). Metatexts do not constitute merely an ancillary or assisting aspect of a reception of a work, but they become an equal part of literary reception. This chapter focuses mainly on metatexts outside the book, epitexts for Genette, which will be further subdivided into affirmative and controversial ones in line with Popovič. According to Genette, epitexts (Greek epi- above, by) are such texts which are not part of the book (censors' reports, reviews, interviews etc.) but have a significant impact on the future reception of the given work. Therefore, I differentiate among the following epitexts: (1) affirmative, i.e. such epitexts that present a positive opinion of the text; and (2) controversial, i.e. such epitexts which present a critical or negative opinion of the text.

Censorship under Franco

For almost forty years (1936–1975) Spain was under a fascist government led by *Generalísimo* Francisco Franco y Bahamonde (1892–1975). All cultural manifestations were closely monitored and controlled by the military authority and the Roman Catholic Church (Merino & Rabadán 2009: 125). It is necessary to investigate the way censorship affected literary production and what it meant for authors or translators to create something in a time when they were not allowed to express their thoughts openly and directly. The so-called *discurso de censura* (Neuschäfer 1994: 10) was created, which describes undesirable topics indirectly and secretly; authors made use of camouflage, feints and pretension. Some of them learned to deceive, or even ridicule, the whole machinery of censorship, thus showing two faces of censorship: its power and its powerlessness.

The omnipresent censorship was an invitation to obedience; everyone had to subject themselves to this manifestation of fascist totalitarianism and Catholic doctrine. Another means of censorship was the press which was to serve the government and the pro-state propaganda. The censorship process had two stages: preliminary censorship or prior to publication (*consulta, censura previa*), which aimed at affecting the text-production, and subsequent or definitive censorship or posterior to publication (*censura definitiva, postcensura*), which was carried out after the text had been completed (cf. Merkle 2010: 19, Neuschäfer 1994: 10, 49). After the new press law was promulgated in 1966, *consulta previa*, obligatory until 1938, became voluntary, but, in fact all literary production was subject to censorship. Fear of a time-consuming supervision process led authors in many cases to make use of self-censorship[5] in order to prevent any possible trouble during *consulta previa* (Rabadán 2000: 20, Merino & Rabadán 2009: 127).

As early as the end of the Spanish Civil War, official censorship began to control information as well as analyse and evaluate the quality of literary works; however; its employees were not literary critics, but censors (members of the pro-Franco political party, the *Falange*, and of the clergy) referred to as *lectores* [readers] in censors' reports. The system of censorship under Francisco Franco became institutionalized very quickly and its executive body turned into an exceptionally well-organized bureaucratic structure. Every act of the censorship authority was thoroughly documented and all documents were archived. The text-production, be it of original works or of translation, was supervised by the so-called *junta de censura*, a censorship committee composed of Church representatives, low-rank officials and men of letters (Merino & Rabadán 2009: 125), who acted in line with Franco's ideology. The mission of the censorship committee lay in repressing all ideas expression and facts which were not to be made public in the public interest (i.e. in the political interest of Franco's regime).

In Spain under Franco, non-democratic press laws were adopted, which became Franco's specific tool of supervision: the first Press Act of 22 April 1938

---

[5] It is very problematic to check the self-censored fragments, however, this "working method" employed by the author, the translator or the publisher cannot be ignored if the findings reach general conclusions.

[*Ley de 22 de abril, de Prensa*]⁶ and the second Press Act of 18 March 1966 [*Ley 14/1966, de 18 de marzo, de Prensa e Imprenta*]⁷ (cf. Neuschäfer 1994, Merino & Rabadán 2009, Cuenca 2013). The application of censorship criteria is based on Articles 2 and 6 of the Press Act adopted in 1938:

Article 2. To fulfil the above function the state is to: [...] Fifth. To carry out censorship until lifted.
Article 6. The Head of the Press Service in each province shall perform the following duties: a) Carry out censorship activities, until these are lifted, according to guidelines issued by the National Press Centre or, as the case may be, by the Civil Governor of the province if the guidelines are related to issues of local or provincial dimension; with regard to war censorship, its performance is subject military authority.⁸

In the sixties, the situation eased and the Press Act of 1938 was amended. From that point on, the censorship procedure was carried out in accordance with the Press Act of 18 March 1966. It follows from Articles 3 and 4 of Chapter 1 on the freedom of the press that the person responsible for publishing a work is not obliged to submit it to the censorship committee; it is only a non-obligatory consultation [*consulta voluntaria*]:

Article Three – Censorship – The Administration may not require preliminary censorship or mandatory consultation, except in cases of emergency and war expressly provided for by law.
Article Four – Non-obligatory Consultation – One. Administration may be consulted on the content of all types of printed texts by anyone who is responsible for its dissemination. The approval or non-action of the Administration exempt it from liability for the dissemination of printed under consultation. Two. The law provides for deadlines that must elapse for the ad-

---

⁶ http://www.derechos.org/nizkor/espana/doc/leypre24abr38.html (30.10.2014).
⁷ https://www.boe.es/diario_boe/txt.php?id=BOE-A-1966-3501 (30.10.2014).
⁸ Artículo segundo.—En el ejercicio de la función expresada corresponde al Estado: [...] Quinto. La censura mientras no se disponga su supresión.
Artículo sexto.—Corresponde al Jefe del Servicio de Prensa de cada provincia: a). Ejercer la Censura, mientras ésta subsista, de acuerdo con las orientaciones que se le dicten por el Servicio Nacional de Prensa, o, en su caso, por el Gobernador Civil de la provincia, cuando éstas se refieran a materia local o provincial; en materia de censura de guerra, el ejercicio de esta censura quedará sometida a la autoridad militar. http://www.derechos.org/nizkor/espana/doc/leypre24abr38.html (04.11.2014).

ministrative non-action to imply approval as well as for the requirements which must be met to submit the printed text for consultation.[9]

Censors' reports are drafted by the Ministry of Information and Tourism [*Ministerio de Información y Turismo*], Directorate General of Popular Culture [*Directorio general de la cultura popular*], Publishing Department [*Departamento editorial*]. Official censorship was officially abolished in 1977. However, according to Merino and Rabadán (2009: 126) and based on my own research, it may be stated that censorship lasted well until 1983, which clearly follows from some analysed files.

Censors' reports

All files drawn up between 1939 and 1983[10] are now deposited at the General Administration Archives (*Archivo General de la Administración* or AGA) in Alcalá de Henares (Madrid) in the culture collection labelled 3(50) in the section on the censorship of books. The censorship system in Franco's Spain was bureaucratic in nature. If a publisher, author or translator intended to publish a certain work, an official application had to be filed and it was necessary to wait for the decision by the censorship *junta*. The whole process was a time-consuming administrative burden (though it is thanks to the administrative acts that so much interesting and extensive material is available to us today). The process consisted of the following stages:

(1) written application [*instancia de solicitud*]

The application through which a publisher applied for permission to publish or import a book was a specific form which had to include: author's name [*autor*], book title [*título*], publishing house [*editor*], number of pages [*volumen*], format [*formato*], number of copies [*tirada proyectada*], price [*precio de venta*]. Unlike

---

[9] https://www.boe.es/diario_boe/txt.php?id=BOE-A-1966-3501 (30.10.2014).

[10] The censorship was officially abolished in 1977, but there are traces of her and files until 1983.

censors' reports in Portugal (cf. Špirk 2011: 208)[11], Spanish censorship did not require the name of the translator to be included; this box is missing.

(2) censor's report [*informe del censor*]

After the censorship committee received a written application, an official file was opened and it was assigned a number [*expediente n.º*]. The first page of the file stated the date of application, book title, author's name, publishing house, number of pages and number of copies. Furthermore, it stated whether a prior report on the given work has been drafted [*antecedentes*] and the person [*lector*] who was assigned with drafting the report [*pase al lector don*]; for censors, only their number, not their name, was stated. This was followed by the actual censor's report [*informe*] which also included a censor's opinion in which the censor had to say whether the analysed work attacked Catholic doctrine; the Church and its representatives; public morals; the regime and its institutions; persons who cooperate or have cooperated with the regime. On the basis of the censor's report, a result [*resultado*] was determined: (not) authorizable [(*no*) *autorizable*], (not) approved [(*no*) *aprobado*], dismissal [*denegación*], dismissed [*denegado*].

(3) final decision [*resolución*]

Then, the applicant was notified of the result of the censorship procedure. By means of the decision, the publisher was notified whether the book was recommended for publication, or not.

Czech literature and Francoist censorship

One of the factors that the Czech and Spanish socio-cultural systems in the period (1939–1983) had in common, was the existence of institutionalised censorship for several decades whose emergence, existence and lifting had a critical impact on the translation of literature (Cuenca 2013). In the case of Spain, the institutional archives on censorship (AGA) are of inestimable importance for the following reasons: they demonstrate the values of the era and they serve as a

---

[11] With regard to files on book censorship (printed works), censors' reports analysing theatre plays required the name of the translator to be stated (cf. Rabadán 2000).

record of translation activities of that time. It is well-know fact that translation activities and their products are mainly part of the target culture's polysystem (the Spanish one in this case) in which the translation process culminates with the final reception and interpretation of the original work.

In the period of official censorship (1939–1983) twenty three Czech books were directly translated and published in Spain (cf. Cuenca 2013: 102–118) and, in addition, nine second-hand translations based on German source text, which are relevant for my research: Filip[12] (1970, 1972), Procházka[13] (1977, 1979, 1983), Kohout[14] (1979), Hašek[15] (1980) and Hofman[16] (1980, 1981). The official censorship focused on these novels not only because they were published in the seventies and eighties, but also because their authors were either in the exile or were opponents of the former Communist Czechoslovakia and the content of their works seemed dangerous for Spanish readers.

Three files evaluating Filip's novels have been obtained from the archival collection (3)50 on culture – censorship of books [*cultura: censura de libros*] deposited in the AGA, the files are designated as follows: 70-1444, 71-9046 and 76-13436 (the first number refers to the year in which the censor's report was

[12] Ota Filip (1930) is a Czech novelist and journalist. His works were banned or censored by the authorities during the communist era government of Czechoslovakia and after the occupation of Czechoslovakia by the Warsaw Pact Armed Forces in 1968, he was sentenced and imprisoned for his dissident activities in 1969–1971 (reason why he moved to Germany in 1974).

[13] Jan Procházka (1929–1971) was a Czech film screenwriter and prose writer. He was one of the radical socialist members of the Czechoslovak Writers' Union, so he was dismissed from the party's Central Committee, of which he was a candidate member.

[14] Pavel Kohout (1928) is a Czech and Austrian novelist, playwright and poet. He was a member of the Communist Party of Czechoslovakia, a Prague Spring exponent and dissident in the 1970s until he was expelled to Austria. He was a founding member of the Charter 77 movement.

[15] Jaroslav Hašek (1883–1923) was a Czech writer, humourist, satirist, journalist, bohemian and anarchist. He is best known for his novel *The Good Soldier Švejk* (1920–1923), an unfinished collection of farcical incidents about a soldier in World War I and a satire on the ineptitude of authority figures.

[16] Ota Hofman (1928–1989) was a novelist and screenwriter, author of books especially for children and screenplays for films for children and youth. The best-known films and serials were on *Mr Tau*.

drawn up, i.e. 1970, 1971 and 1976; the second number indicates the envelope in which the file is to be found) and bear the following call numbers: 66/05356, 73/01185 and 73/05808 (the five-digit number refers to the box in which many envelopes with censors' reports are deposited and the first number indicates in which part of the archives the relevant box is stored; the AGA has three depositories: No. 21 with the oldest files and Nos. 66 and 73). The first file 70-1444 analyses the novel *El café de la calle del cementerio* (1970) [The path to the cemetery], the envelope contains a typed Spanish translation and an application (February 1970) filed by the *Plaza & Janés* publishing house for the approval to publish it. However, the report suggests that sentences be deleted [*tachaduras*] on pages 40, 154, 435, 461 and 564 because they contain sexual and erotic references that attack the morals; therefore, they are crossed out in red in the translation:

> I was fifteen when I enjoyed myself with her on the damned couch; ~~when I touched her breasts, she stretched out how long she was, she was not yet sixteen, I noticed how her nipples could be seen under the bra, then I caressed her buttocks and she squeezed the two oval halves, so they got hard as melons, but they were not cold, but rather warm~~, my hands were quite rough [...]
> [...] because of the success of the pirouette~~, or because the soft hair that came out from Stefka's tight shorts as she stretched her legs~~. Men [...] ~~For that flock of hairs?~~
> [...] I laid my eyes on her nipples, clearly marked under her dress.
> One of them muttered: "Suck my ass!"
> [...] hope and lecherous promises, she discovered his genitals, pulling out his member from inside his military cloak. Then she [...] [17]

---

[17] Quince años tenía yo cuando disfruté de ella en el maldito canapé; cuando toqué sus pechos, se tendió cuan larga era, ella no tenía aún diesises años, noté cómo sus pezones se atiesaban bajo el sostén, luego acaricié sus nalgas, y ella apretó las dos ovaladas mitades, de forma que se pusieron duras como melones, pero no estaban frías, sino más bien calientes, tenía las manos bastante ásperas [...]

[...] por el éxito de la pirueta, o porque Stefka, esparrancar las piernas, le salieron un poco los blandos pelitos de los estrechos shorts. Los hombres [...] ¿Por aquel par de pelitos?

[...] posé mis ojos en sus pezones, claramente marcados bajo el vestido.
Uno de ellos murmuró: "¡Chúpame el culo!"
[...] esperanza y lubricas promesas, descubrió su sexo, sacando su miembro de entre los pliegos de su capote militar. Luego se puso [...]

The finished typesetting [*galeradas*] of pages 18, 72, 204, 216 and 263 (without the above mentioned sentences) are also to be found in the envelope. Finally, some sentences after having been self-censored, the novel is authorized to be published.

File No. 71-9046 focus on the novel *Un loco para cada ciudad* (1972) [Crazy in town]. A typed Spanish translation by José M. Pomares is attached to the application. The file consists of three censors' reports that suggest that sentences be deleted on pages 5, 6, 7, 92, 93 and 233 (marked in red in the translation). Finally only one omission was made (on page 233): "Ilonka is a kind of Virgin from Czenstochau. What happens is that she is not pure. She has committed all the wonderful sins that only a woman can make."[18] The translation is approved on 30 May 1972. In this file there appear two names of *lectores*: Fernando Fernandes-Monzón Altolaguirre (2.10.1971) and Domingo Casanova Trujillo (29.9.1971).

Official file No. 76-13436 states that the novel *Un loco para cada ciudad* (1976) had been considered in 1971 in File No. 71-9046. This report drawn up after Franco's death only notes that "the requirements of the Consignment stock before publication had been met under Article 12 of the Press Act in force".[19]

Official File No. 75-1197 on the novel *La verduga* [Hangwoman], incidentally very thin, only states that the book by Pavel Kohout meets all the requirements of the Consignment stock before publication. The application of this file makes references to the publishing house *Pomaire* and to the name of the censor No. 16, Goméz Nisa.

In the case of children's literature [*infantil, juvenil*], all reports have a green line on the page margin to distinguish them from the prose for adults. Three children books by Jan Procházka were translated into Spanish *La carpa* (1977)

AGA (3)50 66/05356.

[18] Ilonka es una especie de Virgen de Czenstochau. Lo que ocurre es que tampoco ella es pura. Ha cometido todos los maravillosos pecados que sólo puede cometer una mujer.
AGA (3)50 73/01185.

[19] Cumplidos los requisitos del Depósito previo a la difusión, exigido por al artículo 12 de la vigente Ley de Prensa e Imprenta.
AGA (3)50 73/05808.

[The carp], *Viva la república* (1979) [Long live the republic] and *El viejo y las palomas* (1983) [The old man and pigeons]. The censor of file No. 77-14682 had no objections to the story of *The Carp*, he authorized the publication. However, he pointed out that "in the short bibliography at the end a next book by the same author is announced, which is called *Long live the republic* that could, given its title, be questionable".[20] Other three Files Nos. 79-5942, 81-10385 (second edition of *La Carpa*) and 83-1782 stated that the publication of Procházka's books by the *Alfaguara* publishing house had been approved as they met all the requirements of the Consignment stock before publication.

On 27 November 1980 (File No. 80-12230) and on 29 April 1981 (File No. 81-4399) Carmen Aragonés Domarco of the publishing house *Juvenil Alfaguara* applied for approval to publish the book *Llega Pan Tau* (1980) [Pan Tau Comes] and *Desaparece Pan Tau* (1981) [Pan Tau Leaves] and both were approved under the Article 12 of the Press Act in force.

A special case worth studying is File No. 69-3066 that evaluated the German translation of the book *Tanzstunden für Erwachsene und Fortgeschrittene* (1965) [Dancing Lessons for the Advanced in Age] by Bohumil Hrabal. The censor drew up the following report:

[...] it treats with little respect even sacred subjects (Jesus Christ, the Blessed Virgin, the Trinity) and institutions. The situations that some commanders are portrayed in several times do not give a good account of them. Furthermore, we believe that while there are no statements discussing political issues, it would be useful to know the Castilian translation to specify therein the erasures to be, considering otherwise this work as approvable.[21]

---

[20] Por el contrario, se anuncia la próxima publicación de la obra del mismo autor: "Viva la república", que tal vez pudiera merecer reservas, a juzgar por el título.
AGA (3)50 73/06422.

[21] [...] tratando con poco respeto incluso temas sagrados (Jesucristo, la Sma Virgen, la Trinidad) e instituciones. Aparecen en diversas ocasiones algunos jefes militares que no quedan en buen lugar.
Por otro lado lo estimamos que si bien no existe tesis alguna ni se tratan temas que rocen la política, convendría conocer la traducción al castellano para especificar en ella las tachaduras a introducir, considerándosela por lo demás la obra como AUTORIZABLE.
AGA (3)50 66/02825.

It could have become another example of an indirectly translated Czech novel based on a German source text, but in fact the translation into Spanish has never been made.

Case study: *The Good Soldier Švejk*

Critical discourse analysis (censors' reports)

Hašek's novel was considered by Franco's censors to be a polemical work; they did not make it possible to publish the book despite numerous attempts to do so and it was only in 1980 that the novel could be published in Spain. Six files evaluating the Hašek's novel have been obtained from the archival collection (3)50 on culture – censorship of books deposited in the AGA, the files are designated as follows: 50-5870, 69-8670 and 69-8671, 71-8648, 80-5737 and 80-5738 and bear the following call number: 21/09319, 66/03389, 73/01153 and 73/07259. Let us have a more detailed look at specific censors' reports. I include the first three censors' reports in the category of controversial epitexts because in the first case in 1950 the importation of the Argentinian translation into Spain was not allowed and in the following two reports in 1969 and 1971 the publication was not approved; however, the last censor's report (1980) is an affirmative one as it approves the book to be published.

On 11 November 1950 Saturnino Calleja of the *Calleja* publishing house filed an application to import and publish the Argentinian translation. The application process was still governed by the Act of 29 April 1938 [*Orden del 29 de abril de 1938*] and it fell within the remit of the Ministry of Education [*Ministerio de Educación Nacional*], Popular Education Department [*Subsecretaria de educación popular*], General Headquarters of Propaganda [*Dirección general de propaganda*], Censorship of Publications [*Censura de publicaciones*]. As is stated in this censor's report, which forms part of file No. 50-5870, the book attacks the Church and its representatives and morals. The censor further adds that it is a "humorous novel defeatist in nature. It continuously ridicules the army of the Central Powers during the First Great War. It also ridicules the Catholic

Church and its representatives as can be seen in Chapters 9, 10, 11 and 12."²² It is not possible to ascertain the identity of the censor: the signature is illegible and the first page of the file only states that censor No. 12 was tasked with drafting the report. On the basis of the submitted report, cancellation of the importation [*suspensión de su importación*] was proposed.

On 5 September 1969 Jorge de Herralde Gran of the *Anagrama* publishing house asked for a non-obligatory consultation in accordance with the Article 4 of the Press Act of 18 March 1966 and applied for approval to publish Hašek's *Švejk*. He also attached the German intermediary translation to the application. The censor's report refers to *Švejk* as a masterpiece of Czech literature and considers the translation to be good. The censor reports means that

> purely from the literary point of view, I would unconditionally accept the work and not delete a word, but its antimilitaristic spirit, its defiance of the church, its contempt of many authorities, even if Austro-Hungarian authorities, are thought-provoking. It is desirable that a priest and a soldier read the book.²³

The result of the censorship report is dismissal (*denegación*).

On 11 September 1971 the *Ediciones Destino* publishing house applied for approval to publish Hašek's novel under the title *Las aventuras del valeroso soldado Schwejk*. A finished translation into Spanish was attached to the application; however, the name of the translator was missing. It is stated in the official file that this novel had been already considered in 1969 in Files No. 69-8670 (Part 1) and 69-8671 (Part 2), with the *Anagrama* publishing house being the applicant and the publication being dismissed. Censor No. 6 drew up the following report:

---

[22] Novela humorista de tipo terriblemente derrotista. Ridiculiza constantemente al ejército de los Imperios Centrales de la I Gran Guerra. También ridicula a la Iglesia Católica y sus Ministros como puede verse en los capítulos 9, 10, 11 y 12.
AGA (3)50 21/09319.

[23] Por mi parte, desde el punto de vista estrictamente literario, aceptaría sin más esta obra maestra, a la que no se puede tachar ni una coma; pero su espíritu antimilitarista, su fobia a la Iglesia, su desprecio de tantas instituciones, aunque se refiera a las austrohúngaras, da que pensar. Conviene que la novela la lean un sacerdote y un militar.
AGA (3)50 66/03389.

The censor does not know how to assess the book. It tells the story of a Czech soldier during the war between 1914 and 1918. The soldier is an idiot. The sergeants are idiots. The [military] officers are even greater idiots. The generals compete in stupidity and idiocy. Army priests and other priests are gamblers, drunkards, heathens and of course idiots. And everything that goes on in the book is so idiotic that one starts to think whether the author wanted to write a humorous book written by an idiot to be read by idiots.

In any case, the anticlerical nature of the book, the selection of words and heathen, not to say blasphemous, scenes and the ridiculous caricature of generals, officers and soldiers of the Austrian army make it an inadmissible book.
NOT AUTHORIZABLE[24]

The final decision reads dismissal [*denegación*] and the whole file is designated as dismissed [*denegado*].

On 26 May 1980 the *Destino* publishing house applies once more to the Ministry of Culture [*Ministerio de cultura*], Management of the Literary Issues and Libraries [*Dirección general del libro y bibliotecas*], Publishing Promotion [*Promoción editorial*] for approval to publish a translation of Hašek's Švejk. At that time, the Press Act of 1966 was still in force; however, it had been amended by a new decree of 1 April 1977 on the freedom of expression [*Real Decreto-ley 24/1977, de 1 de abril, sobre libertad de expresión*] (articles on censorship and non-obligatory consultation had been repealed). The freedom of expression follows from Article 1 of Chapter 1 on the freedom of the express through the press: "Freedom of expression and the right to disseminate information through printed or audio means shall be subject to no other limitations than those established by the legal system in general"[25]. Official File No. 80-5737 which is, un-

---

[24] El lector no sabe cómo calificar este libro. Cuenta la historia de un soldado checo en la Guerra 1914–18. El soldado es idiota. Los Sargentos son idiotas, los oficiales más idiotas todavía. Los Generales baten el récord de la estupidez y de la idiotez. Los sacerdotes castrenses y no castrenses son jugadores, borrachos, impíos, y naturalmente, idiotas. Y todo lo que pasa en el libro es tan idiota que empieza uno a pensar si el autor no habrá querido hacer un libro humorístico escrito por un idiota para que sea leído por idiotas.

En todo caso, su aspecto anticlerical, sus expresiones y escenas impías y casi blasfemas, y la caricatura ridícula que hace de los Generales, Oficiales y soldados del Ejército austriaco, lo clasifica como libro inadmisible.

No autorizable
AGA (3)50 73/01153.

[25] De la libertad de expresión por medio de impresos

like the other files mentioned above, very thin, points out the fact that the publication had been dismissed in File No. 71-8648. However, censor No. 8 concluded that "it is not necessary to adopt measures under Article 64 of the Press Act of 1966", and that "the work complies with the formal requirements".[26] It was stated in the final decision that "the requirements of the Consignment stock before publication had been met under Article 12 of the press law in force".[27] Finally *Švejk* could be published in Spain for the first time in 1980, i.e. five years after the fall of Franco's regime and three years after censorship had been abolished.

Oral history (interviews)

Interviews as affirmative epitexts may offer an interesting insight into the genesis of translation. Given the topic of this chapter, I would like to emphasize only such answers that are illustrative of the background of the censorship procedure. Andreu Teixidor (of the *Ediciones Destino* publishing house) found the translation of *Švejk* ready and waiting together with other translations to be published; he liked the book and decided to publish it[28]. At that time the censor did not ap-

---

Artículo primero. La libertad de expresión y el derecho a la difusión de informaciones por medio de impresos gráficos o sonoros, no tendrá más limitaciones que las establecidas en el ordenamiento jurídico con carácter general.
http://www.boe.es/buscar/doc.php?id=BOE-A-1977-9008 (12.11.2014).

[26] No procede adoptar las previsiones del artículo 64 de la ley de prensa e imprenta. Requisitos formales completos.
AGA (3)50 73/07259.

[27] Cumplidos los requisitos del Depósito previo a la difusión, exigido por al artículo 12 de la vigente Ley de Prensa e Imprenta.
AGA (3)50 73/07259.

[28] En los sesenta, a finales de los sesenta, entonces yo en los setenta cuando era que me encuentro con el libro ya traducido y compuesto también. Entonces mi gran pregunta fue qué pasa con este libro que había encargado en algún momento y este libro no pasó la censura, no se podía publicar porque no había pasado la censura. [...] Pues yo intenté a principios de setenta y dos, setenta y tres, me acuerdo que, era un proceso divertido, porque aun en aquella época, claro, estabamos en la dictadura, por lo tanto el libro no... tenía que pasar por el depósito previo, etc. y lo mandamos y no pasó.
Interview with Andreu Teixidor on 10 of July 2012

prove the book to be published (see above). Teixidor explained that "he did not want to delete anything and the retranslation could be expensive"[29]; therefore, he waited for the opportunity to publish the translation, which came only in 1980.

Why was the German translation used as the source text? At the time, there were no translators in Spain capable of translating directly from Czech (according to Teixidor the situation changed with the arrival of Monika Zgustová), and therefore translations into other languages were used as source texts. This is confirmed by Alfonsina Janés, the translator, who adds that given the geopolitical situation of the time, it was difficult to get the Czech original. After she had submitted the translation, she did not go back to it or reread it, so she does not know whether any editorial changes were made to it[30].

Micro-textual analysis

In this section, my aim is to compare the Czech original and the two selected Spanish translations by Janés and Zgustová. The German text will be examined to reveal whether the shifts occurred already in the translation from Czech into German, or whether they were in fact introduced by Janés. Selected excerpts from *Švejk* are presented in the following order: the Czech original (Hašek), the German first-hand translation (Reiner), the Spanish second-hand translation (Janés) and the Spanish translation (Zgustová). Excerpts[31] for the micro-textual analysis were selected on the basis that they may have represented problems for the censor. Knowing that Alfonsina Janés made her translation at a time when not only translation but also original literary production were subject to official censorship, and she (or editor) was aware of this situation, we may ask, for in-

---

[29] Pero yo no quería quitar nada, es decir... Lo que pasa es que claro el proceso de retraducir el libro y todo eso era... era caro y complicado y tal y yo ya lo tenía todo preparado y dije bueno lo voy a publicar ya.
Interview with Andreu Teixidor on 10 of July 2012

[30] Por otra parte tenga en cuenta que yo nunca leo mis traducciones, a parte de que ésta concretamente tardó muchos años en salir.
Email correspondence with Alfonsina Janés (12.11.2014)

[31] In my research I analysed more than ten passage, but for the purpose of this chapter and in order not to exceed it, I enclose only one to illustrate the self-censorship. For more details see Vavroušová 2013: 43–56.

stance, whether Alfonsina Janés (or editor) self-censored at some points (cf. Neuschäfer 1994: 49, Merino & Rabadán 2009: 127).

The following excerpt deals with anticlericalism and criticizes the Catholic Church:

Hašek (1921/2008: 111–112)	Reiner (1926/2011: 132–133)	Janés (1980/2010: 115–116)	Zgustová (2008: 130)
Přípravy k usmrcování lidí děly se vždy jménem božím či vůbec nějaké domnělé vyšší bytosti, kterou si lidstvo vymyslilo a stvořilo ve své obrazotvornosti. [...] **Než svatá inkvizice upálila své oběti, sloužila nejslavnější bohoslužby, velkou mši svatou se zpěvy.** [...] Veliká jatka světové války neobešla se bez požehnání kněžského. Polní kuráti všech armád modlili se a sloužili polní mše za vítězství té strany, jejíž chleba jedli.	Die Vorbereitungen zur Tötung von Menschen sind stets im Namen Gottes oder eines vermeintlichen höheren Wesens vor sich gegangen, das die Menschen ersonnen und in ihrer Phantasie erschaffen haben. [...] **Bevor die heilige Inquisition ihre Opfer verbrannte, zelebrierte sie die feierlichsten Gottesdienste und die große heilige Messe mit Gesängen.** [...] Die große Schlachtbank des Weltkriegs konnte des priesterlichen Segens nicht entbehren. Die Feldkuraten aller Armeen beteten und zelebrierten Feldmessen für den Sieg jener Partei, deren Brot sie aßen.	Los preparativos para matar a las personas se han llevado siempre a cabo en nombre de Dios o de un elevado ser hipotético que han inventado los hombres y que han creado en su fantasía. [...] XXX El gran matadero de la Guerra Mundial no podía prescindir de la bendición sacerdotal. Los capellanes castrenses de todos los ejércitos rezaban y celebraban misas de campaña por la victoria del partido cuyo pan comían.	Los preparativos para las matanzas de gente se han llevado a cabo en nombre de Dios o de algún otro hipotético ser supremo que la humanidad haya engendrado en su imaginación. [...] **Antes de quemar a sus víctimas, la Santa Inquisición celebraba la más solemne de las ceremonias religiosas, es decir, una gran misa cantada.** [...] El gran matadero que fue la Guerra Mundial no podía prescindir tampoco de la bendición eclesiástica. Los capellanes castrenses de todos los ejércitos rezaban y celebraban misas de campaña por la victoria del país que les procuraba el pan.

Figure 1: Excerpts of the novel

Information on the Holy Inquisition, a legal institution of the Catholic Church and also the Spanish and Portuguese rulers whose remit was to deal with heresy, is missing in the translation by Alfonsina Janés which omits the sentence[32] *Než svatá inkvizice upálila své oběti, sloužila nejslavnější bohoslužby, velkou mši svatou se zpěvy [Before the Holy Inquisition burnt its victims, it per-*

---

[32] In Monika Zgustová's translation made later when the political censorship did not manifest itself in any way, the sentence is not missing.

formed the most solemn religious service – a High Mass with singing]. This omission may be accounted for in a number of ways:
(1) It is possible that the sentence was missing in the German source text available to the translator. Assuming, however, that the various editions did not differ from each other, it is not very likely because the first German edition (1926–1927) available to us and also the new version from 2011 contained the sentence.
(2) The sentence was not missing in the German source text; the translator failed to notice it by mistake and thus did not translate it.
(3) Applying self-censorship, the translator intentionally did not translate the sentence because Janés made the translation at the end of the 1960s when censorship was very active in Spain (see above).
(4) It is also possible that Janés translated the sentence, but it was later omitted by an editor or a third person that was aware of rules of censorship proceedings. Janés has stated in an email correspondence (October 2014) that after having submitted the translation, she never saw it again[33].

Conclusions

This chapter describes the way the official censorship in Franco's Spain determined literary production (both original and translations). Authors, in our case translators, were aware of unwritten rules and tried to "adjust" their texts because they knew that they would be judged according to certain criteria (cf. Merino & Rabadán 2009: 127).

Having analysed all censors' reports concerning second-hand translations (from German) of novels of Czech literature published under Franco's dictatorship, it can be stated that the most relevant and "interesting" themes for *lectores*

---

[33] No puedo recordar si tuve en cuenta la censura o no, no lo creo, pero es que no me acuerdo de nada. Por otra parte tenga en cuenta que yo nunca leo mis traducciones, a parte de que ésta concretamente tardó muchos años en salir. Y tenga también en cuenta que las editoriales tienen sus correctores, y por lo tanto quizás una persona que conocía los problemas de censura suavizó algunos pasajes sin que yo me enterara.
Email correspondence with Alfonsina Janés (12.11.2014)

were the following ones: (1) all insinuations or passages attacking the fundamental pillars of the regime, i.e. Hašek's *Švejk*; (2) all erotic and sexual parts used to be deleted in order to save and ensure the "pure" mind of the reader. In the first case the publication of the books (translations) was not authorized at all, there was no possibility of changing or deleting controversial parts (sometimes it would be necessary to delete whole chapters). In the other case there was a possibility of "negotiating"; that means that censors only advised (they did not order at all) to delete inappropriate sentences and if the publishing house agreed and made some changes, then the novel could be published. The use of self-censorship was a frequent tool to avoid difficulties with the Establishment; two types of self-censorship have been observed: (1) prior self-censorship, mostly used by the translator or the editor and "hidden" from the censors, (2) post self-censorship, mostly done by the publishing house and performed upon the recommendation of the *lector*. The official censorship was very cautious as well as discreet, only single sentences, or even only some unacceptable words used to be deleted.

From today's point of view it is surprising that the power and influence of the censorship was genuinely omnipotent and benefited from the right to delay the literary communication of unfavourable books by a few years (in many cases the decision depended on one person only) to protect the Spanish public from dangerous and contaminant ways of thinking.

The obtained data were used for a detailed description of the "adventures" of Czech literature under Franco's dictatorship in the Spanish-speaking part of the Iberian Peninsula and, in general, the research may contribute to the clarification of the Czech-Spanish literary relations, not leaving aside the important mediating role of the German language.

References

BOE-A-1977-9008 (1977): "Real Decreto-ley 24/1977, de 1 de abril, sobre libertad de expresión". http://www.boe.es/buscar/doc.php?id=BOE-A-1977-9008 (12.11.2014)

BOE-A-1966-3501 (1966): "Ley 14/1966, de 18 de marzo, de Prensa e Imprenta". https://www.boe.es/diario_boe/txt.php?id=BOE-A-1966-3501 (30.10.2014)

CUENCA, Miguel (2013): "Influence of the Spanish Polysystem on Czech-Spanish Translation during the Second Half of the 20th century". Dissertation. – Prague: Charles University. Faculty of Arts, Institute of Translation Studies. Supervisor: Doc. PhDr. Miloslav Uličný, CSc.

FILIP, Ota (1970). *El café de la calle del cementerio.* – Barcelona: Plaza & Janés. Translated by Martín Ezcurdia.

FILIP, Ota (1972). *Un loco para cada ciudad.* – Barcelona: Plaza & Janés. Translated by José Manuel Pomares.

GENETTE, Gérard (1997): *Paratexts: Thresholds of Interpretation.* Cambridge: CUP. Translated by Jane E. Lewin.

HAŠEK, Jaroslav (1920–23/2008): *Osudy dobrého vojáka Švejka za světové války.* – Praha: Euromedia Group k.s. Knižní klub.

HAŠEK, Jaroslav (1926–27/2011): *Die Abenteuer des braven Soldaten Schwejk.* – Berlin: Aufbau Verlag. Translated by Grete Reiner.

HAŠEK, Jaroslav (1980/2011): *Las aventuras del valeroso soldado Schwejk.* – Barcelona: Destino. Translated by Alfonsina Janés.

HAŠEK, Jaroslav (2008): *Las aventuras del buen soldado Svejk.* – Barcelona: Galaxia Gutenberg: Círculo de Lectores. Translated by Monika Zgustová.

HOFMAN, Ota (1980): *Pan Tau: Llega Pan Tau.* – Madrid: Alfaguara. Translated by Lola Romero.

HOFMAN, Ota (1981): *Pan Tau: Desaparece Pan Tau.* – Madrid: Alfaguara. Translated by Lola Romero.

JANÈS, Alfonsina (2012): "Sobre la traducción de Schwejk", Interview 09.07.2012

JANES, Alfonsina (2014): "Re: Censura y Schwejk", Email correspondence 20.11.2014

KOHOUT, Pavel (1979). *La verduga.* – Barcelona: Ultra-mar. Translated by Yolanda Salvá Yenes.

MERINO, Raquel & RABADÁN, Rosa (2002): "Censored Translations in Franco's Spain: The TRACE Project – Theatre and Fiction (English-Spanish)". *TTR:*

traduction, terminologie, rédaction 15 (2), 125–152. http://www.erudit.org/revue/ttr/2002/v15/n2/007481ar.pdf (09.07.2014)

MERKLE, Denise (2010): "Censorship". In: GAMBIER, Yves & VAN DOORSLAER, Luc (eds.): *Handbook of Translation Studies*. – Amsterdam: John Benjamins Publishing, 18–21.

NEUSCHÄFER, Hans-Jörg (1994): *Adiós la España eterna: la dialéctica de la censura: novela, teatro y cine bajo el franquismo*. – Barcelona: Anthropos.

POPOVIČ, Anton (1975): *Teória umeleckého prekladu: Aspekty textu a literárnej metakomunikácie*. – Bratislava: Tatran.

POPOVIČ, Anton (1983): *Originál/preklad: interpretačná terminológia*. – Bratislava: Tatran.

PROCHÁZKA, Jan (1965): *Viva la república*. – Madrid: Alfaguara. Translated by Javier Lacarra.

PROCHÁZKA, Jan (1977): *La carpa*. – Madrid: Alfaguara. Translated by Antonio Skármeta.

PROCHÁZKA, Jan (1983): *El viejo y las palomas*. – Madrid: Alfaguara. Translated by Anton Dieterich.

PYM, Anthony (1998): *Method in translation history*. – Manchester: St. Jerome Publishing.

RABADÁN, Rosa (2000): "Con orden y concierto: la censura franquista y las traducciones inglés-español 1939–1985". In: RABADÁN, Rosa (ed.): *Traducción y censura inglés-español (1939–1985). Estudio preliminar*. – León: Universidad de León, 13–22.

ŠPIRK, Jaroslav (2011): "Ideology, Censorship, Indirect Translations and Non-Translation: Czech Literature in 20th-century Portugal". Dissertation. – Prague: Charles University. Faculty of Arts, Institute of Translation Studies. Supervisor: Prof. PhDr. Jana Králová, CSc.

ŠPIRK, Andreu (2012): "Sobre Švejk y censura", Interview 10.07.2012

VAVROUŠOVÁ, Petra (2013): "German as a Mediating Language in the Translation of Hašek's Švejk into Spanish". Master's Diploma Thesis. – Prague: Charles University. Faculty of Arts, Institute of Translation Studies. Supervisor: PhDr. Jaroslav Špirk, Ph.D.

Mute, dumb, dubbed: Lulu's silent talkies

Tessa Dwyer
Monash University, Melbourne
tessa.dwyer@monash.edu

This chapter examines the role dubbing has played in shaping modes of practice across the film industry. Focusing on the transition from silent cinema to talkies, it sketches a cultural context for dubbing by detailing the production conditions, textual thematics and reception of two films staring Louise Brooks, The Canary Murder Case *and* Prix de beauté. *In doing so, it connects same-language revoicing or 'voice doubling' to foreign-language dubbing, seeking to identify how language pragmatics and issues of interlingual translation are formative, not anomalous, to screen media dynamics. Introducing the concept of 'to-be-dubbed-ness', it argues that post-synchronised revoicing can impact upon filmmaking at all stages of production and reception, and that it needs to be acknowledged as more than an afterthought. Finally, it traces dubbing's deconstructive edge and its relation to modernist efforts to denature and demystify filmic illusion.*

Introduction

She is primarily remembered as a silent star, yet the ups and downs of Louise Brooks' tumultuous career demand to be read foremost in relation to her voice. Curiously, although featuring in two early talkies – Paramount's *The Canary Murder Case* (St. Clair, 1929) and *Prix de beauté* (Genina, 1930) made at SO-FAR, Paris – her voice is heard in neither. In both, she is dubbed. This technical production detail is often passed over in histories of Brooks and critical analyses of her work, warranting only brief, parenthetical discussion and some disparagement. Below, I proceed to revisit Brooks' vocal machinations in both these films, in order to explore dubbing's varied contours in different national and industrial contexts and its significance, not just for Brooks but also for the transition era as a whole and with it, emergent practices and politics of sound filmmaking still in effect today.

In *The Canary Murder Case* and *Prix de beauté*, dubbing is deployed to very different ends – alternately intralingual and interlingual, domestic and foreign. It was Brooks herself and not the studio or production team behind *The Canary Murder Case* that engineered her vocal substitution as the Canary, whereas the multiple-language dubbing of *Prix de beauté* was planned in pre-production while Réne Clair was still tabled to direct. Hence, one film had dubbing thrust upon it, while the other pro-actively seized upon this tool for its cross-border, translational possibilities. In the following discussion, I consider the connection between these two quite different films and their distinct revoicing strategies, asking how early foreign-language dubbing relates to other concurrent practices of doubling, ghosting and post-synchronisation. This project engages with the language politics specific to cinema as an early global, mass media form, exploring its transnational, translational pull. In isolating issues of dubbing in *The Canary Murder Case* and *Prix de beauté*, distinctions quickly disintegrate between pre- and post-production, text and context, performance and persona, while novel connections emerge, demonstrating the profitability of viewing these films in tandem.

Refusing to speak

Figure 1: Publicity photo of Louise Brooks sporting her famous 'black helmet' bob, from the *Stars of Photoplay* booklet (*Photoplay* magazine, 1930).

As Brooks documents in her autobiographical *Lulu in Hollywood*, in early 1929, she refused to lend her voice to the sound version of *The Canary Murder Case* (2000, 104). The facts around this refusal are little known despite the many claims made on its behalf, not least that it effectively ended Brooks' career, confining her stardom to the silent era alone and investing her iconic 'black helmet' image (Fig. 1) with an unshakable sense of muteness (see Hagener 2004: 112;

Gladysz 2010; Hastie 1997: 5).[1] Before scrutinising and complicating such claims, a reiteration of the story is necessary. This task is far from straightforward, however, for the choice of source naturally affects the telling. Brook's own writings have been privileged as the proper place to begin, despite appearing over fifty years after the incident occurred. Earlier accounts are drawn from reviews and previews from the time of the film's release, some of which exposed Brooks' ghosting prior to the public premiere on February 16, 1929. Two days earlier, for instance, Mollie Merrick wrote in the *Lincoln Evening Journal* (Feb 14, 1929):

> In a recent picture made with Louise Brooks for leading woman, a talkie version was decided upon only after Miss Brooks had sailed for Europe. Margaret Livingston took her place and the substitution took nothing from the picture, they tell me.

While accepting Amelie Hastie's (1997: 5) warning that Brooks' own writings need to be approached with caution, as a "carefully constructed self-representation" inseparable from her other performances, her account remains at least as fascinating as its legacy. In *Lulu in Hollywood*, Brooks reminisces:

> It had pleased me on the day I finished the silent version of The Canary Murder Case for Paramount to leave Hollywood for Berlin to work for Pabst. When I got back to New York after finishing Pandora's Box, Paramount's New York office called to order me to get on the train at once for Hollywood. They were making The Canary Murder Case into a talkie and needed me for retakes. When I said I wouldn't go, they offered me any amount of money I might ask, to save the great expense of reshooting and dubbing in another voice. In the end, after they were finally convinced that nothing would induce me to do the retakes, I signed a release (gratis) for all my pictures, and they dubbed in Margaret Livingston's voice in The Canary Murder Case. But the whole thing–the money that Paramount was forced to spend, the affront to the studio–made them so angry that they sent out a story, widely publicized and believed, that they had let me go because I was no good in talkies (Brooks 2000: 104).

Here, Brooks intimates the stakes involved in her obstinate choice to remain silent in the post-synchronised, all-talking version of *The Canary Murder Case*. The salient points within her account are: i) reshooting was involved as well as

---

[1] Brooks' signature bob was referred to as the 'black helmet', a term that appears in the title of Kenneth Tynan's interview with Brooks published in *The New Yorker* in 1979 and reprinted in *Lulu in Hollywood*. See Tynan (2000).

revoicing, ii) she signed away all rights to her Paramount pictures, and iii) the studio then embarked on a smear campaign centred around her voice and its supposed failings. Earlier in her autobiography, Brooks states categorically that this incident resulted in her blacklisting, claiming that afterwards "[n]o major studio would hire me to make a film" (2000: 58). In commentary on *The Canary Murder Case*, many have seized upon this blacklisting claim, positioning her Paramount refusal as a turning point that signalled the demise of her career.[2] Ostensibly, such readings attach great significance to dubbing. However, despite the prominence afforded this vocal transfer technique, surprisingly little attention is given to its actual operations or industrial and cultural significance. Rather, Brooks' unusual insistence that she be dubbed "by another voice" (2000: 104) is simply treated as further evidence of her rebellious and unconventional character. In this way, her decision to remain silent is personalised and, to a degree, trivialised. Consequently, any importance placed upon dubbing is ultimately defused, subsumed by the Brooks persona.

In the following investigation, I revisit this dubbing incident in order to rethink its significance as a serious industrial intervention that reflects as much on actors' rights in the face of a changing aesthetic and technological landscape, as on any 'Brooksie' quirkiness. To do so, I consider Brooks' blacklisting charge in relation to subsidiary claims around her body/voice doubling and the copyright release she signed. My objective is not to evaluate the truth value or otherwise of such claims, but to consider how they have circulated, and why – directly engaging with the "economy of discourse that encircles (and historicizes) Brooks" (Hastie 1997: 5). Why, for instance, has her blacklisting claim sparked such interest whereas her casual signing away of vocal property rights has been largely ignored? Revisiting this story might aid, I suggest, in identifying how Brooks' self-imposed muteness in *The Canary Murder Case* signals her precarious positioning at a specific historical crossroad between silence and sound. Brooks' rebuttal of Paramount's speech demands and lucrative financial offers deserves to

---

[2] For an exception, see Farmer (2010) who notes the many offers, roles and contracts she turned down, concluding that Brooks' movie career failed because, ultimately, she didn't want to be in movies.

be taken seriously and mined for insight into the varied stakes involved in dubbing, sound recording and synchronisation during the transition period.

One further qualification is needed regarding Brooks' account. When later commentators and scholars defer to Brooks in relation to this incident, an interesting dynamic ensues. As Hastie notes, Brooks' autobiographical writings are often deployed to facilitate a re-vocalising effect – giving back voice to her mute, silent-era performances (1997: 6). Referring specifically to analyses of her most famous silent *Pandora's Box / Die Büchse der Pandora* (Pabst, 1929), Hastie points out how such operations can problematically conflate Brooks with her landmark role as Lulu. Moreover, the tendency to privilege Brooks' own words within analysis of her films becomes doubly problematic in relation to *The Canary Murder Case* given Brooks' pointed, categorical refusal to speak in the film. In this context, the retrospective restoration of Brooks' voice via her writing seems particularly perverse, disrespecting or simply overlooking the significance of her silence on set. This revoicing effect also pervades the numerous reiterations of Brooks' account by later scholars and critics (including myself). In repeatedly recounting and reproducing Brooks' words, her silent resistance is drowned out by a cacophony of commentary that perpetuates exactly the demand for vocal agency and authenticity that Brooks deliberately dodged.

Brooks' refusal to speak for (or dub) herself in *The Canary Murder Case* has caught peoples' imagination, I suggest, because it so profoundly upsets present-day thinking on political enfranchisement and self-worth, when 'having a voice' is common parlance for self-autonomy and agency (see Dunn and Jones 1994: 1). Brooks' silence in this film similarly went against the swell of public opinion on talkies at the time, judging from fan and trade publications. As Donald Crafton notes, as the era progressed, audiences tended more and more to demand a level of 'naturalness' and 'authenticity' from screen voices, identifying voice as "an integral part of the actor" (1999: 513). Indicative of such demands are the numerous sworn statements and affidavits published by stars testifying to the authenticity of their vocal performances. In the same year that *The Canary Murder Case* premiered, for instance, Colleen Moore published a statement in *Photoplay* to accompany the release of *Smiling Irish Eyes* (Seiter, 1929) and *Footlights and Fools* (Seiter, 1929), declaring: "at no place in said talking pictures has a 'double' or substitute been used for my voice" (Crafton 1999: 512). While other actors were fighting with studios to retain control of their voices and to secure fair remuneration and equitable contracts for re-vocalisations of silent films (see "Two Equityites", 1929), Brooks, in contrast, casually signed away all rights to her Paramount films for no financial gain. The multiple-language dubbing strategy of *Prix de beauté*, filmed around six months later, goes some way towards explaining this maverick move.

Mouthing french

Prix de beauté constituted Brooks' second foray into talkies and her third European film. Although post-synchronised in four languages including English, it would seem Brooks' voice was absent from all versions. As *Variety* (Dec 18, 1929) reported under the headline "Louise Brooks Double" – "French Girl did Dialog for American Girl in "Beauty Contest", she was dubbed. The "French Girl" (ibid.) responsible was the uncredited Hélène Regelly. *Variety* goes on to detail some of the method used in the film's foreign-language revoicing: "Miss Brooks' French being limited and dialected, she merely memorized the French phrases, moving her lips accordingly and the ghost-voice recorded." This technique of mouthing in a foreign tongue provided the basis for a number of different revoicing strategies trialled during the early sound period including the Vivigraph method proposed by stage producer Edwin Hopkins (1928) and the Multiple-Language Version (MLV) variant favoured by Erich Pommer at UFA in Berlin, known as the 'optical version' (Wahl 2007: 13). In this section, I treat the dubbing of *Prix de beauté* in some length in order to identify specific processes employed, redress misnomers and better understand Brook's idiosyncratic attitudes.

Adopted for a time at MGM in 1931 (Ďurovičová 2003), the Vivigraph method saw actors speaking lines mechanically in foreign tongues as they repeatedly performed their scenes, with native-speaking dubbing actors then recording these same lines as they also *performed* the scenes on the same sets, in full costume and in front of a paying audience. Proposing that American actors should learn "fairly well" Spanish, French, Portuguese, Italian and German in order to perfect the mouthing of these foreign tongues, yet that they might approach more "difficult" languages phonetically by rote, Hopkins explains:

> There must be in the studio a foreign acting cast for each foreign language to be re-vocalized. They should watch the scene being shot in English and in their own language. They should play the dialogue in their own language in a theatre, before an audience, in order that when they re-vocalize the film they may give the re-vocalization the proper dramatic force and finish. (1928: 851)

This Vivigraph method sought to add authenticity and depth to dubbing voices, which emanated from bodies (invisible yet present) performing the very actions seen on screen. As Nataša Ďurovičová notes, it emphasised the voice's "expressive function" and viewed "corporeal presence as necessarily underwriting voice" (2003). 'Optical versions', on the other hand, aimed above all for accurate lip-sync. Pommer had actors "learn their lines phonetically for every single foreign language version", and their speech was then carefully analysed with the help of metronomes and stopwatches so that it could be plotted in relation to shot-lengths, actions and musical accompaniment (Wahl 2007: 13). Utilising a mechanised form of dubbing in order to avoid the expense of new casts for each language version (standard practice for MLVs) Pommer nevertheless viewed the 'optical version' as a MLV *variant* rather than alternative, and "remained a strict adversary of dubbing" (Wahl 2007: 12). Like the Vivigraph method, 'optical versions' involved reshooting (and re-mouthing) for each language version produced. Hence, revoicing was built into the production process itself, rather than being relegated to post-production. This meant films were open to further elements of cultural customisation as, according to Pommer, a "love scene in Berlin, Paris or London has never the same colouring" (qtd and transl. in Wahl 2007: 12).

From newspaper reports on the revoicing of *Prix de beauté* and its planned language versions, it would seem that the methods employed in this film were both similar and different to Vivigraph and 'optical versions'. Judging by US reports, German reviews, and the only extant sound version of the film – a French-language print held by the Cinémathèque Française – it would appear the film was shot simultaneously in silent and sound versions, with Brooks mouthing her lines in French to facilitate her later revoicing by Regelly. A column from *Screen Play Secrets* reports on Brooks "making German and English films in several languages although confessing she is not proficient in more than her own English" (Green 1930). Additionally, reviews of the German-language version (retitled *Miss Europa*) express extreme dissatisfaction with the film's dubbing. A review in *Kinematograph* (Aug 12, 1930) reports: "As soon as the dialogue begins, it is terrible. It is not possible to dub a dialogue that is spoken in French later into German... because the lip movement does not fit" (qtd and transl. in Hagener 2004: 106). Rather than re-mouth her lines for each language version produced, as in Vivigraph and 'optical version' practices, it would appear that subsequent language versions of the French production were post-synchronised using different dubbing casts. In other words, despite being produced in four language versions, the sound version was only shot once, with other languages then superimposed onto the French lip movements (see Pozzi 2004: 25–27). While this streamlined, pragmatic approach to dubbing seems more in line with present-day practices, *Prix de beauté*'s carefree attitude to lip-sync marks it as belonging to the idiosyncratic category of the 'unsynchronised talkie' (Atkinson 2006), and aligns it with the experimentation specific to transition.

Interestingly, Malte Hagener suggests that the *Kinematograph* reviewer is mistaken in assuming "that the dialogue was spoken in French", countering that "as Louise Brooks did not speak French this at least does not hold true for her" (2004: 106). If the report from *Variety* is to be believed however, it would seem Hagener also makes an assumption. As Vivigraph and 'optical version' methods attest, it is not necessary to have second language expertise in order to mouth foreign dialogue on-screen, and it is likely that Brooks' lips at least were speaking French, even if she herself could not. If the *Kinematograph* reviewer and US press reports are correct, it appears that photography for the German-language version matched that of the French version, complete with French-language lip movements and, according to a review from *Reichsfilmblatt* (Aug 16, 1930), a French acting style to boot (transl. in Hagener 2004: 106). On this basis, it seems likely that the English-language version would have also been dubbed, with Brooks remaining mute. This would have avoided any contrast between Brooks' American accent and an otherwise British-accented dubbing crew substituting for the rest of the French cast.

Modernist tones

In some ways the circumstances surrounding the dubbing deployed in *The Canary Murder Case* and *Prix de beauté* could not be more different. *The Canary Murder Case* utilised same-language voice doubling only as a desperate last resort when Brooks refused to return for retakes, and reluctance towards this device is unequivocally felt, manifesting in an array of masking effects that I go on to detail below. In contrast, *Prix de beauté* displays an attitude towards dubbing that manages to be both serious and carefree at the same time. Foremost, Regelly's revoicing of Brooks is motivated by pragmatics, yet its largely 'unsynchronised' effect means that her voice never sticks but rather, roams self-reflexively around this exotic figure, drawing attention to itself and to dubbing as a device.

This crucial difference in the revoicing that underpins these productions is something to which I will return shortly. For now, I focus in contrast on their connection through Brooks – detailing the dubbing contracts she actively entered into. I wish to suggest a level of self-engineering on the part of Brooks that is only brought into relief when viewing these two films together. Seen side-by-side, added significance attaches to Brooks' decision to make *Prix de beauté* – a French talkie – in the light of the bad press she received in response to her dubbed vocals in *The Canary Murder Case*.

Rather than writing off Brooks' ready willingness to embark on the multiple-language *Prix de beauté* despite Clair's advice that she ditch the project (Paris 1989: 317), I propose to take this decision seriously, reviewing it in relation to her earlier refusal to re-vocalise *The Canary Murder Case*. Rather than dismissing both acts as signs of Brooks' unconventionality or as short-sighted, arbitrary moves made at the behest of either Pabst or her lover George Marshall, I contend Brooks' voice may be more apparent than first appearances suggest, and that issues of agency may, in fact, lie at the heart of these decisions. As she states in *Lulu in Hollywood*, many reviewers and columnists had interpreted her ghosting by Livingston in *The Canary Murder Case* as a sign of vocal failure (2000: 104). Writing for the *Washington Post* (May 13, 1930) for instance, Nelson B. Bell proposed: "the American microphones do not care for Miss Brooks' voice, although she is kept reasonably active in the studios abroad". Whatever the reason behind such interpretations – Paramount smear campaign or typical fan speculation – it is clear that Brooks' reputation suffered when the Livingston cover-up went public. Nevertheless, only a few months after the film's release, she travelled to Paris intending to embark on a foreign-language talkie in which vocal substitution would be unavoidable.³ Rather than view this decision as a failing on Brooks' part, I interpret it as a deliberate statement in support of dubbing and its modernist, cosmopolitan possibilities.

The seriousness of Brooks' decision to remain silent in *The Canary Murder Case* is clearly demonstrated by her concurrent signing of a release 'gratis'. From this action, it is clear that Brooks took dubbing, doubling and duping seriously, indicating in no uncertain terms that she was behind the concept and convenience of vocal substitution, even in same-language contexts. Although possibly motivated in part by revenge, seeking to repay Paramount for refusing to increase her salary (see Paris 1989: 312), this move nevertheless indicates, at base, belief in the dubbing process.⁴ Brooks' approval of dubbing suggests that she saw this device as a useful tool in the filmmaking arsenal – one that enabled the continuation of transnational exchange, despite the new barrier of sound and its so-called 'language problem', and one no different, at heart, to other techniques of filmic illusion such as special effects, lighting and make-up. "Why is it worse to have a voice double than any other?" queries a fan in *Photoplay* (Nov 1929): "We know the stars use doubles for dangerous stunts, and nobody stays away because of it." In the same issue of *Photoplay*, another reader states:

It seems to me the most wonderful progress in the picture industry when we can see the beauty of face and form of old friends, combined with the beauty of voice we like to think theirs. After all, movies are all the romance the majority of us get out of life, so why not let the actors remain ideal in our hearts and minds? (Sutton 1929: 146)

---

[3] News of the film being made in both a silent and sound version was reported in *Cinématographie française* as early as May 1929.

[4] Paris suggests Brooks was motivated foremost by revenge, stating that in refusing to do retakes for *The Canary Murder Case*, "she cut off her voice to spite her face" (1989: 312). He also quotes a letter Brooks wrote expressing dissatisfaction with her dubbing by Livingston, complaining: "a cheap Brooklyn accent she gave me" (qtd in Paris 1989: 311).

It is also possible that Brooks embraced dubbing for its modernist potential, revelling in the effortless way it denatured filmic illusion at its base, stripping back layers of artifice to lay bare its mode of production. In the historical moment in which Brooks found herself during the industry's transition to sound, there was considerable debate around dubbing and its uses in both domestic and foreign-language contexts. Sound recording and synchronisation were much discussed items both in the trade and general press. Against this backdrop, Brooks' Paramount refusal and subsequent decision to embark on *Prix de beauté* indicates an acceptance of dubbing that speaks to an alternate possibility for sound filmmaking than that dictated by romanticist notions of integrity and authenticity. During this period, an actor's voice was still approached as a variable, rather than a fixed entity (Crafton 1999: 513) and Brooks' proactive mobilisation of dubbing points to a vision of sound filmmaking more in line with modernist than romanticist ideals, celebrating rather than denigrating the possibilities inherent within machinic disembodiment.

To gauge how the artifice/authenticity tensions of this era played out in relation to dubbing in particular, an article by sound engineer George Lewin (1931) is especially instructive. First presented at the Fall 1930 Meeting of the Society of Motion Picture Engineers, in the year following *The Canary Murder Case*'s release, this chapter sets out specifically to repair the damage done to dubbing's credibility by such acts of duplicitous body and voice doubling. Asserting that ghosting is now entirely absent from domestic productions, Lewin proceeds to re-apportion the blame, resting it entirely upon foreign tongues. "The old practice of using 'voice doubles' to fake the speech of actors whose own voices were not suited for recording has been completely abandoned", he insists, so that now the "only time voices are really faked is in the preparation of foreign versions" (Lewin 1931: 48). Moreover, for Lewin, foreign-language revoicing does not constitute dubbing proper. He prefers the term "doubling", ascribing this practice duplicitous undertones (Lewin 1931: 38). In contrast, Lewin presents dubbing as an entirely reputable process integral to sound filmmaking. When a film's soundtrack includes the actual voices of the on-screen actors, he argues, then it remains authentic, despite its often highly constructed, manipulated nature – as in the case of song-and-dance numbers. Conceding the constructed nature of playback techniques common to musicals where "the sound is recorded first, without the picture, so that the singers may be placed in any way desired", he insists this is "not a faking process, in the ordinary sense of the word, as the voices we hear are actually those of the people we see" (Lewin 1931: 47).

In his haste to blame the 'foreign' for practices well documented at the time in domestic contexts, Lewin indicates the extent to which anxieties surrounding the actor's voice – its aesthetic and technical suitability – culminated around vocal substitution. In fact, as Ďurovičová (2003) notes, in the early 1930s, voice doubling was far from absent from Hollywood studios. "After 1930", she writes, "voice interchangeability, so insistently denied by the exhibition departments of the majors, was fully permissible in the production departments, with a new clause in the standard studio contract, allowing the producer the right 'to dub or use a "double" in lieu of the artist' (Ďurovičová 2003). Brooks' refusal to reshoot talking scenes for Paramount, and the subsequent release she signed, could well have influenced the insertion of this new standard clause. As Crafton asserts, voice doubling "raised the stakes in the game of who controlled the screen voice" (1997: 509). Scandal surrounding the doubling of stars as they sang, spoke, or played musical instruments raised public awareness of these early talkie tactics which, as Crafton notes, were common yet not publicised (1999: 509). In a *Photoplay* article exposing such double dealings in *Weary River* (Lloyd, 1929), *The Divine Lady* (Lloyd, 1929), *Show Boat* (Pollard, 1929) and *The Canary Murder Case*, Mark Larkin warns: "When you hear your favourite star sing in the Talkies, don't be too sure about it…There's many a slip between the screen and the cutting-room floor!" (1929). Crafton points out, "[w]hile actors' contracts explicitly gave legal control of their voice to the studio, Actors Equity was fighting to at least require the performer's consent to substitute voice-doubles" (1999: 511).

Ironically, Lewin's assurances about the authenticity of sound pictures achieve the opposite effect, only serving to illustrate how artifice lies at the very core of sound/image constructions. Although he promises that the duplicitous potential of motion picture sound recording is only that – a now 'abandoned' possibility – and one that he and his fellow sound engineers will not misuse, the damage appears already done. By describing in detail the manifold ways in which sound recording invites manipulation, Lewin cannot help but underline the uncanny dimension of film sound, despite his request that cinemagoers put their faith in the authenticity of this illusion. Despite fastidiously seeking to separate dubbing from doubling, Lewin's defence ends up emphasising, not minimizing, the centrality of artifice within sound filmmaking. Hence, he unwittingly draws attention to the duplicitous possibilities inherent within this technology and the deconstructive effects embedded within all forms of dubbing whether "ordinary", "straight" or otherwise (1931: 39, 48). As Mikhail Yampolsky argues, the unnatural voice/body combinations produced via foreign-language dubbing are "already contained in the very structure of the sound film", as "dubbing only leads the alienation of the voice from the body to extremely paradoxical and therefore more tangible forms" (1993: 73).

'To-be-dubbed-ness'

Although it is often claimed that Brooks refused to return to Hollywood to voice *The Canary Murder Case* because she was in Europe filming *Prix de beauté* (see "Screen News" 1931) in fact, she was only in New York, and production of *Prix de beauté* began around six or seven months later. The crux of the connection between the production of these two films rests not only on the fact that they both feature Brooks revoiced, but also on the way that each one self-reflexively comments in its style, form and thematic on this device, exhibiting a quality I term 'to-be-dubbed-ness' – a knowing nod to the dubbing process itself. This terms riffs off the concept of 'to-be-looked-at-ness' formulated by Laura Mulvey in her seminal essay "Visual Pleasure and Narrative Cinema". While Mulvey's psychoanalytic approach and object of analysis is quite distinct from my own, it is useful nonetheless for underlining how the production of cinematic images and modes of representation structure reception processes, pointing to levels of self-reflexivity within cinema's layered interchange of looks between camera, audience and characters (1989, 25). Mulvey proposes that women in mainstream cinema are coded as passive sexual objects that are "simultaneously looked at and displayed" and hence "connote *to-be-looked-at-ness*" (1989, 19). Somewhat differently, I deploy 'to-be-dubbed-ness' to explore how post-production processes can inflect filmic conception and construction. In the context of the transition era and the coming of sound, the quality of 'to-be-dubbed-ness' points to the centrality of voice replacement, manipulation and translation within the industry, and goes some way towards acknowledging how dubbing practices and policies have shaped the industry ever since. Although these two films handle dubbing very differently, using it to different ends, both nevertheless envisioned post-synchronisation as integral to their productions *from their outset.*

Judging by reports in the trade and fan press, and the timeline offered by Brooks, it would seem that principal photography for *The Canary Murder Case* took place around September 1928, wrapping up in early October. Brooks sailed for Europe soon afterwards and began production of *Pandora's Box* in Berlin in December (Brooks 2000: 47, 104). It comes somewhat as a surprise then to learn that already in July 1928, *The Canary Murder Case* was advertised in the *Exhibitors Herald and Moving Picture World* as part of Paramount's upcoming selection of "all-talking" features in its "The Whole Show In Sound" program. It was also in July that *Variety* first announced Malcolm St. Clair as director, with production not yet begun. Even allowing for time lags, these reports confound common knowledge surrounding the production of this film. In *Lulu in Hollywood*, Brooks refers to *The Canary Murder Case* as her "last silent film" (2000: 58) and many have subsequently inferred that it was originally conceived as a silent with the decision to transform it into a talkie coming later, after production ended (see Brennan 2010; Paris 1989: 253). According to Dennis Harvey, for instance, it was "reworked as a part-talkie to cash in on the sudden sound craze" (2013).

Paramount's advertising campaign tells another story: prior to the start of shooting, *The Canary Murder Case* was already conceived as a double production to be released in two versions, one silent and the other sound. It was planned and advertised in the *Exhibitor's Herald and Moving Picture World* (July 7, 1928) as a "Paramount picture in sound!" containing "sensational talking sequences" and later, in *Motion Picture News* (Dec 1928), as an "all-star, all-talking" feature with mention made of a silent version as well. A sound version was already planned in pre-production, before the film was shot *as a silent*. Vocal post-synchronisation then was always intended, and traces of this anticipated re-vocalization inflect the film's textual and thematic core. The reason Paramount felt retakes were necessary in the New Year is unclear. During the transition period, expectations around talkies were changing rapidly, and it may be that in the months between principal photography and the film's final release,

Paramount changed it mind about just how its 'all-talking sequences' would play out, and about which techniques the public would tolerate, switching from a loose, largely unsynchronised talkie to one concentrating on matching lip movements.

Pertinently, Davide Pozzi stresses that the Cineteca del Comune di Bologna's recently restored silent version of *Prix de beauté* should not be thought of as the 'original' in comparison to its post-synchronised sound version (2004: 25). Rather, he notes that this film was conceived early on (while Clair was still at the helm) as a double work, to be produced in both sound and silent versions, as press reports at the time affirm (2004: 26). As Brooks did not speak French, interlingual dubbing must have been envisioned from the start. Additionally, like *The Canary Murder Case*, *Prix de beauté* is self-reflexive about this "to-be-dubbed-ness" while language difference and issues of translation permeate all aspects of its production and reception, underscoring interconnection between these processes.

Ghosting the canary

Figure 2: Back view of the Canary as she converses with Charles Spottswoode in *The Canary Murder Case* (1929).

Re-vocalised, with its lengthy, static dialogue sequences, *The Canary Murder Case* is difficult to imagine as a silent. The lack of action received some negative response from reviewers at the time (see e.g. Orndorff 1929), despite otherwise positive press.[5] Meanwhile, *The World* (March 11, 1929) reported: "a good movie plot gone wrong as the result of spoken dialogue". The sound version of *The Canary Murder Case* reveals an almost obsessive interest in dialogue and moving lips. The camerawork is largely static and characters tend to be framed by medium and long shots, in scenarios focused on the exchange of dialogue. This preoccupation with characters 'seen talking' presents considerable problems in relation to the Canary. A conspicuous number of scenes featuring Livingston as the substitute Canary are shot from behind (Fig. 2). When the camera doesn't focus on the back of her head, it frames the conversing Canary in long shots, dimly lit, with her facial features obscured by shadow, side-profiling or screens (Figs. 3, 4, and 5). These tricks did not pass unnoticed at the time. Louella O. Parsons (1929) writes: "Only long shots are permitted of her and even these are far from convincing when she speaks". Similarly, a reviewer for the *Oakland Post-Enquirer* (March 2, 1929) attributes the "not quite perfect synchronization in close ups and the variety of back views and dimly photographed profiles of the Canary" directly to Livingston's doubling. The *Knoxville Journal* (March 5, 1929) reports of the actors: "all of them do passably well except Miss Brooks. Not once is she shown actually speaking. This defect is most glaring in the picture". Margaret L. Coyne finds the "only flaw is the substitution of another voice for that of Louise Brooks – the Canary – making necessary a number of subterfuges to disguise the fact" (1929).

---

[5] For a particularly useful bibliography of press clippings on this film, see the Louise Brooks Society website (www.pandorasbox.com).

Figure 3: Dimly lit long shot of the Canary speaking on the telephone in *The Canary Murder Case* (1929).

Figure 4: An intruder overhears the Canary, seen in silhouette, speaking on the telephone, in *The Canary Murder Case* (1929).

Figure 5: The Canary argues with her ex-husband from behind a screen, in *The Canary Murder Case* (1929).

Charles O'Brien identifies similar tactics at work in other films from the early sound years (2010: 38). Focusing on Hitchcock's *Waltzes from Vienna* (1934), O'Brien notes how the anticipation of the film's dubbing into French actually affected Hitchcock's direction of the 'original' British version (2010: 37). In particular, he refers to the many scenes "whose compositions are contrived to conceal the actors' lip movements and hence facilitate the film's eventual dubbing" (2010: 45). In pointing to the "stylistic impact" of post-synchronised revoicing on the textual fabric of the film – its editing and composition – O'Brien advances a similar idea to that encapsulated in "to-be-dubbed-ness" (2010: 39). Recalling how Mulvey's concept of 'to-be-looked-at-ness' positions women as the passive object rather than active subject of cinema's gaze (1989, 19), the notion of 'to-be-dubbed-ness' foregrounds the ways in which active/passive dichotomies also inflect revoicing, with post-production operations of translation regularly dismissed as inconsequential to filmmaking and film meaning. However, dubbing and related considerations tied to export, translation and transformation affect film production in particularly active and self-reflexive ways. Moreover, concept of 'to-be-dubbed-ness" encourages a consideration of the wider cultural politics of dubbing – how issues of gender, for instance, can inform dubbing decisions and its reception, as I go on to explore in relation to *The Canary Murder Case*.

Sound recording and vocal manipulation are central to the storyline of *The Canary Murder Case* and the novel by S. S. Van Dine on which it is based. Published in 1927, the novel is the second volume in the popular Philo Vance series. In the novel, as in the film, the murderer covers his tracks with the help of a phonograph. After killing the Canary, he sets a phonograph record playing that he has specially recorded in advance. He then leaves her apartment and proceeds to the lobby desk. After a few moments, a scream is heard coming from the Canary's apartment. The murderer and lobby attendant run to her door and enquire after her. From behind her closed door, she assures them that she is fine. However, it is later revealed that this voice (and the earlier scream) originated not from the living body of the Canary but from a machine. The voice is actually that of the murderer, adjusted in falsetto to approximate a female pitch, recorded onto a phonograph disk and then timed in playback to synchronise with his concerned enquiries outside her door.

Today, this plot device appears particularly clumsy. The speech that emanates from the phonograph record is entirely unconvincing as a male voice in falsetto. This rather far-fetched notion that the murderer could convincingly mimic the Canary's voice seems to reflect how in the early years of voice recording the public were fairly unfamiliar with the basic characteristics and limitations of this technology. Amongst ideas circulating at the time around speech recording was that advanced by Theodor Adorno in 1928:

[m]ale voices can be reproduced better than female voices. The female voice easily sounds shrill – but not because the gramophone is incapable of conveying high tones, as is demonstrated by its adequate reproduction of the flute. Rather, in order to become unfettered, the female voice requires the physical appearance of the body that carries it. But it is just this body that the gramophone eliminates, thereby giving every female voice a sound that is needy and incomplete. (1990, 54)

This view is echoed in a passage from Van Dine's novel when Vance exposes the murderer's tricks: "The voice on the record is merely his own in falsetto – better for the purpose than a woman's, for it's stronger and more penetrating" (Van Dine

1927). Vance then explains how the murderer conversed with the recorded voice through the closed door, timing his questions exactly to coincide with his pre-recorded answers by keeping "his eye on his wristwatch". Describing this synchronisation feat as "the simplest part" of the operation, Vance explains:

> The moment he heard the cry, he calculated the intermission on the record and put his question to the imagin'ry lady at just the right moment to receive the record's response. It was all carefully figured out beforehand; he no doubt rehearsed it in his laborat'ry. It was deuced simple, and practically proof against failure. (Van Dine 1927)

In this summary dismissal of the hazards and complexities of post-synchronisation, the novel foreshadows the fate of the film. Ironically, as Paramount was to discover only a year or so later, post-synchronised voices proved a little harder to successfully pull off than anticipated by either Vance or Van Dine. Forced to hire Livingston at great expense to double for the Canary, Paramount's post-synchronisation efforts were widely denigrated.

Exporting Miss Europa

Figure 6: Lucienne working as a typist for newspaper *Le Globe,* in *Prix de beauté* (1930).

Prix de beauté centres upon a female typist Lucienne (Brooks) who works for Paris newspaper *Le Globe* (Fig. 6). According to Lawrence Rainey, Lucienne is an embodiment of that "novel figure" to emerge from the communication revolution of the late nineteenth and early twentieth centuries, "the female clerical worker" (2010):

> ... a figure who not only stood at the centre of a communications revolution transpiring in the real world, but also became a major protagonist within a rapidly changing media ecology that reformulated that world as spectacle; she became both the addressee and the protagonist of plays, postcards, comic strips and cartoons, novels serialized in tabloid newspapers, conduct books, popular songs, poetry, and above all, film.

Lucienne enters a beauty contest, wins the title of 'Miss France' and is finally crowned 'Miss Europe.' Her fiancé and fellow office worker André disapproves and trouble ensues. Even this barebones summary provides some indication of the translational and transnational themes of the film, and how they are brought into relief by the figure of Brooks – the American starlet imported into the role directly from Hollywood with much accompanying publicity. In focusing on *Prix de beauté*'s importation of Brooks this publicity mirrored the film's storyline, which centered around another American import: the beauty contest (see Rainey 2010). In featuring Miss Brooks playing the part of 'Miss France' and then 'Miss Europe', *Prix de beauté* echoes the global posturing enabled by the medium of cinema, articulating its cross-border aspirations and imaginary. Brooks' own 'to-be-dubbed-ness' was widely reported in the US press. In Paris her arrival for the start of production was treated with great fanfare, with her image regularly gracing the covers of magazines such as *Ciné-Miroir* (Oct 18, 1929; May 23, 1930), *Cinémonde* (May 8, 1930) and *Pour Vous* (May 2 and Sep 19, 1929) (Fig. 7). News of Brooks' involvement was reported in the French press as early as March 1929 in *Le Journal des Débats Politiques et Littéraires* and she posed for publicity shots with René Clair in April (Tynan 2000: xxvi).

Figure 7: Louise Brooks on the cover of *Pour Vous* (2 May 1929).

With her flapper looks and lifestyle, Brooks epitomised a type of cosmopolitan style and worldly glamour and her trademark bob was widely imitated in Paris where it also created headlines (see "Louise Brooks et ses Cheveux"; Paris 1989: 335). This publicity informs and overlaps her dubbing in *Prix de beauté*, demonstrating how Brooks' American nationality formed part of her appeal in Europe, as did, no less, her deviation from American values and eschewing of national borders. As Kenneth Tynan notes, during the early sound years, few actors travelled from Hollywood to Europe – the reverse route was far more common (Tynan 2000: xxvi). Consequently, Brooks' celebrity in France and Europe focused on the fact of her importation. In reports surrounding production of *Prix de beauté*, repeated reference was made to her inability to speak French ("Louise Brooks Double" 1929; Green 1930). Hence, audiences were under no illusion that the sound version of *Prix de beauté* would contain Brooks' voice. Rather, she was feted as a star precisely due to her cultural and linguistic *otherness*. Indeed, her inability to speak French could have worked to positively reinforce her exotic 'Americanness', given America's monolingual tendencies. In this sense, Brooks' dubbing in *Prix de beauté* was distinct from that of *The Canary Murder Case*, in that the public was privy to it from the outset.

Prix de beauté is a film thoroughly invested in notions of cultural and linguistic translation. It is a film about film, and the role of mass media within emerging conditions of modernity and globalisation (see Rainey 2010; Cox 2002). Moreover, in both its production and thematic, it reflects upon the pragmatics of language and translation that underpin concepts of the global and its mediascape. The dubbing-dependency of *Prix de beauté*'s sound version, and its four-way interlingual revoicing underscore the complicated strategies required to navigate the latent multilingualism of modernity. It also mobilises the polyvocal possibilities engendered via the machinic, positioning translation at the centre of society's modernist transformations. In this way *Prix de beauté* embraces interlingual dubbing as a mode of modernist awakening, reveling in the possibilities of disembodiment – as its post-sync methods attest. Alternately referred to as a "part-talkie" (Harvey 2013) or "unsynchronized talkie" (Atkinson 2006), it approaches synchronization loosely as a concept more than a constraint. Although Brooks mouths French, her speech rarely coincides with her lip movements. According to Michael Atkinson, *Prix de beauté* flaunts a "ramshackle form" and "patchwork approach" to sound, "often avoiding the actor's [sic] moving mouths altogether and then suturing the narrative with a frenetic soundtrack of dubbing, ambient noise, and music" (2006).

According to Alan Williams, the breakthrough in the success of talkies related more to formal than technological innovation: *The Jazz Singer* (Crosland, 1927) worked when others failed due to its *re*presentational (rather than *presentational*) mode of address – the fact that it included a diegetic audience (1999: 234–5). *Prix de beauté* is similarly *re*presentational in that it sees itself looking. Lucienne is continually framed in still photographs and moving screens, and commented upon by song lyrics, enabling the characters themselves to become her audience. Through the combined efforts of Genina and Clair, the *re*presentational in *Prix de beauté* reaches new heights of self-reflexivity, which culminate in its acclaimed dénouement. Nevertheless, the sound version of this film is regularly regarded as a relic, a clumsy curiosity from a past era caught in-between sound and silence. Its 'part-sync' status has marred its stature, with critics regularly referring to its unsubtle juxtapositions between diegetic and non-diegetic sound, synched speech, foley effects and deadening silence. However, according to Williams, contemporary sound cinema depends upon a similar integration of sync and non-sync segments and he proposes that the 'part-talkie' format is very much extant. "To this day", he writes, "few commercial narrative sound films… are exempt from the part-talkie's alternation of sync and non-sync sequences" (Williams 1999: 237). It is only our familiarity with its techniques, he claims, that disguises its constructedness (Williams 1999: 237). Dubbing's central place in the hybrid, part-talkie format of *The Canary Murder Case* and *Prix de beauté* extends this argument, articulating the significance of language, voice and translation in shaping film practices and conventions.

Swan songs

It is difficult to talk about *The Canary Murder Case* and *Prix de beauté* – either on their own or together – without engaging, to some degree, with endings. Both are regularly viewed as last gasps in Brooks' dying film career, prophetically signalling death while also depicting it literally. My aim here has been to think about the sound, tone and languages in which these last gasps are uttered and heard. While Brooks' dubbing in these films is indeed ironic, given that they were her first talkies, it is also telling. Brooks' absent, dubbed voice in *The Canary Murder Case* and *Prix de beauté* provides an under-examined perspective from which to review the historical conditions and in-flux production practices of her day. It also heralds the contractual role that screen voices were increasingly expected to fulfil as they became welded to notions of interiority, integrity and authenticity. This was the case especially for Anglophone audiences unused to experiencing on any serious scale the ignominies of screen translation. By insisting on her right to remain silent, Brooks upset expectations and infuriated Paramount executives. In response, the Hollywood majors became increasingly intent on securing vocal property rights, and a new clause was inserted into standard studio contracts (Ďurovičová 2003).

Figure 8: The final scene in *Prix de beauté* (1929) depicting Lucienne's death.

Fittingly, the ending of *Prix de beauté* depicts the death of Lucienne in a startling composition that juxtaposes her still, dying profile (placed in the extreme foreground) against her moving image playing in the background. On screen, Lucienne sounds out over her dead body, singing in the realist tradition of the French chanteuse (see Conway 2004) (Fig. 8). By adding singing into the silent-sound mix, this scene strains the limits of speech, articulating a tension evoked by both the absence and presence of the vocal.[6] According to Pozzi, this scene was differently shot for the sound and silent versions of the film (2004: 27). At one point, the frame focuses solely on the film within the film: Lucienne's screen test. The sound version has been carefully constructed so that the borders of the image are visible, complete with a sound strip along the left side (Fig. 9). Here, the conditions, materiality and new technologies of production are self-reflexively brought into focus, gesturing towards a modernist engage-

---

[6] On song and opera in relation to the vocal tensions of silent and sound cinema, see Grover-Friedlander (2005).

ment with the medium that perhaps also informed Brooks' casual deference to dubbing. Forged at a crossroad between the intralingual and the interlingual, Brooks' mute vocals in *The Canary Murder Case* and *Prix de beauté* direct attention to points of overlap between these two modes of voice transfer. In Hollywood, domestic policies around vocal agency both influenced and were themselves shaped by foreign-language practices, prejudices and presumptions. In turn Hollywood policies provided benchmarks for the industry as a whole. Issues of translation cannot be siphoned off from filmmaking 'proper': the intralingual and interlingual develop in tandem, just as did Brooks' dubbing detours.

Figure 9: Full frame image of Lucienne's screen test in *Prix de beauté* (1929) complete with sound strip along the left-hand side (produced for the sound version only).

References

—. (1929): "Louise Brooks Double", *Variety*, December 18, 5.
__. (1929): "Louise Brooks et ses Cheveux", *Mon Ciné*, May 4.
—. (1929): "Two Equityites Refuse Talking Version Jobs", *Variety*, July 10, 7.

—. (1931): "Screen News", *Screenland* 23, 91.

ADORNO, Theodor W. (1990): "The Curves of the Needle" [1928], transl. Levin, Thomas, Y., *October* 55, 48–55.

ATKINSON, Michael (2006): "Louise Brooks's Swan Song to Stardom", *The Village Voice* (Online), March 26. http://www.villagevoice.com/2006-03-28/screens/louise-brooks-s-swan-song-to-stardom/full/ (28.08.2014).

BELFRAGE, Cedric (1930): "Their European Souls" *Motion Picture*, February.

BRENNAN, Sandra (2010): "The Canary Murder Case, 1929: Review Summary" *The New York Times*. http://www.nytimes.com/movies/movie/86550/The-Canary-Murder-Case/overview (27.08.2014).

BROOKS, Louise (2000 [1989]): *Lulu in Hollywood*. – Minneapolis: University of Minnesota Press.

CONWAY, Kelley (2004): *Chanteuse in the City: The Realist Singer in French Film*. – Berkeley: The University of California Press.

COX, Tracey (2002): "Consuming Distractions in *Prix de beauté*", *Camera Obscura*, 17 (2), 41–68.

COYNE, Margaret L. (1929): "New Picture Plays." *Post-Standard*, April 1.

CRAFTON, Donald (1999): *The Talkies: American Cinema's Transition to Sound 1926–1931*. – Berkeley and London: The University of California Press.

DUNN, Leslie C. & JONES, Nancy A. (eds.) (1994): *Embodied Voices: Representing Female Vocality in Western Culture*. – Cambridge: Cambridge University Press.

ĎUROVIČOVÁ, Nataša (2003): "Local Ghosts: Dubbing Bodies in Early Sound Cinema", *Moveast* 9. http://epa.oszk.hu/00300/00375/00001/durovicova.htm (09.10.2009).

FARMER, Robert (2010): "Lulu in Rochester: Louise Brooks and the cinema screen as a *tabula rasa*", *Senses of Cinema* 55. http://sensesofcinema.com/2010/feature-articles/lulu-in-rochester-louise-brooks-and-the-cinema-screen-as-a-tabula-rasa-3/ (25.08.2014).

GLADYSZ, Thomas (2010): "Canary Murder Case screens in Rochester, NY", *The Examiner* (online edition), June 9.

GREEN, Grace (1930): "And *This* Is Paris", *Screen Play Secrets*, July.

GROVER-FRIEDLANDER, Michal (2005): *Vocal Apparitions: The Attraction of Cinema to Opera*. – Princeton and Oxford: Princeton University Press.

HAGENER, Malte (2004): "*Prix de beauté* as a Multiple Intersection. National Cinema, Auteurism, and the Coming of Sound", *Cinema & Cie* 4, 102–115.

HARVEY, Dennis (2013): "Prix de Beauté, 1930", http://www.silentfilm.org/archive/prix-de-beaute (13.09.2013).

HASTIE, Amelie (1997): "Louise Brooks, Star Witness", *Cinema Journal* 36 (3), 3–24.

HOPKINS, Edwin (1928): "Re-Vocalized Films", *Transactions of the Society of Motion Picture Engineers* 12 (35), 845–852.

H., P. L. (1929) "The New Shows Reviewed", *Knoxville Journal*, March 5.

LARKIN, Mark (1929): "The Truth About Voice Doubling", *Photoplay* 36 (2), 32–33, 108–110.

MERRICK, Mollie (1929): "Says English is to be Future's Esperanto", *Lincoln Evening Journal*, February 14.

MULVEY, Laura (1989): "Visual Pleasure and Narrative Cinema" [1975], *Visual and Other Pleasures.* – London: Macmillan Press, 13–36.

O'BRIEN, Charles (2010): "The 'Cinematization' of Sound Cinema in Britain and the Dubbing into French of Hitchcock's *Waltzes from Vienna* (1934)". In: MAZDON, Lucy & WHEATLEY, Catherine (eds.): *J'taime... moi non plus: Franco-British Cinematic Relations.* – New York and Oxford: Berghahn Books, 37–49.

ORNDORFF, Maguerite (1929): "The Canary Murder Case", *Educational Screen*, March.

PARIS, Barry (1989): *Louise Brooks.* – New York: Alfred A. Knopf.

PARSONS, Louella O. (1929): "'Canary Murder Case' Pulsating Mystery Picture", *Los Angeles Examiner*, February 8.

POZZI, Davide (2004): "Quelle version restaurer? Deux cas concrets: *Nana* et *Prix de beaute*", *Cinema & Cie* 4, 22–29.

RAINEY, Lawrence (2010): "Gender, Spectacle, and Machinery: Prix de beauté (1930)", *Space Between: Literature & Culture, 1914–1945* 6 (1), 125–139.

S., A. (1929): "The New Films", *The World*, March 11.

SUTTON, Nina (1929): "A Kind Word for Voice Doubling", *Photoplay*, 36 (6), 146.

SUTTON, Pearle (1929): "Barthelmess Fan Leaps to Rescue", *Photoplay*, 36 (6), 144.

TYNAN, Kenneth (2000): "Introduction: The Girl in the Black Helmet", in BROOKS, Louise: *Lulu in Hollywood*, vii–xivi (reprinted from *The New Yorker,* 1979)

VAN DINE, S. S. (1927): *The Canary Murder Case*. Project Gutenberg Australia: http://gutenberg.net.au/ebooks02/0200351h.html#Toc6247389 (28.08.14).

WAHL, Chris (2007): "'Paprika in the Blood': On UFA's Early Sound Films Produced in/about/for/with Hungary", *Spectator* 27 (2), 11–20.

W. D. (1929) "Mystery Tale Well Staged As Oakland All-Talkie." *Oakland Post-Enquirer*, March 2.

WILLIAMS, Alan (1999): "The Raw and the Coded: Sound Conventions and the Transition of the Talkies". In: BROPHY, Philip (ed.): *Cinesonic: The World of Sound in Film*. – Sydney: AFTRS, 229–243.

YAMPOLSKY, Mikhail (1993): "Voice Devoured: Artaud and Borges on Dubbing", transl. Joseph, Larry P., *October* 64, 57–77.

Politics of film translation: Cinema and nation-building in China (1949–1965)

Fan Yang & Dongning Feng
SOAS, University of London
256296@soas.ac.uk
d.feng@soas.ac.uk

This article examines the relationship between film translation and nation building during the period 1949 to 1965 in China. After the People's Republic of China (PRC) was founded in 1949, the Chinese Communist Party (CCP), as the new ruling party, was faced with the pressing task of rebuilding a country that had been devastated by decades of war and a nation that had been rent by political disunity. Thus, building a "new revolutionary culture" that would reflect, and ultimately legitimise the change, was high on the political agenda. Imported films were part and parcel of such a drive. Two issues are to be addressed in this article: firstly, it discusses how the new government, as a "patron", controls the selection of films to be translated for the purpose of building a new ideology and "revolutionary culture" that would strengthen the status of the CCP as a legitimate ruling party; secondly, it explores how the selected Soviet films were introduced and promoted to be part of the political drive. These films interacted with other forms of expression and contributed to the transformation of Chinese society. The 1980s saw translation studies turning its attention from prescribing linguistic equivalence on the textual level to investigating translation in its historical, economic, and socio-political context in which the translation operates. Within this paradigm, the concept of patronage is often drawn upon by researchers to explore and explain ideology-driven translation activity.

Patronage, ideology and translation

The 1980s saw translation studies turning its attention from prescribing linguistic equivalence on the textual level to investigating translation in its historical, economic, and socio-political context in which the translation operates. Within this paradigm, the concept of patronage is often drawn upon by researchers to explore and explain ideology-driven translation activity.

The notion of patronage is put forward by Lefevere as part of his theoretical paradigm of rewriting. Lefevere (1992) has particular interest in examining "very concrete factors" such as "powers, ideology, institution and manipulation", which govern the reception, acceptance or rejection of literary texts (Lefevere 1992). He defines the manipulation of literary texts undertaken in the service of power as rewriting, and the motivation for such rewriting can be ideological (to conform to or rebel against the dominant ideology) or poetological (to conform to or rebel against the prevailing poetics). Thus, Lefevere and Bassnett argue, "all rewritings, whatever their intention, reflect a certain ideology and a poetics and as such manipulate literature to function in a given society in a given way" (ibid: vii). For Lefevere, translation is "the most obviously recognizable type of rewriting" (ibid: 9), and through translation, on the one hand, the original text is distorted or constrained to a certain ideology or poetics of different audiences; on the other hand, "new concepts, new genres, new devices" can be introduced (ibid: vii).

The rewriting of the original text is controlled by two factors. One factor is professionals including critics, teachers, translators and so on, who operate within the literary system. Professionals decide the poetics of the translated texts. The second factor is patronage, which can be exercised by "powers (persons, institutions), which help or hinder the writing, reading and rewriting of literature" (ibid: 15). Patrons can limit the choice of subjects and the form of rewritten texts, employ translators, and lead to elevating the translator's reputation.

Although Lefevere developed the concepts of patronage and rewriting for investigating literary translation, his ideas are applicable to the investigation of many other types of translation. In the audiovisual translation field, some researchers have exploited the theory to investigate the relationship between patronage and translation in terms of the state's intervention in actual film translation. For example, Chen (2004) finds that in Hong Kong, Cantonese swearwords in American films are often not rendered in their Cantonese equivalents to prevent the film from being given a Category III rating[1] by the authorities. Lanza (2002) shows how both the Franco regime and the Catholic church in Spain had jointly set strict guidelines to manipulate film translation by changing the original dialogue and even the plot of the films. Other scholars went beyond the text and considered the role of patron in terms of controlling the reception of foreign films. For example, Lanza (1997), by presenting a list of ministerial regulations on film translation, highlights cultural control under the Franco dictatorship. Similarly, Szarkowska (2005) argues that the tradition of film dubbing in Italy, Spain and Germany can be traced back to each country's dictatorial regime in history.

While many researchers, like those mentioned above, have investigated the role of patrons in controlling the original text, not enough research has been done to examine the function of rewriting in introducing "the new concept, new genre, and new devices" (Lefevere, ibid: vii). In addition, even though researchers like Lanza (1997) recognise the influence of patrons on imported films, much of the research has been based on the official documents and guidelines to support their arguments rather than analysing the imported films. Against this background, this paper intends to explore the history of film imports in China during the period when foreign films were used as a vital tool to promote the new revolutionary culture and introduce the new political ideology. To operationalise this undertaking, both statistical and thematic analyses are conducted in order to examine how and why these films were selected during a certain period in China. Subsequently, the argument is followed by a review of film paratexts with the intention of identifying how the new authorities promoted politically charged films in China where Hollywood films had once been dominant. It is worth noting that film paratexts can be particularly informative of the ideological forces behind film dissemination and reception. As Gray explains, paratexts

---

[1] According to the Hong Kong Motion Picture Rating System introduced in 1988, Category III means "no persons younger than 18 years of age are permitted to rent, purchase, or watch this film in the cinema."

such as posters, podcasts, reviews, or merchandise can "create texts", "manage them", and "fill them with many of the meanings that we associate with them" (2010: 6).

Background: New patron, new cinema

The didactic function of cinema with its power of persuasion was recognised by the CCP long before it came into power. From the 1930s onwards, the Party began exploiting cinema as a means of political communication and persuasion. During the period of the Japanese invasion, the appeasement policy of the Chinese Nationalist Party (*Guomindang*) led to anti-government sentiment amongst the public. As a major voice in the anti-Japanese war, in many areas the CCP proactively cooperated with left-wing intellectuals and participated in activities aimed against the Nationalist government (Pang, 2002: 19–21). In the film industry, from 1933, some Party members had cooperated with the left-wing filmmakers and promoted the production of documentaries and short movies. In order to steer such activities, the Cultural Committee of the CCP (*Wenhuaweiyuanhui*) established the Film Group (*Dianyingxiaozu*). The members of the group were not only involved in filmmaking but also acted as film critics. During this period, Soviet films were introduced into China, with fifty-five reviews and articles about these films published in the year of 1933 alone (Pang, 2002:145). Nevertheless, Chinese screens were still dominated by Hollywood films. The influence of film as a political force was still limited. Notwithstanding the cooperation with left-wing intellectuals in the anti-government movement, the CCP was far more radical than the objectives of left-wing intellectuals, with its principal aim of overthrowing the Nationalist Government, which was rocked by widespread corruption, economic crisis and poverty and political turmoil. However, because of lack of funding, activities involving the use of films as political communication were restricted mainly to introducing Russian progressive films into the country and translating film theories; and there were very few domestic films made with "revolutionary" content.

Therefore, when the CCP came to power in 1949, the political function of the cinema was soon reconfirmed by the Party and put on the agenda of national regeneration. Immediately after the first film studio, the Northwest Film Studio, was established in 1948, when China was still in the last stage of a three-year civil war between the Communists and the Nationalists, the Propaganda Department of the CCP Central Committee released a document entitled *Instructions on Film Industry* stipulating that Marxism and Leninism were to be the guiding principles in filmmaking. One year later, in 1949, the CCP published the first national film policy called *Decisions on Strengthening the Film Industry*, which officially defined film-making as "a widely acceptable propaganda tool". Following this, with more state-owned studios and film journals, and the establishment of censorship (Clark, 1987: 34–35), China's cinematic landscape soon changed, firstly, by breaking down the dominant position of Hollywood films, and secondly by producing so-called home-made "revolutionary" films.

Meanwhile, a centralised film industry was established under the control of the central government, which ensured that all domestic and imported films complied with Party guidelines. With respect to foreign film importation, the Film Import and Export Department was established in 1950, affiliated to the state-owned China Film Management Bureau, which took charge of importing foreign language films. From then on, foreign film companies, especially Hollywood companies could no longer set distribution branches and directly work with the distributors in China. It was replaced by a central purchasing system (*Tongxiaotonggou* 统销统购), in which the state was the major importer and buyer of foreign language films. Regarding film dubbing, in 1946, years before the official founding of the PRC in 1949, the Communist Party took over Japanese Manchurian Motion Pictures in Changchun and established the Northeast Film Studio. After that, the Beijing Film Studio, the Shanghai Film Studio and the August First Film Studio (*Bayi Film Studio*) were successfully established between 1949 and the early 1950s. These four film studios had a dual function: besides making films, they also doubled as dubbing studios in charge of all of foreign language films and documentaries introduced into China. Following dubbing by these studios, the Movie Examination Institution, created in March 1949 under the control of the Propaganda Department (it later came under the authority of the Ministry of Culture following the official establishment of the PRC), was responsible for censoring and approving the imported films before they were screened (Zhu and Rosen, 2010: 23–24). In the distribution sector, new film theatres and mobile projection units were set up to bring films, including foreign films, to the rural population (Zhu and Rosen, 2010: 23).

To understand the actions of the Chinese film industry at that time, it is necessary to view the situation in a global context in the early twentieth century, when the role of film as an effective political medium expanded dramatically worldwide. Regimes as diverse as Soviet Russia, the United States, and Fascist Italy, had all produced propaganda films in order to maintain morale in wartime, and win the hearts and minds of people (Fox, 2007). Nevertheless, unlike these regimes, in the 1950s and the 1960s, since the domestic film industry was still in its infancy and had yet to recover from the destruction of the Second World War, the newly founded PRC was unable to produce domestic films in large numbers that would reflect the emergent official ideology and inform people about the fundamental changes in Chinese society. In this situation, foreign language films, especially the films about socialist realism, had become a *proxy* to fulfill this purpose. This paper covers two symbolic historical moments in contemporary Chinese history, i.e., the inception of the People's Republic of China (PRC), and the start of the Cultural Revolution, which lasted ten years.

Statistics on film selection

Although this paper focuses on the period 1949–1965, in order to identify the trend of film imports and the underlying factors influencing it, this section will present an analysis of the statistics concerning film translation in China in an extended period between 1949 to 1991, namely, from the founding of the PRC to the end of the Cold War (see figure 1). During this period, film imports are largely politically directed.

During the period of 1949–1991, the Changchun Film Dubbing Studio (*Changchun dianying yizhipian chang*) and the Shanghai Film Dubbing Studio (*Shanghai dianying yizhipian Chang*) were two major institutions responsible for translating and dubbing foreign films. After these two studios started film translation and dubbing in 1949 and 1950 respectively, in 1969 the August First Film Dubbing Studio (*Bayi dianying yizhipianchang*) began dubbing foreign documentary films. In 1972, the Beijing Film Studio also established a dubbing unit called the Beijing Film Dubbing Studio (*Beijing dianying yizhipian chang*). From 1949 to 1991, all imported films to China had to be dubbed by these official dubbing studios before being released for public screening. Thus, the trend of film dubbing throughout these years also reflects the trend of film importation.

Regarding the criterion of data selection, this research only includes feature films that were translated for public consumption. The data analysed in this paper have been gathered from films dubbed by the Changchun Film Dubbing Studio, the Shanghai Film Dubbing Studio and the Beijing Film Dubbing Studio. Films dubbed by the August First Film Dubbing Studio are not included because most of them were documentary films. During the period between 1966 and 1979, some foreign feature films were screened exclusively in closed circles of officials in various positions, known as "reference films" (*neicanpian*内参片) (Cao, 2010; Huang, 2013). For example, in the late 1970s, although around 37 American films were imported to China, none of them had been shown in public cinemas. The data related reference films are excluded from this research.

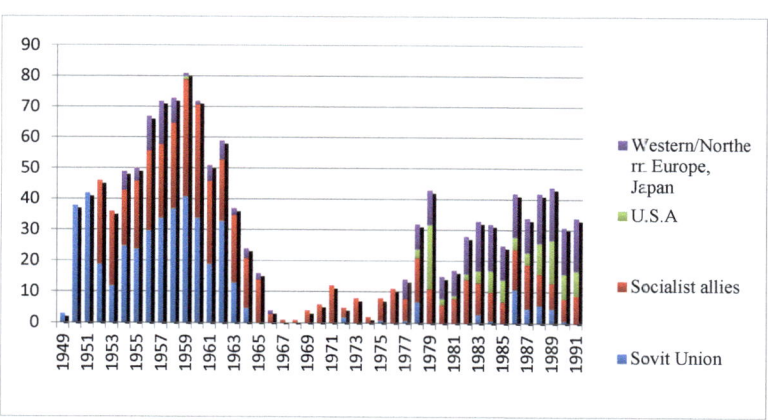

Figure 1. The number of dubbed foreign films in China from 1949 to 1991
(Source: the Shanghai Dubbing Studio and the Changchun Film Dubbing Studio[2])

---

[2] Data from the Shanghai Film Dubbing Studio are accessed from a fieldwork at the Studio in 2010. Data from the Changchun Film Dubbing Studio is accessed from a book Heroes behind the Screen: 1949–2008 published by Changchun Film Dubbing Studio in 2008.

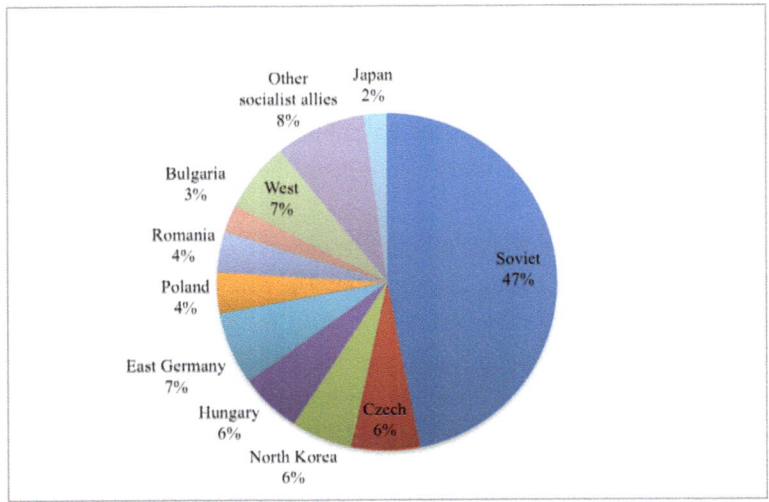

Figure 2. The proportion of countries or origin (1949–1965)

China's film imports between 1949 and 1991 can, generally, be divided into three periods. The first period was from 1949 to 1965, which saw large-scale import of foreign films: with the highest number of imports, 41 in 1959, and the lowest, 12 in 1953. Among a total of 873 films imported in this period, nearly half of them (around 47%) came from the Soviet Union. Soviet films were imported annually in large volumes until 1963 after which the number suddenly dropped to 5, the lowest number in fifteen years.

Whilst the first three years of the PRC saw Soviet Union films taking the largest share of foreign film screening in China (with only one North Korean film, *My Hometown* [1950]), the years following 1952 witnessed a diversified source of foreign film imports. The majority of films came from countries of the Soviet bloc such as Hungary, East Germany as well as North Korea. Films from these countries made up around 44% of total imports. Here are some examples: in 1952, the films that were dubbed for public screening in China included the East German film *The Condemned Village* (1952), the Hungarian film *Befrietes Land* (1951), the Polish film *Unvanquished City* (1950), the Czech film *Divá Bára* (1949) and the Romanian film *Life Triumphs* (1951).

In contrast to the sharp rise in film imports from the Soviet Union and its satellite states, only one American film, *Salt of the Earth* (1945, 1959 in China), was imported during this period. This was a dramatic change given that American films had been dominating the Chinese film market when China was under the Nationalist rule for nearly two decades (1912–1949). Even during the civil war (1945–1949), in Shanghai, 1083 American films were shown in cinemas (Zhang, 2004: 95). Other imported western films included one Finnish film, *According to the Law* (n.d.); two Norwegian films, *Nine Lives* (1957; 1958 in China) and *In a Night like This* (1958, 1959 in China), and 15 British films: *The Pickwick Papers* (1952, 1955 in China), *The Great Expectations* (1946, 1956 in China), *Laughter in Paradise* (1951, in 1957), *Oliver Twist* (1948, 1957 in China), *The Million Pound Note* (1954, 1958 in China), *A Night to Remember* (1961 in China), *Conspiracy of Hearts* (1960, 1963 in China), and others. Additionally, 16 Japanese films were imported such as *Hakone Fuuunroku* (1952, in China 1954), *Because of Love* (1955, 1956 in China), *Darkness in the Noon* (1956, 1957 in China), and *Matsukawa Derailment* (1961, 1961 in China).

The second period covers the years between 1966 and 1976, i.e. the period spanning the Cultural Revolution, which brought a drop in imports of all foreign films. In 1962, 33 films from the Soviet Union were imported to China, but in 1963 that number suddenly fell to 13, and then to 5 by 1964. In the following six years, no Soviet film was imported. Although some Soviet films appeared in Chinese cinemas between 1971 and 1978, annual imports never again reached double digits. The number of imported films from the countries of the Soviet bloc was also in decline. From 1966 to 1969, only 9 films were imported to China from those countries. From 1970 onwards, although there was a slight increase in film imports from Soviet bloc countries, most of film imports came from Albania.

The third period of film imports extends from 1976 to 1991, in which only a few Soviet films were imported. Also, film imports from other socialist' allies such as North Korea, Hungary and East Germany remained at a stable low point, i.e. roughly 10 per year. By contrast, there was an increase in western films. In 1979, the number of American film imports rocketed to 21. Since then, around 10 American films were imported to China every year. Moreover, film imports from Britain, France and Italy also increased.

Film imports and international relations

The above statistical analysis can inform the role of the new government's international relations in film imports. Although this research focuses on the first period (1949–1965), examination of the extended period from 1966 to 1991 can further prove the point.

First of all, the large import of films from the Soviet Union and its satellite countries were characteristic of the China's relationships with these countries. In the 1950s through to the early 1960s, within the spectrum of the Cold War period, China launched the "leaning to one-side" diplomatic policy[3] (see Zhu, 2001), and sought an alliance with the Soviet Union against the "imperialist states" led by the United States. The close Sino-Soviet relationships appeared to have made impact on the importation of films from Soviet Union and other socialist countries in China.

However, from the late 1950s to the early 1960s, due to decreasing support from the Soviet Union to help China recover from the aftermath of the Great Leap Forward (1958–1961), and the Soviet Union's reluctance to support China to recapture Taiwan in the late 1950s as well as the China-India border disputes in 1962 (Lanteigne, 2009: 4), Sino-Soviet relations deteriorated. Towards the end of the 1960s, further exacerbated by the border disputes, Sino-Soviet relations had completely collapsed. Perhaps in response to the Sino-Soviet split, film imports from the Soviet Union suddenly declined in 1963. Further evidence of the link between film imports from socialist countries and international relationships can be found in the 1970s, when films were increasingly imported from Albania, an ideological ally of China at the time in 1970s (see Yang, 2000).

Secondly, it was evident that international relations also had an impact on China's film imports from western countries and Japan. In the 1950s, influenced by the "leaning to one-side" policy, a large-scale campaign was initiated by the CCP to proscribe all American films (Niu, 1998). At the end of the 1970s, the Chinese government made efforts to develop strategic relations with the USA,

---

[3] Leaning to one side policy is China's policy of leaning towards the Soviet Union in the 1950s (see Zhu, 2001).

which in 1979 led eventually to the official establishment of diplomatic relations between the two countries. It was hardly a coincidence that the number of American film imports soared when the relations between the two countries thawed.

The easy access of films from Finland, Norway and Australia to China could also have been influenced by the political climate at the time, since they were neutral countries during the Cold War period. Moreover, during the same period, despite some conflicts, Chinese leaders began to put in efforts to establish non-governmental diplomatic relations with Japan. For example, they signed non-governmental trade agreements with Japanese companies and organisations, sent trade delegations to Japan for goodwill visits, and received Japanese trade delegations to China (Hsiao, 1977; Johnson, 1986). Thanks to the recovering Sino-Japan relationship, in the 1950s and the 1960s, film imports from Japan had seen a steady pace.

One should note that, in the first three decades of the PRC, the Communist government forged its international relations in a very pragmatic way, aimed at strengthening the country and its status as a legitimate ruling government. For example, the "leaning to one-side" policy was made based on the CCP's assessment of the post-war global order and China's interests in it. From 1949 onwards, China had concerns about the threat posed by America to Chinese interests in view of the United States' continuous support of Taiwan, now considered as a renegade region of China. Allying itself with the Soviet Union would provide China with a stronger security position to fend off any threats from the United States and its allies. Besides, after eight years of war against the Japanese invasion, followed by four more years of civil conflict, the "leaning to one-side" policy provided various economic benefits to China during post-war reconstruction. Now the opportunity for China had come to rebuild its economy and a new nation. In addition, as previously stated, when the Soviet withdrew their support, from the mid 1960s China adjusted its foreign policy and started to develop international relations with America in the hope of winning support to prevent the potential threat from the Soviet Union.

Film imports and socialist ideology

The above statistics demonstrate China's pragmatism in forging international relations with other countries, and how the international relations affected film imports. However, film imports did not entirely rest on international relationship alone. Firstly, although a number of films were shown in China one or two years later after they were screened in the Soviet Union, many others were outdated, which had been published ten or twenty years ago in the Soviet Union. Back in the 1930s and the 1940s, it was a period when socialist realism was the dominant language of art endorsed by the Soviet authorities in film production. This form of socialist realism believed that art should be realistic in style, and didactic in intention. As such, it is used to portray the heroic deeds of workers and working people, industrial and agricultural landscapes and achievements to romanticise the Soviet State, thus turning the arts into a form of government propaganda (Krishnan, 2012). The embracing of socialist realism as an artistic form was encouraged in the Stalin era (1928–1953) (ibid). The period between 1928 and 1932 brought with it Stalin's (1978–1953) first "five-year plan", in which the state restructured agriculture and industry and implemented the centrally planned economy (Millar, 1974). As an aftermath of this, the 1930s saw the production of many films that portrayed Soviet revolutionary leaders and Russia's historical heroes. After the Great Patriotic War (1941 to 1945), Stalin created the cult of personality with a great number of films praising the positive role Stalin played during and following the war. The film *Stalingrad* (1947) is one of the outstanding examples of this. Stalin's death in 1953 was a turning point in Soviet history as Stalin's rule was subsequently denounced by his successors. At the time, Soviet film production took the turn to feature stories of the ordinary people in the war with a more realistic significance. The years from the 1950s to the late 1960s were known as the "thaw" period in which Soviet filmmakers were allowed greater freedom of expression of ideas and views (Woll, 2003: 4). With a temporary relaxation of censorship and relative cultural liberalism during the early stages of the "thaw period" in the Soviet Union, several key "thaw" films were produced. Examples included *The Forty-First* (1956), *The Cranes Are Fly-*

ing (1957), *Ballad of a Soldier* (1959), *Destiny of a Man* (1959), and *Clear Heaven* (1961).

Along with the relaxation of the Soviet government's control of art and culture, an increasing number of films began to revise Stalinist ideology (Woll, 2000: xi). However, the years from the 1950s to the early 1960s saw China still importing many Soviet films made in the Stalin era. Moreover, even though it had imported some important "thaw" films, only *Destiny of a Man* (1959) and *The Cranes Are Flying* (1957) were released for public viewing for a short period of time; the other three were all designated "reference films" without public screening (Cao, 2006).

Secondly, the statistics show that in the 1950s and the early 1960s China also imported films from Western Europe and the USA whose ideology and political systems were seen as contradictory to that of China's. For example, the Australian film *Three in One* (1957, 1958 in China), the American film *Salt of the Earth* (1954, 1959 in China), the British films *The Million Pounds Note* (1954), *Great Expectations* (1946, 1956 in China), and *Oliver Twist* (1948, 1957 in China), the French film *Fanfan la Tulipe* (1952, 1956 in China) and the Italian film *The Bicycle Thief* (1948) were all imported to China for public viewing during this period.

The selective import of Soviet Union films and the screening of western films both indicated that international relations are not the only factor that determines film imports in the years between 1949 and 1965. In order to find out other factors that could influence film imports, a thematic study was carried out on films imported from 1949 to 1965. Four kinds of themes could be recognised: anti-imperialism, anti-feudalism, anti-capitalism and films that glorified socialism. Categorisation of these four themes were mainly based on film critiques published in film journals at that time and film descriptions offered by the Shanghai Film Dubbing Studio. One could easily find words and expressions such as "anti-imperialism", "anti-feudalism", "anti-capitalism", and "glorification" in critiques and descriptions on films screening during the period under research. Besides, the categorisation also corresponded to the new government's policy on film imports and translation. It was the Party's consistent belief that the films cannot be separated from its broader political agenda and objectives. In 1948, the CCP Central Committee Propaganda Department sent an instruction to the Northeast Film Bureau's Propaganda Department, in which it was reiterated: "we accept all films that are anti-imperialist, anti-federalist, and anti-capitalist." (Central Policy Research Office of the CCP, 1949) During the 1950s, the Chinese leaders delivered a number of speeches highlighting the importance of film translation. For example, in 1952, the first "five-year plan" put the dubbing of foreign language films as a political task to be accomplished.

Most anti-imperialist Soviet films were made against the backdrop of the Second World War, either centred on the Great Patriotic War, such as *Menige Alexander Matrosov* (1947) and *Stalingrad* (1947), or guerrilla wars, like *Marite* (1947), *Konstantin Zaslonov* (1949) and *Teen Guerrillas* (1951). Besides, some Western Europen films also belong to this category of theme. *Voyage of the Damned* (1976) for example, tells the story of a group of Jews escaping from the persecution of the Nazis. Anti-feudalist films portray the hardship endured by the peasants under the control of feudal landlords. Examples included the Hungarian film *Treasured Earth* (1948), the Indian film *Two Acres of Land* (1953), the Soviet films *Gadfly* (1956) and *Idiot* (1958), and some Western films such as *Fanfan la Tulipe* (1952). Anti-capitalism was one of the main themes of the Soviet films made during the Cold War. Besides, some European films could also be seen as anti-capitalist films. One prime example was the Italian neo-socialist film *The Bicycle Thief* (1948), famous for its denigration of the dark nature of capitalism. British films that were adapted from Dickens' works provided other good examples. During the late Qing Dynasty, Dicken's novels have been known for their exposure of Britain's social ills (Zarrow, 2005: 51). When it came to the 1950s in China, films adapted from his novels were deemed to be a reflection of Dickens' sharp observation and criticism of British capitalist society, and they were, as such, considered good teaching material to feed into the broad narrative of building a new socialist nation. Hence, *The Pickwick Papers* (1952, 1955 in China), *Great Expectations* (1946, 1956 in China; 1978), *Oliver Twist* (1948, 1957 in China) and *The Million Pound Note* (1954, 1958 in China) were continuously screened in the 1950s in China. Similarly, the American film *Salt of the Earth* (1945, 1959 in China) and Japanese films such as *Matsukawa Derailment* (1961, 1961 in China) were all considered to belong to this category exemplifying the struggles of workers against the capitalists, and reflecting the dark nature of capitalism. Lastly, there were films glorifying or praising socialist reality. Normally, such films described how progressive intellectuals, workers and farmers contributed to socialist construction, or how people took part in the struggle against the capitalist-imperialist enemy. Accordingly, industrial and agricultural landscapes were popular subjects celebrating the achievements of the Soviet state. A notable example of this category was *Dream of a Cossack* (1951, 1951 in China) which tells the story of a soldier named Tutarinov who returns to his hometown and takes an active part in re-building a hydropower station with the others in his village.

Nearly every film translated during this period fell into one of the four categories mentioned above. Thus, it can be concluded that as long as films belonged to one of these four categories, they were considered to be in line with China's grand vision and were able to gain access to the Chinese screen, even if they came from Western countries. This criterion for film selection corresponded to the central government's objectives of nation-building. After the CCP had overthrown the Nationalist Government, the Party's major political mission shifted from fighting against the Nationalist Party to securing the Party's legitimacy as the ruling authority, and transforming China from a semi-feudal and semi-colonial society into a new socialist one (Zimmerman, 2010: 51). From 1949 to 1967, in order to achieve the defined objectives, a series of policies had been put in place covering areas such as diplomatic relations, economic development and social reforms. With respect to diplomatic relations, the Party endeavoured to pursue international recognition and support. On the economic front, it outlined a series of "five-year plans" aiming at reviving China's war-torn economy. In regards to domestic politics, the Party had a vision to reform the class system and improve people's living standards (Wang, 2009). But what concerned the central leadership most was how to prevent the revolution from losing its momentum, namely, how to stamp out the remnants of the Nationalist regime and uphold the leadership of the CCP. In September 1949, the Chinese People's Political Consultative Conference (CPPCC) was held in Beijing as both a celebration of the communists' victory in the war against the Nationalist Party, and a preparatory session to proclaim the founding of the New China. At the conference opening, Mao Zedong made a speech emphasising the advantage of a "democratic dictatorship" in protecting the fruits of the revolution (Mao, 1949b) and the necessity to continue the struggle against the imperialist and domestic reactionaries who were the opponents of a socialist China. In his New Year's message, Mao (1948) also called upon the CCP "to carry the revolution through to the end". He wrote:

> If the revolution is to be carried through to the end, we must use the revolutionary method to wipe out all the forces of reaction resolutely, thoroughly, wholly and completely; we must unswervingly persist in overthrowing imperialism, feudalism and bureaucrat-capitalism; and we must overthrow the reactionary rule of the Kuomintang on a country-wide scale and set up a republic that is a people's democratic dictatorship under the leadership of the proletariat and with the worker-peasant alliance as its main body. (Mao, 1948)

In addition, throughout 1949, Mao had repeatedly warned the communists against the "sugar-coated bullets" of the bourgeois classes that would corrode our Party and corrupt our people (Mao, 1949a).

Against this background, screening foreign films of the "three-anti" categories was believed to contribute to China's mission of nation-building in three ways. Firstly, the selected foreign films had corroborated the achievements of the CCP in the revolution. In 1949, the Central Propaganda Department's *Decisions on Strengthening the Film Industry* highlighted this point: "it is important to strengthen the film industry, so as to promote the achievements made by the Party in the new democratic revolution and national construction"[4]. (Chen, 1989) The achievement is known to be the overthrow of "the three mountains": namely, imperialism (*diguozhuyi*), feudalism (*fengjianzhuyi*), and bureaucrat-capitalism (*guanliaozibenzhuyi*), which were the forces that infringed Chinese sovereignty, oppressed the peasants and controlled Chinese economic life.

As mentioned above, from the 1930s, filmmaking in the Soviet Union began to adhere to socialist realism. Through showing revolutionary history in other socialist countries, and the revolutionary experiences of foreign leaders such as *Lenin in October* (1937, 1949 in China), *Lenin in 1918* (1939, 1951 in China), the films of socialist realism literally brought the heroic figures of the war into the limelight eulogising their courage in the fight against the power of imperialists, feudalists and capitalists. This rhetoric was to work well with the initiatives of the CCP in the early stages of nation-building. Therefore, many films of so-

---

[4] My translation.

cialist realism were shown in China. For the same reason, the Soviet "thaw" films were banned in China, since they questioned the Stalinist ideology, and this tendency was seen as a form of revisionism by the Chinese leadership. For example, critics usually interpreted the flying cranes in the film *Cranes Are Flying* (1957, 1958 in China) as a metaphor for hope and renewal of society (Shrayer, 1997).

Besides promoting the achievements of the CCP, showing selected foreign films was instrumental to consolidating the legitimacy of communism as a "correct" ideology leading China to success and prosperity. From the Opium War in the 1840s onwards, China struggled to shake off Western dominance of its economy and politics. The progressive forces in China saw Soviet Russia as an aspiration and communism as a way to free China. Exhibiting socialist realism films was one of the building blocks used to achieve their vision. The main idea of socialist realism prescribed that all forms of art should portray some aspects of the human struggle for social progress. Exhibiting the "three-anti" films delivered an underlying message, namely, that by providing a "comparison" with various other political forces and a new political vision, the Chinese communists deserved the right to lead the country. Also, films that glorified the life of socialist countries contributed to the legitimacy of the leadership of the CCP. Through the contrast between past social evils and "progressive" socialist ideology, a message was delivered to audiences that socialism was far superior to other forms of society. The portrayal of western people suffering from capitalism also had a similar function, which would send out a similar political message to Chinese audiences.

Lastly, the peaceful life and prosperity of socialist society presented in Soviet movies, such as *Dream of a Cossack* (1950, 1950 in China), provided a perfect model for China, namely, "a good future that Chinese people could visualise and aspire to in the future" (Chen, 2004). The former state leaders, from Mao Zedong to Liu Shaoqi (1898–1969), all endorsed the Soviet Union as a model for China to learn from. In 1954, when Zhou Enlai (1898–1976), former premier of the PRC, talked with Nikita Khrushchev (1894–1971) about the first "five-year plan" of socialist construction in China, he said, "today's Soviet Union is the future of China".

The promotion of foreign films

Translating foreign films into Chinese did not only mean screening these films in China. Another purpose was to lead the Chinese audience to "read" and understand these new cultural products. The early 1950s had seen many viewers reluctant to accept Soviet Union films (Clark, 1987: 35). Some audiences wrote to the film journal *Popular Cinema* and asked why the cover of journals had been changed to the Soviet style (Chen, 2004). Some audiences complained that they could not understand the Soviet films (Liu, 2008). However, despite the short period of resistance, more and more Chinese audiences began to embrace these Soviet films. An article in *The People's Daily* carried a report on the popularity of Soviet Union films in China. It showed that in 1948 there were 1.3 million viewers of Soviet films; whilst in 1949 that number had soared to around 7 million. In 1953, five Soviet films were screened between 15,600 and 37,600 times attracting audiences of between 15 million to over 32 million (Chen, 2010). Moreover, many audiences admitted that they were inspired by Soviet films and that these films influenced their lives. For example, there were teachers who regarded the teacher in the film *A Country Teacher* (1949) as a role model; and after watching *Far from Moscow* (1950), many youngsters volunteered to serve in the remote border areas of China.

As mentioned earlier, paratexts are beneficial to promoting and influencing the consumption of a film. The CCP made great efforts to promote Soviet films. In order to make full use of imported films, the central government created many unusual channels to bring these films to Chinese audiences. For example, besides being screened in film theatres, they were also shown in subway stations so that the poor were not excluded due to their inability to pay (Xu, 2010). Publishing comic book adaptations of films was another way to promote these foreign films in China. In 1950, the central government established the Beijing People's Art Publishing House and the Shanghai People's Art Publishing Company. From then on, comic books, known as *Lianhuanhua* in Chinese, became a popular medium of propaganda (Lent, 2012).

Publishing film programmes, known as *dianyingshuomingshu* in Chinese, was a way to bring these films to Chinese viewers. Using photographs and written information, film programmes, similar to today's movie trailers, aimed to give the potential audiences a first impression of the film. But, unlike movie trailers which often leave room for audiences to imagine the film content, film programmes did not only reveal film content but also intensified the political message of the film. Take the French film *Fanfan la Tulipe* (1952) as an example. In order to use the film for political propaganda, the programme asserted that the meaning of the film was "uncovering the absurdity and impudence of French feudalism"[5]. Such a way of interpreting the film is different from how Chinese people review the film nowadays. On two Chinese film review websites, Douban.com and Mtime.com, none of the reviews of this film mentions its anti-feudal significance. Instead, Mtime judges the film to be a "film mocking the knight-errant"[6].

In addition to film programmes, film journals were another important medium used by the authorities to get across the message of films to audiences in China (Chen, 2004). On the one hand, journals such as *Popular Cinema* (*dazhong dianying* 大众电影) and daily newspapers such as *The People's Daily* (*renmin ribao* 人民日报) disseminated translations of Soviet film theory and practice. On the other hand, through publishing film reviews and replying to readers' letters, film journals made efforts to establish ties between the foreign films and the reality of China. By doing so, some critics showed how some Chinese viewers admitted to being inspired by the heroes and heroines in foreign films, which had a life-changing impact on them. Some persuaded the audiences to associate the struggles and the prosperous socialist life portrayed in foreign films with Chinese reality, and inspired them to work for a better Chinese society. For example, in 1950 *The People's Daily* posted a film critique of the North Korean anti-imperialist film *My Homeland* (1949), which read as follows:

In view of the colonised people's struggles, we do admire them. Even though it was not translated, many people had been touched by the film when it was premiered in Beijing. It is because China and North Korea had experienced a similar historical hardship, and finally they were united and fought together. When our nation was in danger before and after the 9.18

---

[5] My translation. See the photo of the progammes of *Fanfan la Tulipe (*1952) at http://book.kongfz.com/item_pic_8575_188728051/

[6] See http://movie.mtime.com/14930/

Incident when Japan invaded China, the Korean people had been enslaved by Japan for nearly 20 years. (Zhong, 1950)[7]

In response to the readers, the journal editors tried to project a "good life" image of China's future, informing readers that the prosperous futures depicted in the Soviet Union films would also be part of China's future. In this environment, "the Soviet Union's today is our tomorrow" used as a slogan had been frequently invoked to conjoin China and the Soviet Union.

Conclusion

This article has examined the selection and promotion of foreign films during the period 1949–1964. During this period, China translated a large amount of foreign films aimed at promoting the achievements of the CCP leadership and socialist ideology as well as building up a socio-political vision of China. Regarding film selection, the article has identified two major factors influencing the selection of foreign films in this period. One factor was China's relationships with other countries in the Cold War: for example, in the 1950s and early 1960s, the close political-cultural ties between China and the Soviet Union. It propelled the CCP to bring in so-called *progressive films* from abroad, especially Soviet films to fill a cultural void in Chinese society. The other factor was the Party's intention of using film as a nation-building vehicle. It drove the party to import films which had anti-imperialist, anti-capitalist and anti-feudalist significance, and those glorifying socialism. Both factors prompted the new communist government to import foreign films to enhance their efforts to build a new ideology and to advance the CCP as a legitimate ruling party in China. On another note, these films contributed to building a modern Chinese identity and continue to inform China's future, as China's recent development has eloquently demonstrated.

---

[7] My translation.

References

CAO, Lei (2006): "远去的回响" [Remote echoes] – Shanghai: Shanghai Lexicographical Publishing House.

CAO, Lei (2010): "文革中神秘的内参片", [Mysterious internal movies in 1970s], *Memories and Archives* (08), 18–21.

CHEN, Chapman (2004): "On the Hong Kong Chinese Subtitling of English Swearwords", *Meta* 49 (1), 135–47.

CHEN, Huangmei (ed.) (1989): "当代中国电影" [Contemporary China Film] – Beijing: China Social Sciences Press, 31.

CHEN, Tina Mai (2004): "Internationalism and Cultural Experience: Soviet Films and Popular Chinese Understandings of the Future in the 1950s", *Cultural Critique* (58), 82–114.

CHEN, Tina Mai (2010): "Film and gender in Sino-Soviet cultural exchange, 1949–1969". In: LI, Huayu (ed.): *China Learns from the Soviet Union, 1949–present.* – Maryland: Lexington Books, 421–445.

CLARK, Paul (1987): *Culture and Politics Since 1949.* – Cambridge: Cambridge University Press

FOX, Jo (2007): *Film Propaganda in Britain and Nazi Germany: World War II Cinema.* – Oxford: Berg.

GARY, Jonathan (2010): *Show Sold Separately: Promos, Spoilers, and Other Media Paratexts.* – New York: New York University Press, 6.

HE, Yinan (2007): "Remembering and Forgetting the War: Elite Mythmaking, Mass reaction, and Sino-Japanese Relations, 1950–2006", *History & Memory.* 119 (2), Fall/Winter, 43–74.

HUANG, Nicole (2013): "Listening to films: Politics of auditory in 1970s China", *Journal of Chinese Cinemas*, 7(3), 197–206.

HSIAO, Gene T. (1977): *The Foreign Trade of China: Policy, Law, and Practice.* – Berkeley/Los Angeles: University of California Press.

JOHNSON, Chalmers (1986): "The Patterns of Japanese Relations with China, 1952–1982", *Pacific Affairs*, 59 (3), Autumn, 402–128.

KRISHNAN, Maya (2012): "Transformation of the human consciousness: the origins of socialist realism in the Soviet Union". In: FITZHUGH, Will (ed.): *The*

LANTEIGNE, Marc (2009): *Chinese Foreign Policy: An Introduction.* – London: Routledge.

LANZA, Camino Gutiérrez (1997): "Spanish Film Translation: Ideology, Censorship and the National Language". In: *The Changing Scene in the World Language.* American Translators Association Scholarly Monograph Series. Vol. IX, PP.35–45, – Amsterdam/Philadelphia: John Benjamins Publishing.

LANZA, Camino Gutiérrez (2002): "Spanish Translation and Cultural Patronage: The Filtering and Manipulation of Imported Material during Franco's Dictatorship". In: TYMOCZKO, Maria & GENTZLER, Edwin (eds): *Translation and Power* – Amherst/Boston: University of Massachusetts Press.

LENT, John A. (2012): "Lianhuanhua", *São Paulo* 1 (2), 4–24.

LEFEVRE, André (1992): *Translation, Rewriting and the Manipulation of Literary Fame* – London: Routledge.

LIU, Dishan (2008): "苏联电影在中国五十年代的考察" [Soviet films in China in the 1950s], *影史探问 [A Survey on Film History]*, vol 4, 55–60.

MAO, Tsetung (1948): "Carry the Revolution Through to The End". In: *Selected Works of Mao Tse-tung*; Vol. IV.
https://www.marxists.org/reference/archive/mao/selected-works/volume4/mswv4_48.htm (05.12.2014)

MAO, Tsetung (1949a): "Cast Away Illusion, Prepare for Struggle". Selected Works of Mao Tse-tung: Vol. IV.
https://www.marxists.org/reference/archive/mao/selected-works/volume-4/mswv4_66.htm (05.12.2014)

MAO, Tsetung (1949b): "The Chinese People Have Stood UP!". In: *Selected Words of Mao Tse-tung*; Vol. V.
https://www.marxists.org/reference/archive/mao/selected-works/volume-5/mswv5_01.htm (05.12.2014)

MILLAR, James R. (1974): "Mass Collectivisation and the Contribution of Soviet Agriculture to the First Five-Year Plan: A Review Article", *Slavic Review* 33(4), 750–766.

NIU, Jun (1998): "The origins of Sino-Soviet alliance". In: WESTAD, Odd Arne (ed.): *The Rise and Fall of the Sino-Soviet Alliance, 1945–1963*. New York: Stanford University Press, 47–89.

PANG, Laikwan (2002): *Building a New China in Cinema: The Chinese Leftwing Cinema Movement, 1932–1937*. – New York/Oxford: Rowman&Littlefield.

CENTRAL POLICY RESEARCH OFFICE OF THE CCP (1949): "中共中央宣传部关于电影工作给东北局宣传部的指示" [The CPC Central Committee Propaganda Department's instruction for Northeast Bureau's Propaganda Department on Film Work]. "一九四八年以来的政策汇编" *[Collection of Policies Since 1948]*. – Beijing: the Central China Bureau of CCP Central Committee, 249.

SHRAYER, Maxim D. (1997): "Why Are the Cranes Still Flying?", *Russian Review* 56(3), 425–439.

SZARKOWSKA, Agnieszka (2005): "The Power of Film Translation" *Translation Journal*, vol.3, no.3. Retrieved 5th November 2014 from http://translationjournal.net/journal/32film.htm

WANG, Zhengxu (2009): "Nation building, state building, and the road to democracy: political development in 60 years of the People's Republic", *Briefing Series*, Volume 54. http://china.praguesummerschools.org/files/china/7china2012.pdf (05.12.2014)

WOLL, Josephine (2000): *Real Images: Soviet Cinemas and the Thaw*. – London: I. B. Tauris.

WOLL, Josephine (2003): *The Cranes Are Flying: The Film Companion*. – London: I. B. Tauris.

XU, Xiaxiang (2010): "农村电影放映队与农民的再造" [Rural film projection teams and the re-making of peasants], 二十一世纪 [Twenty First Century] (12), 47–55.

YANG, Kuisong (2000): "The Sino-Soviet Border Clash of 1969: From Zhenbao Island to Sino-American Rapprochement", *Cold War History*, 1(1), 21–52.

ZARROW, Peter G. (2005): *China in War and Revolution, 1895–1949*. – London: Routledge Curzon.

ZHANG, Yingjin (2004): *Chinese National Cinema*. – New York/London: Routledge.

ZHOU, Tiedong (2012): "新中国电影对外交流" [New China's Film foreign exchange], 电影艺术 [Film Arts] (01), 113–118.

ZHONG, Dianfei (1950): "朝鲜人民的第一部影片——'我的故乡'" [The first film of North Korean people – *My Hometown*], 人民日报 [People's Daily] 25th August, Volume 5.

ZHU, Tianbiao (2001): "Nationalism and Chinese Foreign Policy", *The China Review*, Vol.1.No.1 (Fall 2001), 1–27.

ZHU, Ying & ROSEN, Stanley (eds) (2010): *Art, Politics and Commerce in Chinese Cinema*. – Hong Kong: Hong Kong University Press.

ZIMMERMAN, James M. (2010): *China Law Deskbook: A Legal Guide for Foreign-invested Enterprises* (3rd edition). – Chicago: Amer Bar Assn.

Freddi's preliminary norms: Italy's censorship bureau

Irene Ranzato
Università di Roma Sapienza
irene.ranzato@libero.it

This article will focus on the Ufficio di Revisione Cinematografica (Bureau of Film Revision), more commonly known in the Italian film industry as ufficio censura (censorship bureau), which was created in 1913 and has been operative since, and whose task is to authorise the screening of films before their distribution in the territory. After a section delineating its origins and main legislative measures, I will discuss the bureau's policies during the fascist period mainly through the illustration of some of the decisions taken by Luigi Freddi, a prominent figure in Italian cinema, who, although not ignored by historians for his political and cultural importance, has been surprisingly and comparatively neglected by researchers in Translation Studies. I will argue that his decisions, reflections and actions could shed further light on the complex role of preliminary norms (Toury 1995: 58) in that particular socio-historical context.

Censorship provisions in fascist Italy[1]

Mussolini and his fascists did not invent either censorship or propaganda in Italy. Both had a very long history in the country (Laura 1961: 4–10). Preventive censorship had been practised extensively by the Catholic Church, especially from the Council of Trent onwards. Ecclesiastical censorship on forms of entertainment was not uniform. On the one hand, it showed an attitude of strict refusal to accept cinema in particular and entertainment shows in general, as occa-

---

[1] Parts of this section are also explored in Ranzato 2016, Chapter 3.

sions and places of vice and immorality.[2] On the other hand, religious authorities could be more open and tolerant provided that films were inspired by moral principles (Brunetta 1975: 60). Pope Pius XI in his encyclical of 21st December 1929, *Divini illius magistri*, warned about the dangers of, among others, cinema shows, but also encouraged the possibility to act through these new media to educate people and give them moral guidance by producing morally edifying theatre and cinema shows (Pio XI 1929).

In the 20th century, the first legislative measures on censorship arrived shortly after the circulation of the first audiovisual products. In 1910, a disposition of the Ministero degli Interni [Home Affairs] gave the prefects the faculty of authorising or rejecting public screenings. A few years later, on 20 February 1913, a memorandum from the Prime Minister, Giovanni Giolitti,[3] gave the prefects the necessary details on the criteria to use in granting or refusing the authorisations for films to be screened. According to the dispositions, it was necessary to ban those films which "make representatives of the public forces appear hateful and make criminals appear as nice people" and it advised to look out for: "the shameful excitation of sensuality, provoked by scenes where the vividness of the images immediately nourishes the lowest and most vulgar passions, and other films which stir hatred between social classes or are an offence to national decorum" (in Laura 1961: 5, my translation).

This text is important because it is the first that gives explicit indications on the nature of the prohibitions, and it is remarkable because it already contains two fundamental principles of the type of control which was going to be exerted from then on: moral censorship (criminals should not be nice and sexuality should be banned because it stirs vulgar passions) and political censorship (exaltation of the public forces, harmony between social classes, affirmation of national dignity). It is equally interesting to note that the provisions perceived that, unlike other modes of expression, cinema has a "vividness" whose effects are more important than those excited by other kinds of representations.

---

[2] This attitude dated back to the pre-Tridentine times and was traditionally linked to patristic studies such as Tertullian's *De Spectaculis* (*On the Spectacles*, written between 197 and 202 AD, in Cargill n.d.).

[3] Giovanni Giolitti (1842–1928) was the Prime Minister of Italy for five times until 1921.

Together with the problem of which contents to censor came the concern over form and ways of verbal expressions. Linguistic correctness became an issue with the arrival of an industrially and culturally significant cinema, that is, with the passage from short to medium and long feature films, in the 1910s. As films became longer, intertitles were also longer and more frequent, sometimes ridden with linguistic mistakes. It became a commonplace for critics and members of the general public to make comments in newspapers not only on the mistakes but also on foreign, 'exotic' words seen (and later heard) on screen. These are for example the words of a reader of *La Grande Italia*, a weekly magazine, who in 1911 perfectly anticipates the linguistic xenophobia of the fascist *ventennio*[4]:

I'd like to remark a fact which has lately become disgusting for viewers and humiliating for our national pride. I'd like to mention several Italian companies and especially a notable one from Turin, which in all of their productions never forget to include that exotic 'something' without which they would not be welcome with clients [...] abroad. So we see that dear police [in English in the text] popping up everywhere in capital letters, and those signs, those notices written in any language but ours. (in Raffaelli 1991: 166, my translation)

These were the first signs of a longing for the 'purity' of Italian which would be considered typical of the fascist years.

After Giolitti's memorandum, censorship was given a proper legislative organisation. L'Ufficio di Revisione Cinematografica [Bureau for Cinematographic Revision] was set up on 1 May 1913 with the specific brief of monitoring and amending the iconic and verbal content – intertitles at the time – of silent films. It carried out an operation of cleansing the films it examined, a task which contributed to conditioning the evolution of the Italian language from the very beginning of cinema and shows how that form of regulatory intervention in linguistic matters, long thought to be unique to the fascist government, was in fact very much alive at the time of Giovanni Giolitti (Raffaelli 1991: 164). The Law of 25 June 1913, n. 785 gave the State the power of control over film content. The Regio Decreto [Royal Decree] of 31 May 1914, n. 532 instituted a censor-

---

[4] It is one of the customary ways in which historians refer to the period Italy was ruled by the fascist government of Mussolini, which lasted roughly twenty years, between 1922 and 1943.

ship commission which was entirely administrative, composed of officers of the public security or police chiefs. This way, it was the Ministero degli Interni that censored films.

A *Regio Decreto-Legge* of 9 October 1919, n. 1953 set up in addition a preventive form of censorship: the stories and screenplays of the Italian films in production would have to be examined and authorised before filming.

The following law, passed on 22 April 1920, n. 531, is also notable because it changed the composition of the censorship committee. This was to be composed not only of public security officers (which went from 4 to 2 members) but also of a judge, a mother of children, an expert in artistic and literary matters, a publicist, and a member to be chosen from among educators or representatives of humanitarian associations for the moral protection of people, young people in particular. For the first time, policemen became a minority on the board and, even if all the other members were to be nominated by the Ministero degli Interni, censorship showed a sign of opening up, in a slightly more liberal sense, to artistic demands. This evolution towards a more liberal system would be brutally interrupted by fascism.

When in October 1922 fascism came to power, it inherited a sufficiently repressive body of legislation. Nonetheless, the new government felt the need to make it stricter and it was the Prime Minister himself, Benito Mussolini, who proposed the adoption of new bills. The *Regio Decreto-Legge* of 24 September 1923, n. 3287 was the most important document on the subject in the whole fascist period and it would be the point of reference for all the following provisions.

The document reiterated the existence of a double censorship – on screenplays and on finished films – and the obligation to submit a project for censorship revision before and after the film was shot. Censorship was always based on ethical criteria on the one hand, and on political criteria on the other. What was completely different now was the way in which censorship actually worked and how the control commission was composed. In fact, the latter continued to exist only in the case of appeals. In ordinary practice, screenplays and films were to be revised by individual executives and officers of the Ministero degli Interni, thus essentially by public security people. This was a very significant change. The commission virtually disappeared, as the material was now revised by 'individual' officers of the Ministry. The mildly liberal turn taken by the former government in choosing people who were not politicians or policemen was then nullified (Gili 1981: 15–19).

After the fundamental 1923 change, the alterations made in the following years were more limited and concerned mainly the composition of the control commission. Following the protests from various sectors of society – cinema professionals, intellectuals, and Catholics from whose ranks the mother and the member belonging to the world of education and the humanitarian organisations usually came –, the first degree commission for the control of screenplays and films was restored in 1924, after only one year after its abolition. And though it became stricter and more repressive through each successive stage of legislation, its oscillations also reveal interesting tendencies and the two souls of the fascist government: one utterly repressive, the other more sensitive to cultural demands.

The mainstay of the Italian fascist political economy was its drive for autarchy, that is, for an economic self-sufficiency and independence from foreign cultural influence. The answer of the authorities to the threat of the possible penetration of films spoken in foreign languages was a total prohibition on screening them in Italy. As for original productions, when foreign words did appear in Italian films under fascism, they would be used ironically, as a populist critique of bourgeois snobbism. In *La contessa di Parma* (Alessandro Blasetti, 1937), for example, we can hear the following exchange (translated into English in Ricci 2008: 63):

The Model: I'm a mannequin in the Maison Printemps!
The Owner: Ha! Printemps! Pri-ma-ve-ra [Spring] Primavera! Can't you hear how much better it sounds? You are a model in the Primavera store.

The whole film is punctuated by negative, ironical comments on how ridiculous it is to 'speak foreign' and how one should use the 'correct' Italian equivalent: "In italiano si dice indossatrice!" [= in Italian, fashion model is *indossatrice*!].

From 1929 to 1931 the absence or the purely experimental character of dubbing gave way to incredible solutions and many sound films were actually muted and screened without sound. According to Gili (1981: 34), the justification of such a policy – wanted, as it seems, by Mussolini himself – was that this way it was possible to prevent Italians from learning foreign languages by going to the cinema.

These 'muted' films were left with only the music track and the sound effects track while the film sequences were continuously interrupted by intertitles, sometimes very long ones, containing the translation of the dialogue. Among these films, to name but a few of the most famous, were *Der blaue Engel* (*L'angelo azzurro*, 1930) by Josef von Sternberg, *Halleluja!* (*Alleluja*, 1929) by King Vidor, and *Sous les toits de Paris* (*Sotto i tetti di Parigi*, 1929) by René Clair.

The problem was finally solved when dubbing became technically viable in 1931. The films were then dubbed into Italian either in their country of origin, normally the USA, or in Italy. But the government was quick to react and the *Regio Decreto-Legge* of 5 October 1933, n. 1414 prohibited the importation of films that had been dubbed elsewhere than in Italy. It was now possible for the censor to view the film in the original version and to 'suggest' the alterations in the dialogue that needed to be introduced in the dubbing so as to modify the unpleasant sequences. With this policy the government achieved a greater control over the 'purity of the language', which added to other, more overtly political advantages: manipulation of content, deletion of unwanted references and, in some cases, addition of more 'pleasant' references. The government could, from then on, exert without difficulty a linguistic control which aimed first of all at the disappearance of Italian dialects, regionalisms and accents in the final dubbed version. US films – the majority of the films imported – were to be dubbed in an abstract Italian, thus contributing to the effort of cultural homogenisation and regional uprooting which was one of the aims of fascism. From this point of view, as pointed out by Gili (1981: 35–37), the foreign film to be dubbed was a more flexible and controllable product than an original Italian film.

This system was ideological in design because it enacted an ongoing imperative of fascist cultural policy, i.e. the defence and promotion of national identity. Indeed, dubbing attempted to protect the Italian public from exposure to foreign influence through the manipulation of language and images, and in this respect it can be seen as the cinematic equivalent to the central goal of the Istituto Nazionale Fascista di Cultura [Fascist National Institute of Culture], founded in

1926. Under the directorship of Giovanni Gentile, the institute was set up to "preserve for our intellectual life its national character according to the genius and the tradition of our race, and also to favor its expansion abroad" (in Mack Smith 1959: 418). The ideological character of the state-mandated dubbing cannot be overstated, as Ricci (2008: 63) points out: "Such was the force of the purification campaign that even in the face of extreme technical limitations, the dubbing requirement remained in place".

With the law of 10 January 1935, n. 65, the process of fascistisation was completed and censorship was by now entirely administrative and politicised: no more educators, no professionals, no experts and no more mothers or judges in the censorship committee.

To sum up, from 1923 to 1939, the various law decrees gave more and more power to censors who were recruited from the ranks of officers of some Ministries, and to the representatives of organisms directly linked to the regime, like the Fascist Party and the Fascist University Groups. Cinema enjoyed very little freedom and, as argued by Gili (1981: 21–25), the self-censorship applied by authors and producers – who did not want to risk their money and then see their film banned – probably worked as a mechanism of self-regulation even before the actual control by the commission.

Luigi Freddi

A journalist and close collaborator of Benito Mussolini, Luigi Freddi was a leading figure in the military, political and cultural life of fascism, from 1915, the year of his early involvement in Mussolini's paper *Il Popolo d'Italia*, to the various prestigious positions he covered within the fascist party, as a member of the fascist government and beyond. After an enlightening trip to Hollywood, he was nominated Direttore Generale per la Cinematografia [General Director for Cinematography] in 1934 and was responsible for the regime's 'vision' of cinema, both for what concerned Italian original productions and foreign products to be distributed in Italy. He was also, and most notably, the champion of preventive censorship. He saw the advantages of a full preventive censorship from the very early stage of screenplay writing and, from the moment he became General Director, he applied it in the strictest possible way (Gili 1981: 28–30). Even if he had great respect and admiration for the Hays code,[5] what Freddi had in mind was especially the German system because it privileged the political aspect of censorship, as he thought censorship was essentially a political institution. He saw the participation of 'simple' citizens in the commission (mothers, art experts etc.) as a serious mistake, as it was, in his opinion, only a demagogic concession to call people who did not have a sense of the moral, social and educational policies of the State to perform a task which was essentially technical (Gili 1981: 40).

For what concerns film dialogue, Freddi had an early phobia of dialects (1929) and he vehemently opposed regionalisms and foreign words in favour of a more standard Italian. All English language films were to be translated into 'pure' – that is, non-accented, non-dialect – Italian. The suppression of accent and dialect in the Italian cinema during the 1930s gives us a key to understand why the national cinema of neorealism, developed between the 1940s and the 1950s, was considered a radical break from the past. Neorealism's use of non-professional actors speaking accented and dialect Italian, which defined them in terms of their diverse regional identity, was also a reaction against the very specific tenets of fascist cultural policy (Talbot 2007: 60–64). The fascist linguistic stance, however, had a permanent influence on the language of dubbing, which substantially maintained the linguistic features elaborated in the thirties: the full respect of the Roman-Florentine pronunciation, a substantial adherence to the grammatical norm, the use of the conditional (which in Italian is considered, as the subjunctive, more educated, thus not commonly used in the most popular dialectal forms), the adoption of a standard and widely comprehensible lexicon. Dubbing has been minimally influenced, from the post-war years till recently, by the vast and profound linguistic transformations experienced by cinema audiences on one side and by national film productions on the other. Italian dubbing remained virtually unaltered, both in cinema and on television, until the beginning of the 1970s. Only then can we register a remarkable turning point in dub-

---

[5] Particularly strict censorship guidelines in vigour in the USA from 1930 to 1968, originally created by William H. Hays, President of the Motion Picture Association of America.

bing, when dialects started to appear in the translation of the big American productions. The first important film where characters speak Sicilian is *The Godfather* (Francis Ford Coppola, 1972).[6] From then on, film dialogue has been marked at times by expressions in dialect and the linguistic gap between national productions and foreign, imported productions has not been as wide as in the previous decades (Raffaelli 1996: 27–28).

When Luigi Freddi, after a long disagreement with the Minister of Popular Culture, left his position as General Director for Cinema in 1939, cultural transformations were beginning to affect the general debate on censorship. There was a new generation of artists and intellectuals, even within the fascist structures, whom the regime had difficulty keeping under control. The industry journals *Cinema* and *Bianco e Nero* published articles which questioned the conformism of Italian film production, and a slow evolution of censorship policies in a more liberal sense was soon under way (Gili 1981: 58–59). This new turn was favoured by political events such as Italy being at war and Mussolini approaching his fall and being thus weaker and less alert.

However, Freddi's fall into disgrace lasted a short period and at the beginning of the 1940s he was again at the head of various institutions, including Cinecittà studios. He continued his relentless activity as an organiser of cinema productions even after the war and, in 1949, he wrote a book of memoirs in two volumes, *Il Cinema*, an invaluable source for the history of cinematography.

Freddi as gatekeeper

Although never ignored by historians and by scholars interested in the history of cinema for his political and cultural importance (Cannistraro 1975, Brunetta 1979, Gili 1981, Siniscalchi 1994 and, more recently, Gulì 2008, Mereu 2013

---

[6] Another popular American film, Disney's *The Aristocats* (Wolfgang Reitherman, 1970), played with different accents in Italian: the main cat character, Romeo, speaks in *Gli Aristogatti* with a heavy Roman accent (in original the cat is of Irish descent, but its accent is not as marked as in the Italian version). But this is an animation film, so the impact was far less shocking than that exerted by the realistic setting and characters of *The Godfather*.

and 2016a, Catolfi 2015), Freddi has been surprisingly and comparatively neglected by researchers in Translation Studies. I will argue that his decisions, reflections and actions could shed further light on the complex role of preliminary norms (Toury 1995: 58) in a particular socio-historical context.

Freddi was in fact, as mentioned above, the principal instigator of preventive censorship, arguably the historico-political concretisation of what Toury meant by preliminary norms, which, according to the scholar, have to do with two, often interconnected considerations, related to translation policy and directness of translation. "Translation policy", the point that mainly interests us here, "refers to those factors that govern the choice of text-types, or even of individual texts, to be imported through translation into a particular culture/language at a particular point in time" (ibid.). According to Toury, there are two major sources for the study of translational norms, textual and extratextual. Although scholars should privilege the former, as texts are primary products of norm-regulated behaviour, semi-theoretical or theoretical pronouncements made by translators, editors, publishers and all those connected with the process of translation can be precious sources of information as long as they are taken as pre-systematic (ibid.: 65–66).

A careful analysis of Freddi's writings, especially those included in his book of recollections on cinema (1949), offers indeed an exemplification of the difficulty of including this kind of extratextual sources in translation analyses, but also how invaluable these multifaceted and sometimes sophisticated reflections can be for Translation Studies scholars.

Freddi illustrates, by quoting from his official reports on films evaluated for distribution in the country, the practical application of "preliminary norms" in film censorship during fascism. He chooses his examples because they represent "extreme cases" relative to moral, political and artistic problems (ibid.: 163). The complexity of Freddi's thinking and the literary quality of some of his pieces of criticism are evident, for example in his long argumentation which constitutes his report on *La grande illusion* by Jean Renoir (1937):

A characteristically political film, the expression of that defeatist, quietist, anti-heroic mentality which is hanging from the white rag of pacifism. A form of mentality which is much worse than what, in bygone years, the antimilitarist one used to be: the latter had a polemical and active spirit, which could hoist an anti and show by doing so a combative attitude. While the quietist mentality of pacifism at all costs is a coward mentality which ignores even the fight for one's own pseudo-ideas. In this film it finds an expression veiled by an infinite precaution, wrapped in a skillful subtlety of nuances, glossed over, so to speak, by a very thin film, but with no heroic cracks. So much so that, for most of the audience, the film hasn't unveiled its goals: it has only left undoubted traces on the soul, which, on second thoughts, reveal their true nature. Traces of disrupting, corrosive elements which act in an almost surgical manner, by slow penetration. Jean Renoir, the author of the film, is a leftist director: not only for his intellectual sympathies, but for his active, direct participation in the operations of red propaganda. And in his film one has to admit that such propaganda is carried out with enormous ability and refined measure. (Freddi 1949: 166, my translation, as with the following excerpts from the same book)

Going on to enumerate the literary (Barbusse, Remarque, Gide) and cinematographic (Pabst, Trivas, Milestone) influences "on the inside more than on the outside" (ibid.: 167) of the film, that is acknowledging that the echoes are not superficial, but they are internal, exerting their influence on the spiritual attitude of the characters, Freddi chooses some sophisticated turns of phrases in order to substantiate his arguments. He finds in the film

a desperate effort to achieve a full realism, a fleshy objectivism which should not only create an atmosphere, and thus be not only descriptive, but also profoundly and creatively inside things and settings. The thing is that the effort is often interrupted and rendered vain by the ideological substratum; and where one feels that the director is about to achieve a poetical momentum or even where he has achieved a human enlightening, there appears the project which shifts the expression from the cinematographic to the intellectual-literary plane. There appears, in short, that unbalance between the film's intention and its realisation, between political inspiration and esthetic inspiration, which gives the whole work a curious uplifting tendency, immediately dragged down by propagandistic purposes. (ibid.: 167–168)

Freddi's political analysis of the film, and his negative evaluation, do not undermine the judgement of the film critic. In his six-page long report of *La grande illusion*, there is also room for technical considerations:

Photography is excellent for its realistic tone, for its clear and simple objectivity. Stroheim's interpretation is perfect, he is an actor of excellent means, perhaps without equals in the cinematography of the whole world, for his expressive abilities through elements of minimal force and maximum result: the idea of the orthopedic brace on his neck, in the second part of the film, is one of the best ever seen on the screen as means to define a character. Gabin is also very good, although he is a little too similar to himself; all the others are fully expressive, human and perfectly clear on the whole and in tone. Parlo has indeed justified, with her naive simplicity, a humanly unjustifiable type. But all this, for the ethical reasons expressed above, is actually an *aggravating circumstance*. (ibid.: 168)

As the omnivorous cinéphile that he was, at the end of the report (ibid.: 169) Freddi recognises in *La grande illusion* elements of plagiarism in the plot as a whole, but even, daringly, in some descriptive details.

The spirit of the cinéphile is also evident in Freddi's mention of *Scarface* (H. Hawks and R. Rosson 1932), a masterpiece that the Italian audiences could not see at the time, as he admits, because of his intervention. A "wild film", scripted with such "diabolical skill" that it takes viewers' breath away (for an in-depth analysis of *Scarface*'s dubbing, see Mereu 2016b).

I would like to emphasise how the very quality of Freddi's style of writing, full of literary images ("hanging from the white rag of pacifism", "a fleshy objectivism", and so on), his undoubted technical knowledge and the true passion for the films and authors he reviews, which surface at every line of his reports, make it extremely difficult to determine the presence of a clear-cut policy as regards the selection of works which would ultimately gain access to the Italian territory.

In his report of *La maison du Maltais* by Pierre Chenal (1938), on the other hand, Freddi interestingly notes how the perverse influence of this film, described with his usual literary graphicness, would be especially dangerous and poisonous for audiences of "second, third and fourth reruns", whose power of discernment is almost nonexistent (ibid.: 171). Freddi's concern for the different types of audiences which would crowd cinema theatres is omnipresent as not all audiences, he maintains, and certainly not those of suburban or provincial cinemas, could resist the "morbid effectiveness" of certain products (ibid.).

Besides these films, which he contributed, or better, prompted to ban from viewing, Freddi devotes six pages of report to a film that he, on the contrary, saved from banishment: *Modern Times* by Charlie Chaplin (1936). After pointing out how the arrival of the film in Italy had stirred hostility for reasons of pure commercial competition, Freddi states in his report that he has personally viewed the film also for the interest "this poet of the screen" deserves (ibid.: 172), dividing his analysis into esthetic and politico-moral considerations.

If there are absolutely cinematographic films which have nothing to do with theatre, these are Charlot[7]'s films. It is clear that the author doesn't let himself be carried away by technical progress, but uses new technical means as tools, within those limits and with that measure which are always necessary, to express his world. See, for example, the film's photography which never overpowers the narrative storyline with its figurative virtuosity, but remains discreetly, almost shabbily, in the background, giving spiritual emphasis to the setting, the characters and the action. Charlot's photography is never affected, and, if one can make a comparison, it is closer to Verga's rough and essential style than to the elegant images of, for example, someone like D'Annunzio[8].

The same with editing: scissors are much in use and one passes naturally from one scene to the other by cuts, without the feats of acrobatics of montage by analogy, so cherished by small and estheticising directors who overuse it. Only a few simple dissolves from time to time to punctuate a necessary passage of time. (ibid.: 172–173)

Freddi praises Chaplin also for his refusal to use dialogue in films, using sound to achieve his artistic means, without following the 'trend' of talkies. In his long report of convinced praise of Chaplin's film, Freddi lists the numerous reasons for granting it permission to be screened in Italy. He concludes that, as the main target of the story is the American world, there is nothing, really, one should censor (ibid.: 177). Finally, Freddi recalls how Mussolini saw the film and liked it very much, suggesting only to cut the scene in which Charlot, in prison, involuntarily feeds himself with cocaine.

Again, it is difficult not to be surprised at how closely and, I would add, lovingly, the reviewer looked at the object of his analysis and how his conclusion to recommend the film for distribution is, after all, counter-intuitive: Charlie Chaplin's leftist sympathies were well known.

In reviewing *Le Quai des brumes* by Marcel Carné (1938), Freddi explicitly mentions the necessity to devise a (preliminary) norm which could be valid for similar cases in the future (ibid.: 178). He describes the film with his customary, imaginative language:

---

[7] Chaplin's *Tramp* is known in Italy by its French nickname, Charlot, often identified, as in this case by Freddi, with the director himself.

[8] Both celebrated Italian literary authors, Giovanni Verga (1840–1922) was an Italian realist writer and Gabriele D'Annunzio (1863–1938) a writer, poet, playwright who had a strong influence on fascism.

The sea, too, is transformed in a sort of smoky swarm of dark silhouettes of ships wandering about, as sad as coffins.
Everything is sad; life is a curse: it weighs on men like the frozen and oppressive cape of a punishing demon. Satan and death are sitting on top of men's dreams; fields do not grow flowers but withered sticks; only black, slimy, insidious mud covers the paths men tread, doomed by a fatal curse; dreary rain lines with dirty tears the face of the sky; when the sun appears, Nelly sees him, pale and consumptive on the small bed where she left her virginity. Life is no longer the great stream with its rests and storms, but a dirty rivulet into which the sludge from the poors' houses drains, with floating peels, crusts and the filthiest waste, foregrounded with the fiercest self-indulgence.
That is what the film says, with a ruthlessness made even harsher by perfect acting and an exasperating realism. (ibid.: 179–180)

Here, Freddi writes, it is not a part, already defined and condemned, of society that is portrayed, but the whole of society, with a depiction made even more powerful by an undeniable artistic excellence (ibid.: 181). While in American gangster movies, he argues that the "practical and constructive Puritan conscience of the Anglo-Saxons is always present, in this film there is the subtle cynicism of Voltaire, of his Candide, by which everything is at the same level or can be indifferently the same: rose and mud, prostitution and virginity" (ibid.).

In spite of the hard condemnation and the recommendation for banning, "the film is, probably, at least in its kind, a masterpiece. But that is what worries more" (ibid.).

If we can detect a norm-governed behaviour in these and other instances quoted by Freddi, it can be summarised as this: the more a film is artistically valuable, the more dangerous it is for the spirit of a nation to be poisoned by its decadent morality, thus the more necessary it is to ban great works of art, if their contents are pernicious. However, the examples of *Modern Times*, cited above, and Freddi's advocacy of gangster movies, make it clear how, after all, the tastes and idiosyncrasies of the film critic (with a clear penchant for 'Anglo-Saxon' films), a cinéphile who was no less intellectual than the 'clique' he sarcastically criticised, render the work of analysis of these extratextual testimonies particularly tortuous although extremely fascinating.

Conclusions

Films to be distributed in today's Italy, of either foreign or local production, need to be submitted to a censorship commission at the Direzione Generale per il Cinema [General Directorate for Cinema] of the Ministero per i beni e le attività culturali (MIBAC) [Ministry for Cultural Heritage and Activities]. The legislation which rules its activities fundamentally dates back to 1962, the year in which law 161 on the revision of films and plays was approved. As in earlier times, the censorship commission is variously composed of a magistrate or law scholar, educators, psychologists, cinema professionals (distributors and producers), cultural experts in cinema, representatives of parents' associations, and if there are animals in the film, also representatives of animal rights' associations. Censorship is mainly concerned with the protection of minors and after its verdict distributors have twenty days to make an appeal or make the necessary cuts to the film. No film can be screened in the theatres without a 'certificate of revision', that is the formal approval of the cinematographic revision commission.

Italy is, luckily, not governed by a dictatorship any longer, if not the more lenient, but not less stifling, dictatorship of bureaucracy. A number of documents, checked by a series of Ministry's executives, need to be delivered together with a copy of the film to be submitted for revision. Before this is shown to the commission, which will judge its contents, others will painstakingly and fastidiously check if the title and end titles on screen match exactly those typewritten on the documents. If the two lists, the one on paper and the one on screen, do not match even by one word, if foreign words have slipped into the title credits of a film, if not all the title credits are translated into Italian, the film will not pass revision unless titles are changed, no matter how small and inconsequential the detail is. Linguistic xenophobia thus resists, at least in this preliminary phase of the censorship process, a legacy, undoubtedly, from the fascist and pre-fascist periods.

A careful study of Italian censorship reports, now lovingly collected by the Italia Taglia project (http://www.italiataglia.it/), is arguably not only precious for the information it provides on cuts, deletions and manipulations of films of all periods, but also to determine the norm-regulated behaviour which has influenced the process of selection of films to be distributed in the country.

References

BRUNETTA, Gian Piero (1975): *Cinema italiano tra le due guerre: fascismo e politica cinematografica*. – Milano: Mursia.

BRUNETTA, Gian Piero (1979): *Storia del cinema italiano 1895–1945*. – Roma: Editori Riuniti.

CANNISTRARO, Philip V. (1975): *La fabbrica del consenso. Fascismo e mass media*. – Bari: Laterza.

CARGILL, John (n.d.): "Tertullian De Spectaculis (Of Spectacles)". Transl. by T. R. Glover. www.the-faith.org.uk/tertullian1.html. (27.05.2016)

CATOFLI, Antonio (2015): "Censura e doppiaggio nelle forme narrative del cinema italiano, nel cruciale passaggio al sonoro degli anni Trenta". In: BIBBÓ, Antonio, ERCOLINO, Stefano & LINO, Mirko (eds.), *Censura e auto-censura*. Between, V(9), http://ojs.unica.it/index.php/between/article/view/1396 (27.05.2016)

FREDDI, Luigi (1929): "Dei dialetti", *Il popolo d'Italia*, 14 August.

FREDDI, Luigi (1949): *Il Cinema*. – Roma: L'Arnia.

GILI, Jean (1981): *Stato fascista e cinematografia: repressione e promozione*. – Roma: Bulzoni Editore.

GULÍ, Roberto (2008): "Cinema sonoro e fascismo". In: *Italia Taglia, progetto di ricerca sulla censura cinematografica in Italia*, www.italiataglia.it/cinema_sonoro_e_fascismo (27.05.2016)

ITALIA TAGLIA, Progetto di ricerca sulla censura cinematografica in Italia: http://www.italiataglia.it/, MiBACT, Cineteca di Bologna. (27.05.2016)

LAURA, Ernesto G. (1961): "Vicende legislative della censura in Italia". In: *La censura cinematografica*. – Roma: Edizione Bianco e Nero, 4–17.

MACK SMITH, Denis (1959): *Italy: A Modern History*. – Ann Arbor: University of Michigan Press.

MEREU KEATING, Carla (2013): "'100% Italian': The Coming of Sound Cinema in Italy and State Regulation on Dubbing", California Italian Studies, 4(1), http://escholarship.org/uc/item/7f86023v (27.05.2016)

MEREU, Carla (2016a): "Italians in film: Opposing and negotiating heteroconstructed images of Italiannes". In: VAN DOORSLAER, Luc, FLYNN, Peter & LEERSSEN, Joep (eds.): *Interconnecting Translation Studies and Imagology*. – Amsterdam: John Benjamins Publishing, 127–142.

MEREU KEATING, Carla (2016b): "'The Italian Color': Race, Crime Iconography and Dubbing Conventions in the Italian-language Versions of Scarface (1932)". In: DÍAZ CINTAS, Jorge, PARINI, Ilaria & RANZATO, Irene (eds.): *Ideological Manipulation in Audiovisual Translation, special issue of Altre Modernità*, http://riviste.unimi.it/index.php/AMonline/issue/view/888. (27.05.2016)

PIO XI (1929): Divini illius magistri. www.vatican.va/holy_father/pius_xi/encyclicals/documents/hf_p-xi_enc_31121929_divini-illius-magistri_it.html (27.05.2016)

RAFFAELLI, Sergio (1991): *La lingua filmata. Didascalie e dialoghi nel cinema italiano.* – Firenze: Le Lettere.

RAFFAELLI, Sergio (1996): "Un italiano per tutte le stagioni". In: DI FORTUNATO, Eleonora & PAOLINELLI, Mario (eds.): *Barriere linguistiche e circolazione delle opere audiovisiva: la questione del doppiaggio.* – Roma: Aidac, 25–28.

RANZATO, Irene (2016): *Translating Culture Specific References on Television: The Case of Dubbing.* – New York/London: Routledge.

RICCI, Steven (2008): *Cinema & Fascism, Italian Film and Society, 1922–1943.* – London: University of California Press.

SINISCALCHI, Claudio (1994): "Introduzione". In: FREDDI, Luigi: *Il cinema. Il governo dell'immagine.* – Roma: Centro Sperimentale di Cinematografia, Gremese.

TALBOT, George (2007): *Censorship in Fascist Italy, 1922–43.* – London: Palgrave Macmillan.

TOURY, Gideon (1995): *Descriptive Translation Studies and Beyond.* – Amsterdam/Philadelphia: John Benjamins Publishing.

Filmography

The Aristocats (*Gli aristogatti*), Wolfgang Reitherman, 1970, USA.
Der blaue Engel (*L'angelo azzurro*), Josef von Sternberg, 1930, Germany.
La contessa di Parma, Alessandro Blasetti, 1937, Italy.
The Godfather (*Il padrino*), Francis Ford Coppola, 1972, USA.
La grande illusion (*La grande illusione*), Jean Renoir, 1937, France.
Halleluja! (*Alleluja*), King Vidor, 1929, USA.
La maison du Maltais, Pierre Chenal, 1938, France.
Modern Times (*Tempi moderni*), Charlie Chaplin, 1936, USA.
Le Quai des brumes (*Il porto delle nebbie*), Marcel Carné, 1938, France.
Scarface (*Scarface-Lo sfregiato*), Howard Hawks and Richard Rosson, 1932, USA.
Sous les toits de Paris (*Sotto i tetti di Parigi*), René Clair, 1929, France.

The influence of policy on subtitling for the deaf and hard of hearing in Poland

Renata Mliczak
University College London
renata.mliczak.13@ucl.ac.uk

This article explores the influence of policy at different levels on the development of subtitling for the deaf and hard of hearing (SDH) in Poland in terms of both quantity and quality. The initial parts of the article concentrate on the beginnings of SDH in the USA and the UK as the first countries that introduced accessible services on television. Government policies, which have an effect on the amount of subtitling on television and broadcasters' internal policies aiming at maximising the quality of SDH, are presented and discussed. Policies issued by monitoring bodies, ensuring that broadcasters abide by the law in terms of provision of SDH on television, are also examined. Next, the situation in Poland is presented as far as governmental policies and broadcasters' internal policies are concerned. It is followed by a diachronic analysis of Polish SDH in an attempt to ascertain how practice informed policies. Particular attention is paid to editing and the presentation of subtitles on television. The impact of research into accessibility in Poland is also briefly discussed as it has the potential of playing a significant role in enhancing legislation related to SDH in the future.

Introduction

In a world of fast developing audiovisual media, subtitling for the deaf and hard of hearing (SDH) is often the main (if not only) tool for people with hearing loss to access information and entertainment. The rights of the hearing impaired have been widely reflected in international policies such as the UN Convention on the Rights of Persons with Disabilities (UNCRPD) and the EU's Audiovisual Media

Services Directive, which calls for equal access to audiovisual content for all citizens of the European Union, including the deaf and hard of hearing.

Pioneered in the USA in the 1940s, SDH found its way to Europe in the 1970s, with the UK setting the pace at the forefront. SDH can now be accessed on many television channels across Europe and beyond, and its use continues to grow. Rising awareness of access services accompanied by the legislative actions of the EU and individual member states have encouraged some sectors of the audience to demand more subtitles by lobbying broadcasters and distributors.

The present article addresses the impact that different policies have had on the provision of SDH. "Policy" is here understood as "a principle or course of action adopted or proposed as desirable, advantageous, or expedient; esp. one formally advocated by a government, political party, etc." (Oxford English Dictionary) and is discussed focusing on two areas: on the one hand, policies put forward by governments and other regulatory bodies, which usually deal with the quantity of subtitling by setting statutory quotas for broadcasters and, on the other hand, policies developed in-house by individual television channels, or other groups, concerned with the standards according to which SDH is, or should be, prepared. Both types of policies are essential to promote the provision of SDH.[1]

The first part of the paper concentrates on the history of SDH in the USA and the UK. Policies influencing the use of SDH in those countries are presented and discussed as they have inspired the changes related to accessibility in Poland. The most influential government policies are highlighted and some of the policies centred on subtitling standards are investigated. Next, the Polish situation is analysed from a diachronic perspective. The main focus of this article lies on the evolution of SDH on the Polish public service television network *Telewizja Polska* (TVP), the broadcaster with the longest history of producing SDH in the country and the highest volume of subtitling on the national television market. TVP subtitlers were also the first ones to develop SDH standards based

---

[1] There are different types of policies (treaties, conventions, directives, etc., but also guidelines or standards), which incur different responsibilities on the target groups, varying from voluntary to obligatory observance. In this article, the main focus is on the results that certain policies have had on the provision of SDH.

on years of experience, communication with the target audience and advice from professionals involved in education of the deaf and hard of hearing. The evolution of SDH on Polish television is illustrated with examples and, where appropriate, comparisons are made with US and English subtitling policies. The article concludes with an overview of the most salient research conducted to date into subtitling for hearing impaired audiences in Poland and comments on the influence of researchers, subtitlers and regulatory bodies on the provision of SDH in the country.

SDH policies in the USA

The advent of synchronised dialogue in films, commercially marked by the release of Alan Crosland's feature film *The Jazz Singer* in October 1927, was a great technological step forward in the history of cinematography. Even though there were barely two minutes of spoken dialogue in the film and the rest continued in the form of intertitle cards, *The Jazz Singer* became a huge commercial success and marked the end of the silent movie era (History of Information n/d). Paradoxically, it meant a step backwards in terms of access services for the deaf and hard of hearing as it turned out that they could no longer enjoy the cinema since the new form of dialogue was not supported by the intertitles or any other graphic form of assistance. Technology, or rather the lack of it, made it impossible for the hearing impaired to follow sound-based films. It was then that Emerson Romero, a deaf actor himself, came across the idea of making films accessible again to deaf viewers. In 1947 he managed to insert the text in between the frames, following the same method used in the silent film era (DCMP 2010). It meant, however, that the flow of the film was continually disrupted. Another method, invented by a Belgian company, followed. It consisted of printing captions onto a master copy of a film, corresponding to what is known today as "open subtitles / captions".[2] The invention of this method allowed the newly created company Captioned Films for the Deaf (CFD) to grow their business.

---

[2] Subtitles / captions that are an integral part of the images and cannot be switched on or off.

The funds were provided by The Captioned Film Act, which was passed in 1959 (Robson 2004).

As new forms of media appeared on the market, CFD was renamed Captioned Media Program (CMP) and has continued its work ever since. It provides hearing impaired people with free loans of captioned films and specialises in captioning educational and special interests materials, relying on consumer suggestions. Part of their remit is also to help new captioning agencies by sharing best practice on the creation of captions. CMP captioning guidelines, known as Captioning Key for Educational Media, can be accessed online (Web 1). It is a most valuable policy focused on the production of educational captions. It extends the range of AV materials accessible to deaf and hard of hearing audiences beyond feature films introducing them into schools and other educational settings.

In 1971 all the major parties involved in captioning (producers, federal agencies, consumers, teachers and other professionals) met at the first National Conference on Television and discussed the future of captioning. The major achievement of the conference was the decision to develop a system of closed captioning initiated by the National Bureau of Standards (NBS). It meant assigning a portion of the video system unused in regular transmissions (Vertical Blanking Interval) to captions (Norwood 1988). The following year the National Association of Broadcasters worked out a roadmap for introducing closed captioning on television. The association discussed the need for developing decoders as well as costs involved in captioning television programmes. That led to the establishment of an independent organisation that would deliver captioning services to broadcasters at a low cost (DCMP 2010). That is how in 1979 the National Captioning Institute (NCI) was formed. The first year of NCI was extremely successful in terms of the volume of captioning. In March 1980, NCI captioned up to 20 hours of entertainment programmes per week, mostly for prime time viewing (Cronin 1980). The majority of the captioners at NCI were the former employees of the Caption Centre at WGBH (Western Great Blue Hill) television station – the first television captioning agency, created in 1972 (NCI n/d), producing open captions for television throughout the 1970s. The National Conference on Television itself, as well as all the steps that followed, are a good example of a roadmap for securing the development of captioning.

Awareness of the need for access to audiovisual information by people with sensory impairments was rising in the country and numerous acts were passed to ensure that the number of captioning hours on television would steadily increase. The most influential acts include The Television Decoder Circuitry Act of 1990, which required that 13 inch or larger screens had to have an in-built decoder able to display captions, and The Telecommunications Act of 1996, which was the first one to stipulate a mandatory volume of closed captioning on television (Robson 2004). A year later, the Federal Communications Commission (FCC: online) set a schedule for distributors to increase the amount of captioning. In 2014, a symptomatic shift in the policies of the FCC, away from focusing on captioning quotas on television to promote the enhancement of quality, can be observed. The new rules focus on accuracy, synchronicity, programme completeness and placement of captions (*ibid.*).

A very similar shift in policy can be observed in the evolution of SDH standards since the early years of its provision on television. At first, the primary interest of captioners was centred on the amount of captioning they needed to do. Due to the high volume of work required they did not seem to find the time to conduct research on the quality of subtitles and the needs of the target audience. In the first years of their operations, WGBH captioners simplified the text substantially as they believed that deaf people's reading skills were significantly lower than those of hearing audiences. As Jeff Hutchins, one of the first captioners at WGBH, commented years later: "we rewrote the news stories almost completely. […] We removed all passive voice sentence construction. We removed nearly all idioms and eliminated contractions. We converted clauses into short, simple, declarative sentences" (quoted in Jensema, Burch 1999:5). When NCI was established a few years later, in 1979, most of the WGBH captioners were employed there. Naturally, they continued applying the same captioning techniques, i.e. heavy editing of the captions in order to make them easier to understand by the majority of hearing impaired viewers. Whenever captioners were faced with a caption editing problem, "they would just talk about it among themselves, reach an agreement, and their decision would become caption policy" (*ibid.*). It was only in the following decade that research results on reading speed, preferences of hearing impaired audiences and linguistic skills started to be used in an attempt to guide captioners, resulting in more verbatim captions (*ibid.*).

This short historical overview shows that the beginnings of captioning in the USA were primarily about overcoming technological challenges and increasing the amount of captioned materials. Another conclusion, however obvious it may seem, can be drawn from the first steps towards captioning, namely, the active role of some influential lobbying government institutions, who, on behalf of the deaf and hard of hearing, fought to secure their right to access information and entertainment. In this sense, the willingness to cooperate between the government and the networks was essential in fostering a stable development of captioning services. It goes without saying that had it not been for the funding and relevant policies issued by the government, and the expertise of engineers working for networks and manufacturers, the ideas of Emerson Romero would not have found ground for growth.

SDH policies in the UK

Two years after Romero's attempts to reuse the silent movie intertitle technique, Arthur Rank showed a captioned film at a cinema in London. He etched the captions on the glass slides that were placed in the projector (DCMP 2010). They were shown on a smaller screen next to the one onto which the film was being projected. A technician operating the projector needed to synchronise the appearance of the slides with the film dialogue. It was a rather tiresome process and turned out to be a one off event (*ibid.*). It was not until 1979 that the BBC first screened a documentary about deaf children, *Quietly in Switzerland*, with subtitles[3] delivered via Ceefax teletext (BBC 2008). The technology issue having been relatively well resolved, in a similar manner to what had been adopted in the USA, the British government now needed to play a proactive role in securing the increase of subtitled content on television. Starting with the 1990 Broadcasting Act, followed by the 1996 Broadcasting Act and the Communica-

---

[3] The term "subtitles", and more specifically "subtitles for the deaf and hard of hearing" (SDH), is used in the UK and the rest of Europe and corresponds to "captions", which is more often used in the USA, Canada and Australia.

tions Act in 2003 (Ofcom n/d), television channels were obliged to gradually increase the volume of subtitled programming. Until December 2003 the Independent Television Commission (ITC) was the body responsible for providing TV channels with guidance on the technical standards for subtitling. In 1999 ITC released a detailed document to serve as a guideline for broadcasters regarding the preparation of closed subtitles.[4] In 2003 the Office of Communications (Ofcom n/d) became the new communications sector regulator and since then its remit has been to ensure that different subtitling targets are being met by the various channels. It is worth mentioning here that the UK is an exception on the European broadcasting landscape in the sense that the BBC already committed itself in 1999 to subtitling 100% of their programmes[5] by 2008, and succeeded in their endeavour (BBC 2008). What is more, as Remael (2007: 25) observes: "In almost all [Western European] countries, public television is far ahead of commercial channels, with the exception of the UK, where public and commercial channels alike provide SDH". Whilst the first policies concentrated on the amount of SDH provided, Ofcom's policies today, still ensuring that the volume of subtitled programming increases on all channels, focus on the quality of subtitles. As most complaints on the part of the viewers are related to live subtitles, Ofcom has recently decided to explore this area in greater detail. Thus, in April 2014 Ofcom published its first report on the quality of live subtitling on television (Ofcom 2014).

As regards SDH standards, the first guidelines for television subtitling were released in 1981 and later updated in the form of a handbook written in 1984 by Baker, Lambourne, and Rowston. The guidelines put forward by Ofcom draw

---

[4] ITC (1999: online) acknowledged their sources in the following terms: "Much of the detail has been taken from an earlier handbook produced by the Independent Broadcasting Authority following research conducted at Southampton University. [...] Further information on the use of subtitles has also been included as a result of a research project conducted on behalf of the ITC and BBC during 1990 and 1991 by Bristol University and the ITC research into Subtitling for Deaf Children 1996".

[5] On the following channels: BBC One, BBC Two, BBC Three, BBC Four, CBeebies, CBBC and BBC News. BBC One, BBC Two, BBC Three, BBC Four, CBeebies, CBBC and BBC News.

heavily from this original handbook. Today some broadcasters prefer to have their own in-house guidelines, such as in the case of the BBC or Channel 4.

The information presented so far justifies why the UK is rightly considered by many as the leader in Europe regarding the provision of subtitling for the deaf and hard of hearing. Without doubt, most European countries have led their own battles to overcome technological challenges and to fully understand the needs and expectations of hearing impaired viewers; however, the UK stands out as a reference for other countries having laid the foundations for television subtitling and compiling standards based on research and many years of professional practice.

SDH policies in Poland

SDH policies in Poland are discussed here from two perspectives: the first subchapter focuses on national policies regulating the quantity of SDH in the country; the second one analyses policies dealing with the quality of Polish SDH. Polish public service television is presented as the broadcaster with the longest history of SDH production and the best example of the evolution of SDH policies on quality.

National SDH related policies

Even though the Polish constitution (Article 32 of the Act of 2 April 1997) refers to the equal treatment of all citizens by public institutions, which would include access to programmes broadcast by public service television for people with hearing loss, it does not name this specific group of people and therefore, to date, has not had any visible impact on the provision of accessible audiovisual media to deaf and hard of hearing Poles.

In terms of increasing the 'visibility' of citizens with hearing impairments, two international documents have played a significant role. The first one was the Convention on the Rights of Persons with Disabilities (CRPD), signed by Poland in 2007 and ratified in 2012. The convention is the first international treaty that refers to the cultural and linguistic identity of deaf people and mentions their right to education in their natural language. It also specifically refers to the access of the hearing impaired to audiovisual media:

> States Parties recognize the right of persons with disabilities to take part on an equal basis with others in cultural life, and shall take all appropriate measures to ensure that persons with disabilities:
> a. Enjoy access to cultural materials in accessible formats;
> b. Enjoy access to television programmes, films, theatre and other cultural activities, in accessible formats;
> c. Enjoy access to places for cultural performances or services, such as theatres, museums, cinemas, libraries and tourism services, and, as far as possible, enjoy access to monuments and sites of national cultural importance (CRPD n/d).

In the five years between the signing and the ratification of the convention, the Polish government was busy introducing the necessary changes to Polish law that would allow the country to be fully prepared to comply with the numerous responsibilities specified in the document in relation to the rights of people with disabilities. One such change came with the signing of the Act on Sign Language and Other Systems of Communication on 19 August 2011, which gives the target groups the right to receive information in a way that is understandable to them. The Amendment to the National Broadcasting Council Act of 25 March 2011, which was passed following the recommendations of the Audiovisual Media Services Directive (AVMSD 2010/13/EU), is the first piece of legislation regulating the provision of accessibility services on television. It stipulates that television broadcasters are obliged to provide at least 10 per cent of their broadcasting time with accessible services including audio description (AD), sign language interpreting (SLI) and SDH. Nonetheless, however significant the act may be for the provision of accessible services, it is only the beginning of a journey to equal access to AV media for hearing impaired citizens.

As the Act mentions only one percentage of accessible services, there are no clear figures as to how much providers are required to deliver for each of these services. The National Broadcasting Council is a constitutional body responsible for the defense of the freedom of expression, the right to information and the safeguarding of the public interest on radio and television (NBC n/d). It works on securing satisfactory solutions for viewers and proposing achievable targets for the broadcasters. It may also impose fines on the broadcasters failing to abide by the requirements of the law. However, one of the criticisms of the system of fines is that for some broadcasters it may be cheaper to pay the fine than prepare accessible services.

Since the implementation of the Amendment of 25 March 2011, the National Broadcasting Council has taken some steps to improve the situation on SDH in Poland. The first important action was the agreement of broadcasters from June 2013, which clarified the terminology related to subtitling, audio description and sign language interpreting and stressed the importance of highlighting programmes which can be watched with accessible services (National Broadcasting Council 2013). The part of the agreement clarifying the terminology was a result of a survey conducted by the National Broadcasting Council three months after the implementation of the Amendment to the National Broadcasting Council Act of 25 March 2011 when it was revealed that many broadcasters did not realise what accessibility involved. Some of the stations in their reports included scrolling texts at the bottom of the screen as a service helping the hearing impaired access information on a par with subtitling.[6]

In the regulatory strategy document for the years 2014–2016 (National Broadcasting Council 2014), the National Broadcasting Council states that it will postulate legal changes to the Act of 2011 to secure an increase in the amount of accessible services on Polish television with a view to reaching 50% by 2020. As representatives of the Council explained at the conference on accessibility of television in September 2014, the organisation is not entitled to take any legal action; it may only make recommendations to broadcasters and proposals to the Ministry of Culture and National Heritage. It shows that the Polish legal system regulating audiovisual services needs amending in order to empower the regulatory body. Again, Ofcom might serve here as a point of reference in terms of the direction Poland should take in its efforts to improve audiovisual accessibility.

Apart from recommendations on the amount of accessible services on television, the National Broadcasting Council can also propose standards of accessible services, including guidelines of SDH preparation. However, even though guide-

---

[6] Information revealed during the presentation of National Broadcasting Council at the conference on "The role of television in breaking down the barriers" on 26 March 2012.

lines already exist for Polish SDH, written by the first subtitlers in TVP (Künstler, Butkiewicz 2012) on the basis of their extensive experience, the Council has not yet approved them as a national set of standards.

The following subchapter describes the work of the pioneering subtitlers, from the beginning until the present day, and discusses the various policies they have followed and amended over the years.

SDH policies of Polish public service television

When it comes to securing the right to access information on television, which must of course include the deaf and hard of hearing, Polish public service television *Telewizja Polska* (TVP) sets the example. In 1994, TVP introduced SDH in Poland and was the first network ever to do so in the country, 17 years before it actually became mandatory for broadcasters to provide accessible services.

Rio Grande (John Ford, 1950) was the first film, aired 1 January 1994, ever to be broadcast with closed SDH, via teletext, on Polish television. In the early years, subtitlers worked only on feature films, but other genres followed soon suit and in 2008 programmes with SDH included all series and feature films, shown immediately after the main daily news, as well as selected documentaries and shows (Künstler 2008). In 1993, TVP started providing semi-live[7] subtitles for the main news programme on a daily basis. At the time of writing this article there were no speech recognition programmes that could be used for real-time television subtitling with respeaking in Polish.

Formerly, the knowledge of subtitlers regarding the purpose of their work was quite limited. As Künstler (2008: 117, my translation), a member of the editorial staff of subtitlers at TVP at that time, states: "There was no research into the reception of subtitles in Poland" and most subtitlers assumed that the expectations of Polish TV viewers were no different to those from other countries. They also relied on European research revealing that 1 in 7 Europeans had hearing problems and was, as such, a potential consumer of subtitles. They knew they were delivering a service that could be beneficial to other groups of viewers

---

[7] In these cases, the script is prepared shortly before the actual broadcast takes place and a subtitler cues the subtitles during the news.

such as people learning Polish, children learning to read and anyone who, for different reasons, watched television in a noisy environment.

Staff at the SDH editorial centre started preparing subtitles on the basis of their own common sense and the feedback obtained from cooperation with scholars of deaf studies. Throughout the years, general subtitling rules were reviewed in order to better cater for the needs of the viewers. However, as no relevant research had been conducted in the country, subtitlers themselves tried to determine the likes and dislikes of their audience by analysing the opinions of viewers as reflected in letters sent directly to the TV channels or in messages posted on the blog of the SDH editorial centre. As the opinions voiced were very subjective and differed substantially among viewers, depending on their level or the onset time of their hearing loss, preparing SDH files proved to be a very demanding task.

The first detailed insight into Polish SDH production was published by Künstler in 2008 in *Przekładaniec*, a Polish journal for translation and intercultural communication. The result of 14 years of professional SDH experience at TVP, the article compiles a detailed list of all the technical as well as linguistic challenges surrounding the production of SDH. For the first time, the general public, researchers, trainee subtitlers and the hearing impaired themselves had the opportunity to read about the problems faced by TVP subtitlers.

Research into accessibility started becoming more popular towards the mid-1990s. Awareness of the rights and needs of sensory impaired people was increasing and, the passing of the Amendment to the National Broadcasting Council Act in 2011 triggered a surge in SDH activity. A new set of guidelines for SDH was commissioned by the foundation *Fundacja Kultury Bez Barier* (Culture Without Barriers) and subsequently drafted by Künstler and Butkiewicz in 2012. Although not an official guide in the sense of the standards recommended by British Ofcom, it is certainly the most current guide on SDH in Poland, and can be easily accessed online (Web 2). The fact that there are no official guidelines in the country may be a reason for some of the inconsistencies found among both public and private broadcasting stations.

Case Study

This chapter discusses some of the major differences found between subtitles for the deaf and hard of hearing produced in the early years of SDH on TVP and those created in more recent years. Two periods of SDH production have been identified, namely, the early period (1994–1996) and the more contemporary one (2010–2012). The main hypothesis driving this analysis is that each of these two periods is characterised by a different SDH policy, which can be observed at various levels. To gauge the potential differences, this study focuses on the visual presentation of subtitles as well as on their linguistic makeup and the text editing decisions taken by subtitlers.

The material comes from the subtitling files on 10 feature films, five from each period, including three Polish productions and two foreign ones from each group:

Films subtitled in 1994–1996	Films subtitled in 2010–2012
1. *Jańcio Wodnik* [Johnie the Waterman] (Jan Jakub Kolski, 1993)	1. *Sto Minut Wakacji* [One Hundred Minutes of Holidays] (Andrzej Maleszka, 1998)
2. *Wierna Rzeka* [The Faithful River] (Tadeusz Chmielewski, 1983)	2. *Hi Way* (Jacek Borusiński, 2006)
3. *Szaleństwa Panny Ewy* [Follies of Miss Eva] (Kazimierz Tamas, 1984)	3. *Miłość Nad Rozlewiskiem* [Love at the Lake] (Adek Drabiński, 2010)
	4. *Material Girls* (Martha Coolidge, 2006)
4. *Tobruk* (Arthur Hiller, 1967)	5. *The Good Shepherd* (Lewin Webb, 2004)
5. *Wildflower* (Diane Keaton, 1991)	

Figure 1: Case study films

The files, courtesy of TVP, have been studied with the help of WinCAPS, a piece of professional subtitling software developed by Screen Systems. This has made a detailed analysis of the main technical features of subtitles possible, such as reading speeds and line lengths, and has also facilitated watching the subtitles with the video content.

The analysis is divided into four parts: (1) degree of editing of subtitles, (2) subtitle layout, (3) display times/reading speed, and (4) typical features of SDH such as use of colours, sound effect labels and the like.

Editing

The comparison between the degree of editing of subtitles from the early years and those of the more contemporary period reveals significant differences. Initially, subtitlers tried to facilitate the reading of subtitles for viewers not proficient in the Polish language by simplifying the written text on screen. To make the subtitled programmes available to people with hearing loss, the use of simplified vocabulary and syntax was common practice, as foregrounded by Künstler (2008: 122, my translation), who states that in the early years lexical changes "consisted of swapping ambiguous expressions and metaphors which did not have equivalents in Polish Sign Language, for straightforward words". The early practice of Polish SDH is reminiscent of the policy adopted by the captioners in the USA during the first years of television captioning, who applied similar editing strategies, simplifying the text by resorting to reformulation and paraphrase rather than by straightforward deletion (Jensema, Burch 1999).

Some extreme editing was performed on the film *Pan Wołodyjowski* [Sir Wołodyjowski], an adaptation of the homonymous historical novel written in the 19th century, in which there is heavy use of archaisms. Feedback from target viewers was very positive claiming that the archaic language typical of Sienkiewicz's writing, however beautiful it may be for Polish people without impaired hearing, is very abstract and difficult to follow for the deaf and hard of hearing (Lamprycht 1995). A detailed analysis of the subtitling files from the early years shows that the editorial staff of TVP used paraphrasing strategies only in instances in which archaic words or vocabulary less typical of everyday language was being used. In all other cases, the omission of whole words or fragments of dialogue was preferred.

Undoubtedly, the task of adapting subtitles in order to make non-standard language understandable for hearing impaired viewers is a more onerous task than the creation of a near-verbatim version. The attitude of the TVP team of subtitlers clearly shows that they gave priority to what they thought to be the needs of their audience, irrespective of the time and cost implications. Fluent communication with the viewers during the years has enabled subtitlers to familiarise themselves with the expectations of their audience and has led to some adjustments to their service. This is why today, based on the input provided by the deaf and hard of hearing conveyed through individual comments as well as empirical research (Künstler 2008, Szarkowska, Laskowska 2014), there is a clear trend towards near-verbatim SDH, requiring minimal editing, as literal verbatim is problematic due to spatial and time constraints. As opposed to paraphrasing techniques, red pencil editing is preferred in the form of omission of words and phrases that are not indispensable for understanding the message. One of the main reasons why the hearing impaired prefer near-verbatim subtitling is that they do not want others to decide for them what information they may find useful. As Neves (2005: 142) claims: "The demand for verbatim transcriptions has become a banner for Deaf associations and movements, who consider any kind of editing as a form of censorship". Moreover, a substantial number of the target audience uses lip reading as a means to decipher the meaning of dialogues. If subtitles faithfully reflect what the characters say, it is easier for the viewers to combine lip reading and subtitle reading skills.

When analysing editing strategies, interesting differences can be observed between Polish SDH and Polish interlingual subtitling of foreign productions. In the latter case, editing seems to be less controversial as viewers cannot rely on reading lip movements or on identifying fragments of dialogue (Szarkowska 2013). However, the matter is not a straightforward one. Most foreign productions on Polish television are voiced-over and subtitles for the deaf and hard of hearing are prepared on the basis of voiced-over scripts rather than on a direct translation of the original dialogue. In voiceover it is standard for the voice talent to start reading the translation a few seconds after the character on screen has started speaking and to finish shortly before the character on screen finishes. When subtitling a voiced-over production, the timing of subtitles can either follow the speech of the Polish *lektor* (voice talent) or the dialogue of the characters. Subtitling professionals tend to prefer synchronising subtitles with the voices of the characters in an attempt to avoid situations where a character is seen/heard talking on screen and there is no subtitle to represent that as the timing follows the Polish voiced-over sound.

Layout

Editing challenges are also closely related to subtitle layout. As a rule, subtitles in Poland have always been placed at the bottom of the screen except when textual inserts are already part of the original programme, in which case subtitles are then raised. Since the very beginning, TVP has used speaker-dependent placement, which means that subtitles are positioned as close to the character speaking as possible. Today, however, some subtitlers prefer to position all subtitles in the centre to save time. This practice contributes to the lack of consistency in SDH presentation.

In addition to placement to identify speakers on screen, TVP also assigns colours to characters for the duration of a film: yellow, green, cyan and white. When necessary, labels are also used to identify characters. Only two characters can speak in one subtitle and the text lines are separated by an empty line to indicate that it is a dialogue exchange (Figure 2). In TVP, no dashes are used to represent a dialogue subtitle:

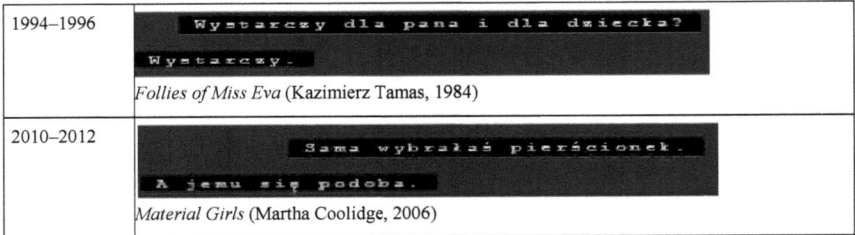

Figure 2: Dialogue within a subtitle

In the early years, it was not uncommon for subtitles to take up four or even five lines. Today however, subtitles fill a maximum of two lines, and only in live news programmes, such as *Wiadomości [The News]*, can, sporadically, three lines be occupied:

1994–1996	Cześć, Sammy. Lisa Mae mówiła, że Calvin Martin polował w nocy na oposy. U Guthriech słyszał to wycie. (10:04:54:04 06:00 10:05:00:04 14cps)
	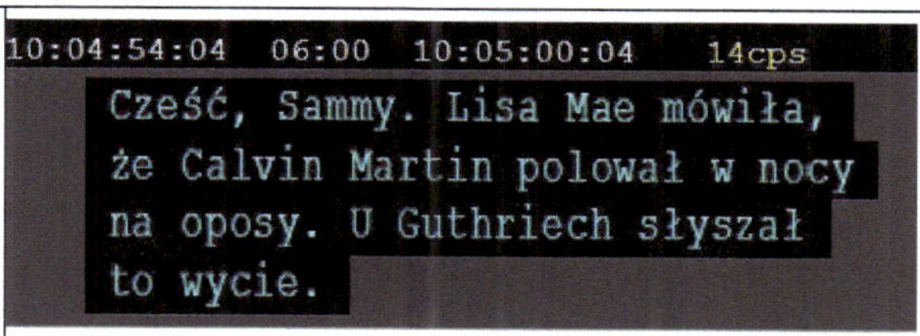 *Wildflower*, (Diane Keaton, 1991) 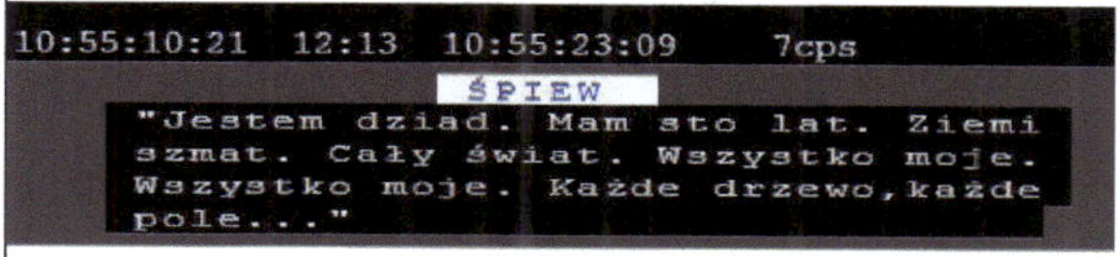
	ŚPIEW "Jestem dziad. Mam sto lat. Ziemi szmat. Cały świat. Wszystko moje. Wszystko moje. Każde drzewo, każde pole..." (10:55:10:21 12:13 10:55:23:09 7cps)
	Johnie the Waterman (Jan Jakub Kolski, 1993)
2010–2012	Dokąd lecisz? Na wakacje do Wenecji. (10:03:35:15 02:23 10:03:38:13 10cps)
	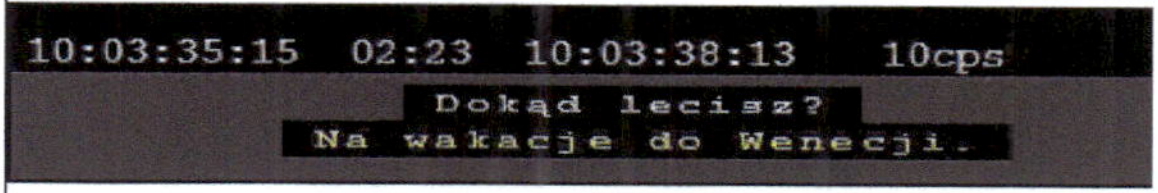 *One Hundred Minutes of Holidays* (Andrzej Maleszka, 1998) 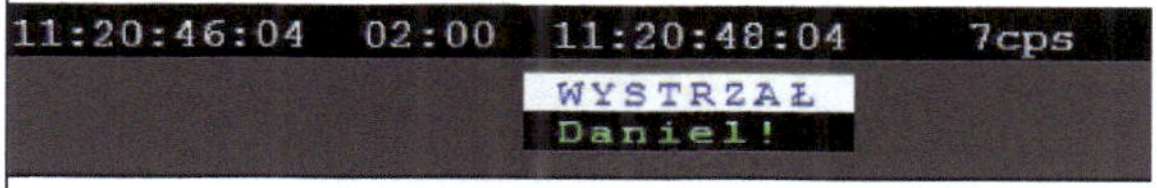
	WYSTRZAŁ Daniel! (11:20:46:04 02:00 11:20:48:04 7cps)
	The Good Shepherd (Lewin Webb, 2004)

Figure 3: Number of lines

Timing

A close technical analysis reveals significant differences when it comes to temporal features such as the duration of subtitles and reading speed. In this respect, subtitles from the early years were often left on screen for over 10 seconds, and sometimes even exceeding 15 seconds, as shown in Figure 4 where the subtitles remain on screen for 15 seconds and 5 frames:

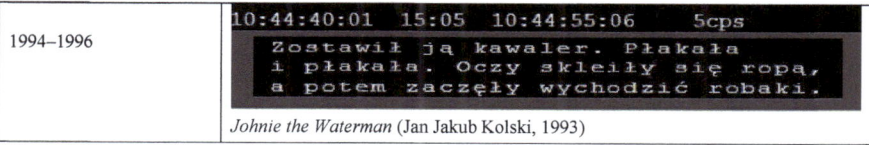

Figure 4: Longer lasting subtitles and lower reading speed

The fact that TVP subtitlers allowed for such a long duration of subtitles seems to be in line with their conception of the target audience using subtitles. Thus, if the target audience was assumed to need simplified text, it was also thought appropriate to reduce the reading speed so that they would have more time to read the text. In general, the reading speed of subtitles used to be much lower than the values found in contemporary subtitles, which in turn means that subtitles had to be heavily edited down.

From the analysis of the early files a very interesting finding comes to light, namely, that the reading speed of subtitles used in national productions (Polish films with Polish SDH) used to be much lower than in foreign films (foreign films with Polish SDH).

Even though the maximum reading speed was set at 12 characters per second (cps) (Künstler 2008), numerous subtitles in foreign films exceeded it, some reaching over 20 cps, as illustrated in Figure 5:

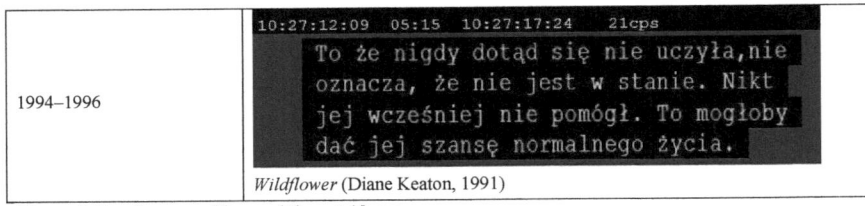

Figure 5: Reading speed beyond the set 12 cps.

It is worth noting that in Poland the maximum reading speed for television subtitling has been set at 12 cps ever since the advent of SDH and has not changed over the years. By contrast, SDH started in the UK with the recommendation of keeping the speed at a maximum of 120 words per minute (wpm)[8] (Baker, Lambourne, Rowston 1984). Subsequent updates of guidelines have substantially increased the speed to 140 wpm in pre-recorded programmes, and even as high as 180 wpm in exceptional circumstances (ITC 1999; BBC 2009).

---

[8] Equivalent of 10 cps (as measured in WinCAPS subtitling software).

Specific features

SDH specific features, such as character identification, description of sounds, music, tone and mood, seem to be included nowadays in a more consistent manner, adhering closely to the guidelines produced by SDH experts (Künstler, Butkiewicz 2012). More descriptions of sounds are included in recent subtitles in an attempt to allow the target audience to 'feel' the atmosphere of the film. It is also less common to find subtitles describing the visuals or actions, e.g. "air raid" [*nalot*] in Tobruk (Arthur Hiller, 1967) or "Ellie reads a letter from Sammy" [Ellie czyta list od Sammy'ego] in Wildflower (Diane Keaton, 1991), rather than the sounds themselves. The development of subtitling to date has been towards the production of less orthotypographically cluttered subtitles and dialogue exchanges uttered in anger, for instance, formerly written in either capital letters or within a few exclamation marks (sometimes both strategies were combined), whereas today it is more common to use one exclamation mark to close the sentence, as it is done in the case of standard subtitles for hearing audiences.

The results presented so far show how subtitlers modified their practice as they gained experience over the years. Empirical evidence shows that they also regularly amended the techniques they applied on the basis of the feedback they received from the target audience and other interested parties. Changes in practice have materialised through new policies on Polish television subtitling that, over the years, have evolved from a rather interpretative stance towards original dialogue exchanges to a near-verbatim rendition of the speech, from "slower" to much "faster" subtitles that very rarely stay on screen for more than 6 seconds; and from a less prescriptive implementation of specific SDH features to a more systematic and conscientious approach. Nonetheless, as already mentioned, some inconsistencies still remain in SDH production and, arguably, they can only be dealt with if a regulatory body, such as the National Broadcasting Council, takes a firm stance and obliges broadcasters to adhere to a set of pre-defined guidelines that foster high levels of quality. Until then, the risk remains that some television networks both public and private, will restrict their accessibility services to merely meet regulatory obligations concerning the volume of subtitling they are required to produce, as specified by the Act of 25 March 2011, and thus circumvent any other responsibilities.

Conclusion

Subtitling for the deaf and hard of hearing in the USA and the UK was initiated by the target viewers themselves as well as those aware of their needs (in the case of Poland it was the public service television network), but the catalyst that has really boosted the provision of SDH in most countries has been legislation. Broadcasters, as some of the most important stakeholders in the provision of SDH, exert their power to determine which programmes are subtitled and the professionals engaged to carry out the tasks, be they subtitling agencies or self-employed subtitlers. For SDH to develop in an organic way and for high standards to be maintained, regulatory bodies need to supervise its delivery. A major role in enhancing the social and scientific standing of the service is also played by researchers and recipients themselves who can provide qualitative feedback on the service they get as well as take action to promote the development of better subtitles. All human agents involved in creating SDH can, potentially, contribute to the design and implementation of new policies which can ensure both the quantity and the quality of SDH provision.

In recent years, many important developments have taken place in Poland as regards SDH. The first steps to securing the obligatory provision of SDH by all broadcasters have been taken. There are generally available standards of SDH created by the subtitlers from TVP. However, these are yet to be endorsed by the National Broadcasting Council.

Research, undoubtedly helping to raise awareness of the needs of the deaf and hard of hearing regarding audiovisual media access for a wider audience, including broadcasters, has advanced considerably. The first noteworthy study on SDH in Poland was part of the European Union project entitled Digital Television for All (DTV4ALL), conducted in 2010 by the University of Warsaw in collaboration with the Interdisciplinary Center for Applied Cognitive Studies (ICACS) at the Warsaw School of Social Sciences and Humanities (SWPS). The aim of the project was to establish standards for SDH on the basis of eye-tracking tests and questionnaires on viewer preferences related to accessibility (Szarkowska et al. forthcoming). Other important studies include SDH in multilingual films; SDH on digital TV; and more recently, viewer preferences regarding television subtitling. All the research results are available on the website of Audiovisual Translation Lab (AVT Lab: http://avt.ils.uw.edu.pl/en/sdh/) and aim to improve current practices.

It is felt that a more active role should be adopted by the National Broadcasting Council in terms of creating a roadmap for SDH policy. However, the actions of the Council need to be supported by a more stable policy on SDH provision at a national level in order to bring satisfying results for the deaf and hard of hearing, similar to the policies followed by the USA and the UK, prime examples of continuous improvement to subtitling for people with hearing impairments.

References

ACT ON SIGN LANGUAGE AND OTHER SYSTEMS OF COMMUNICATION OF 19 AUGUST 2011.
http://dziennikustaw.gov.pl/du/2011/s/209/1243 (10.08.2014)

AMENDMENT TO NATIONAL BROADCASTING COUNCIL ACT OF 25 MARCH 2011.
http://orka.sejm.gov.pl/opinie6.nsf/nazwa/3812_u/$file/3812_u.pdf (10.08.2014)

AVMSD (2010): http://eur-lex.europa.eu/legal-content/EN/TXT/PDF/?uri=CELEX: 32010L0013&from=EN

AVT LAB http://avt.ils.uw.edu.pl/en/sdh/ (10.08.2014)

BAKER, Robert, LAMBOURNE, Andrew & ROWSTON, Guy (1984): *Handbook for Television Subtitlers.* – Winchester Hampshire: Engineering Division Independent Broadcasting Authority.

BBC (2008): "BBC Vision celebrates 100% subtitling".
http://www.bbc.co.uk/pressoffice/pressreleases/stories/2008/05_may/07/subtitling.shtml (08.08.2014)

BBC (2009): "Online Subtitling Editorial Guidelines".
http://www.bbc.co.uk/guidelines/futuremedia/accessibility/subtitling_guides/online_sub_editorial_guidelines_vs1_1.pdf (21.08.2014)

CRONIN, Barry J. (1980): "Closed-Caption Television: Today and Tomorrow", *American Annals of the Deaf* 125 (6), 726–728.

CRPD (2006): "Convention on the Rights of Persons with Disabilities". http://www.un.org/disabilities/convention/conventionfull.shtml (10.08.2014)

DCMP (Described and Captioned Media Programme) (2010): "How Bird Hunting in North Carolina Saved Captioning".
http://www.dcmp.org/caai/nadh36.pdf (09.08.2014)

DÍAZ-CINTAS, Jorge, REMAEL, Aline (2007): *Audiovisual Translation: Subtitling*. – Manchester: St Jerome Publishing.

FCC: "Closed Captioning on Television Closed Captioning on Television". http://www.fcc.gov/guides/closed-captioning (19.08.2014)

HISTORY OF INFORMATION: "The First Full-Length Film with Synchronized Dialogue".
http://www.historyofinformation.com/expanded.php?id=3522 (09.08.2014)

ITC (1999): "Guidance on Standards for Subtitling".
http://www.ofcom.org.uk/static/archive/itc/itc_publications/codes_guidance/standards_for_subtitling/index.asp.html (09.08.2014).

JENSEMA, Carl & BURCH, Robb (1999): *Caption Speed and Viewer Comprehension of Television Programmes.* – Washington: U.S. Department of Education.

KARAMITROGLOU, Fotios (2000): *Towards a Methodology for the Investigation of Norms in Audiovisual Translation. The Choice between Subtitling and Revoicing in Greece.* – Amsterdam: Rodopi.

KÜNSTLER, Izabela (2008): "Napisy dla Niesłyszących – Problemy i Wyzwania" [Subtitles for the deaf – Problems and challenges]. Przekładaniec. O Przekładzie Audiowizualnym [Translation Journal: On Audiovisual Translation] 20: 115–24. http://www.ejournals.eu/Przekladaniec/2008/Numer-20/

KÜNSTLER, Izabela & BUTKIEWICZ, Urszula (2012): "Napisy dla osób niesłyszących I słabosłyszących – zasady tworzenia" [Subtitles for deaf and hard-of-hearing people – guidelines]
http://dzieciom.pl/wp-content/uploads/2012/09/Napisy-dla-nieslyszacych-zasady-tworzenia.pdf (10.08.2014)

LAMPRYCHT, Janina (1995): "Z myślą o niesłyszących" [Thinking of non-hearers]. Comment in Gazeta telewizyjna [Television Magazine] 27.05–02.06.1995.

NATIONAL BROADCASTING COUNCIL:
http://www.krrit.gov.pl/krrit/informacje-o-krrit/ (10.08.2014)

NATIONAL BROADCASTING COUNCIL (2013): "Porozumienie nadawców w sprawie sposobu realizacji obowiązków wynikających z art.18a ustawy o radiofonii i telewizji dotyczących udogodnień w programach telewizyjnych dla osób z niepełnosprawnością wzroku i dla osób z niepełnosprawnością słuchu" [Broadcasters' settlement in terms of fulfilling the obligations arising from article 18a of the National Brodcasting Council Act on accessible services in television programmes for people with sight impairments and people with hearing impairements]:
http://www.krrit.gov.pl/Data/Files/_public/Portals/0/Nadawcy/aktualnosci/porozumienie_nadawcow.pdf

NATIONAL BROADCASTING COUNCIL (2014): "Strategia regulacyjna na lata 2014–2016" [Regulatory strategy for the years 2014–2016]:
http://www.krrit.gov.pl/Data/Files/_public/Portals/0/sprawozdania/strategia_final.pdf

NEVES, Josélia (2005): *Audiovisual Translation: Subtitling for the Deaf and Hard-of-Hearing*. – Unpublished PhD Thesis London: Roehampton University. http://rrp.roehampton.ac.uk/artstheses

NCI: "History of Closed Captioning". http://www.ncicap.org/about-us/history-of-closed-captioning/ (08.08.2014).

OFCOM (2012): "Ofcom's Code on Television Access Services".
http://stakeholders.ofcom.org.uk/broadcasting/broadcast-codes/tv-access-services/code-tv-access-services-2013/ (08.08.2014)

OFCOM (2014): http://media.ofcom.org.uk/news/2014/ofcom-publishes-first-results-on-quality-of-tv-subtitles/ (19.08.2014)

REMAEL, Aline (2007): "Sampling subtitling for the deaf and the hard-of-hearing in Europe". In: DÍAZ-CINTAS, Jorge, ORERO, Pilar & REMAEL, Aline (eds.): *Media for All: Subtitling for the Deaf, Audio Description, and Sign Language*. – Amsterdam/New York: Rodopi, 23–52.

ROBSON, Gary D. (2004): *The Closed Captioning Book.* – Amsterdam: Focal Press.

SZARKOWSKA, Agnieszka, KREJTZ, Izabela, KŁYSEJKO, Zuzanna. & WIECZOREK, Anna (forthcoming): "Eyetracking tests in Poland". In: ROMERO-FRESCO, Pablo (ed.): *The Reception of Subtitles for the Deaf and Hard of Hearing in Europe.* Peter Lang.

SZARKOWSKA, Agnieszka, LASKOWSKA, Monika (2014): "Jakie powinny być napisy? Raport z badania preferencji widzów na temat napisów telewizyjnych" [How should subtitles look like? Results of viewers' preferences on television subtitles] http://avt.ils.uw.edu.pl/files/2014/09/Wyniki-ankiety-o-napisach_Polska_FINAL.pdf

SZARKOWSKA, Agnieszka (2013): "Towards interlingual subtitling for the deaf and the hard of hearing", *Perspectives: Studies in Translatology* 21(1), 68–81.

THE TELEVISION DECODER CIRCUITRY ACT (1990):
http://transition.fcc.gov/Bureaus/OSEC/library/legislative_histories/1395.pdf

WEB 1: http://www.dcmp.org/captioningkey/captioning-key.pdf

WEB 2: http://dzieciom.pl/wp-content/uploads/2012/09/Napisy-dla-nieslyszacych-zasady-tworzenia.pdf

TRANSKULTURALITÄT – TRANSLATION – TRANSFER

Bd. 1   Cornelia Zwischenberger: Qualität und Rollenbilder beim simultanen Konferenzdolmetschen. 434 Seiten. ISBN 978-3-86596-527-1

Bd. 2   Sarah Fünfer: Mensch oder Maschine? Dolmetscher und maschinelles Dolmetschsystem im Vergleich. 150 Seiten. ISBN 978-386596-548-6

Bd. 3   Dörte Andres/Martina Behr (Hg.): Die Wahrheit, die reine Wahrheit und nichts als die Wahrheit. Erinnerungen der russischen Dolmetscherin Tatjana Stupnikova an den Nürnberger Prozess. 242 Seiten. ISBN 978-3-7329-0005-3

Bd. 4   Larisa Schippel (Hg.): Magda Jeanrenaud: Universalien des Übersetzens. 332 Seiten. ISBN 978-3-86596-444-1

Bd. 5   Sylvia Reinart: Lost in Translation (Criticism)? Auf dem Weg zu einer konstruktiven Übersetzungskritik. 438 Seiten. ISBN 978-3-7329-0014-5

Bd. 6   Sophia Scherl: Die deutsche Übersetzungskultur in der zweiten Hälfte des 18. Jahrhunderts. Meta Forkel-Liebeskind und ihre Übersetzung der *Rights of Man*. 152 Seiten. ISBN 978-3-7329-0020-6

Bd. 7   Thomas Kammer: Basiswissen für Dolmetscher – Deutschland und Spanien. 204 Seiten. ISBN 978-3-7329-0035-0

Bd. 8   Dorothee Jacobs: Basiswissen für Dolmetscher – Deutschland und das Vereinigte Königreich Großbritannien und Nordirland. 192 Seiten. ISBN 978-3-7329-0036-7

Bd. 9   Sophia Roessler: Basiswissen für Dolmetscher – Deutschland und Italien. 212 Seiten. ISBN 978-3-7329-0039-8

Bd. 10 Annika Selnow: Basiswissen für Dolmetscher – Deutschland und Frankreich. 192 Seiten. ISBN 978-3-7329-0040-4

Bd. 12 Alice Leal: Is the Glass Half Empty or Half Full? Reflections on Translation Theory and Practice in Brazil. 334 Seiten. ISBN 978-3-7329-0068-8

Bd. 13 Kristina Werner: Zwischen Neutralität und Propaganda – Französisch-Dolmetscher im Nationalsozialismus. 130 Seiten. ISBN 978-3-7329-0085-5

Bd. 14 Larisa Schippel/Magda Jeanrenaud/Julia Richter (Hg.): „Traducerile au de cuget să îmblînzească obiceiurile …". Rumänische Übersetzungsgeschichte – Prozesse, Produkte, Akteure. 368 Seiten. ISBN 978-3-7329-0087-9

Bd. 15 Elena Kalašnikova (Hg.): „Übersetzer sind die Wechselpferde der Aufklärung". Im Gespräch: Russische Übersetzerinnen und Übersetzer deutscher Literatur. 254 Seiten. ISBN 978-3-7329-0097-8

Frank & Timme

TRANSKULTURALITÄT – TRANSLATION – TRANSFER

Bd. 16   Dörte Andres/Martina Behr (eds.): To Know How to Suggest … Approaches to Teaching Conference Interpreting. 260 Seiten. ISBN 978-3-7329-0114-2

Bd. 17   Tatiana Bedson/Maxim Schulz: Sowjetische Übersetzungskultur in den 1920er und 1930er Jahren. Die Verlage *Vsemirnaja literatura* und *Academia*. 182 Seiten. ISBN 978-3-7329-0142-5

Bd. 18   Cécile Balbous: Das Sprachknaben-Institut der Habsburgermonarchie in Konstantinopel. 90 Seiten. ISBN 978-3-7329-0149-4

Bd. 19   Cornelia Zwischenberger/Martina Behr (eds.): Interpreting Quality: A Look Around and Ahead. 334 Seiten. ISBN 978-3-7329-0191-3

Bd. 20   Mehmet Tahir Öncü: Basiswissen für Dolmetscher – Deutschland und die Türkei. 232 Seiten. ISBN 978-3-7329-0154-8

Bd. 21   Marc Orlando: Training 21st century translators and interpreters: At the crossroads of practice, research and pedagogy. 158 Seiten. ISBN 978-3-7329-0245-3

Bd. 22   Christian Trollmann: Nationalsozialismus auf Japanisch? Deutsch-japanische Beziehungen 1933–1945 aus translationssoziologischer Sicht. 154 Seiten. ISBN 978-3-7329-0281-1

Bd. 23   Ursula Gross-Dinter (Hg.): Dolmetschen 3.0 – Einblicke in einen Beruf im Wandel. 226 Seiten. ISBN 978-3-7329-0188-3

Bd. 24   Lieven D'hulst/Carol O'Sullivan/Michael Schreiber (eds.): Politics, Policy and Power in Translation History. 256 Seiten. ISBN 978-3-7329-0173-9

Bd. 25   Dörte Andres/Julia Richter/Larisa Schippel (Hg.): Translation und „Drittes Reich". Menschen – Entscheidungen – Folgen. 352 Seiten. ISBN 978-3-7329-0302-3

Bd. 26   Julia Richter/Cornelia Zwischenberger/Stefanie Kremmel/Karlheinz Spitzl (Hg.): (Neu-)Kompositionen. Aspekte transkultureller Translationswissenschaft. 404 Seiten. ISBN 978-3-7329-0306-1

Bd. 27   Barbara den Ouden: Translation und Emotion: Untersuchung einer besonderen Komponente des Dolmetschens. 438 Seiten. ISBN 978-3-7329-0304-7

Bd. 28   Larisa Schippel/Cornelia Zwischenberger (eds.): Going East: Discovering New and Alternative Traditions in Translation Studies. 540 Seiten. ISBN 978-3-7329-0335-1

Bd. 29   Dörte Andres/Klaus Kaindl/Ingrid Kurz (Hg.): Dolmetscherinnen und Dolmetscher im Netz der Macht. Autobiographisch konstruierte Lebenswege in autoritären Regimen. 280 Seiten. ISBN 978-3-7329-0336-8

Frank & Timme

TRANSKULTURALITÄT – TRANSLATION – TRANSFER

Bd. 30 Martina Behr/Sabine Seubert (Hg.): Education is a Whole-Person Process. Von ganzheitlicher Lehre, Dolmetschforschung und anderen Dingen. 516 Seiten. ISBN 978-3-7329-0324-5

Bd. 31 Simone Kellner: Basiswissen für Dolmetscher und Übersetzer – Österreich. 108 Seiten. ISBN 978-3-7329-0370-2

Bd. 32 Simon Zupan/Aleksandra Nuč (eds.): Interpreting Studies at the Crossroads of Disciplines. 204 Seiten. ISBN 978-3-7329-0045-9

Bd. 33 Hilke Effinghausen: Zwischen Neutralität und Propaganda – Spanisch-Dolmetscher im Nationalsozialismus. 178 Seiten. ISBN 978-3-7329-0394-8

Bd. 34 Lars Felgner: Nonverbale Kommunikation beim medizinischen Dolmetschen. 428 Seiten. ISBN 978-3-7329-0386-3

Bd. 35 Annika Schlesiger: Berufsschutz für Übersetzer und Dolmetscher in Deutschland. Vergangenheit – Gegenwart – und Zukunft? 200 Seiten. ISBN 978-3-7329-0408-2

Bd. 36 Lena Skalweit: Dolmetscher und ihre Ausbildung im Zeitalter der europäischen Expansion. Osmanisches Reich und Afrika. 312 Seiten. ISBN 978-3-7329-0371-9

Bd. 37 Samantha Blai: Basiswissen für Dolmetscher und Übersetzer – Deutschland und Polen. 306 Seiten. ISBN 978-3-7329-0446-4

Bd. 38 Jette Knapp: Basiswissen für Dolmetscher und Übersetzer – Deutschland und USA. 248 Seiten. ISBN 978-3-7329-0447-1

Bd. 39 Thomas Baumgart/Mona Gerlach: Basiswissen für Dolmetscher und Übersetzer – Deutschland und Spanien. 254 Seiten. ISBN 978-3-7329-0465-5

Bd. 40 Amrei Bahr/Katja Hagedorn: Basiswissen für Dolmetscher und Übersetzer – Deutschland und das Vereinigte Königreich Großbritannien und Nordirland. 236 Seiten. ISBN 978-3-7329-0467-9

Bd. 41 Saskia Isabelle Riemke/Eleonora Pepe: Basiswissen für Dolmetscher und Übersetzer – Deutschland und Italien. 276 Seiten. ISBN 978-3-7329-0468-6

Bd. 42 Miriam Heike Schroers: Basiswissen für Dolmetscher und Übersetzer – Deutschland und Frankreich. 280 Seiten. ISBN 978-3-7329-0485-3

Bd. 43 Charlotte P. Kieslich: Dolmetschen im Nationalsozialismus. Die Reichsfachschaft für das Dolmetscherwesen (RfD). 428 Seiten. ISBN 978-3-7329-0515-7

Bd. 44 Viktoria Fedorovskaja/Tatiana Yudina: Basiswissen für Dolmetscher und Übersetzer – Deutschland und Russland. 264 Seiten. ISBN 978-3-7329-0487-7

F Frank & Timme

TRANSKULTURALITÄT – TRANSLATION – TRANSFER

Bd. 45 Ke Liu: Basiswissen für Dolmetscher und Übersetzer – Deutschland und China.
228 Seiten. ISBN 978-3-7329-0527-0

Bd. 46 Antonina Lakner: Peter de Mendelssohn – Translation, Identität und Exil.
414 Seiten. ISBN 978-3-7329-0491-4

Bd. 47 Sabine Seubert: Visuelle Informationen beim Simultandolmetschen.
Eine Eyetracking-Studie. 402 Seiten. ISBN 978-3-7329-0572-0

Bd. 48 Kimberly Dinnissen/Rob Soons: Basiswissen für Dolmetscher und Übersetzer –
Deutschland und die Niederlande. 270 Seiten. ISBN 978-3-7329-0583-6

Bd. 49 Martina Behr: Dolmetschen: Komplexität, Methodik, Modellierung.
288 Seiten. ISBN 978-3-7329-0635-2

Bd. 50 Aleksey Tashinskiy/Julija Boguna/Andreas F. Kelletat (Hg.):
Übersetzer und Übersetzen in der DDR. Translationshistorische Studien.
292 Seiten. ISBN 978-3-7329-0698-7

Bd. 51 Kate Reiserer: Vier Übersetzerinnen und ihre neun Ehemänner.
Ehe und Übersetzung in der Romantik. 154 Seiten. ISBN 978-3-7329-0755-7

Bd. 52 Larisa Schippel/Julia Richter (Hg.): Translation und „Drittes Reich".
Translationsgeschichte als methodologische Herausforderung. 370 Seiten.
ISBN 978-3-7329-0661-1

Bd. 53 Aleksey Tashinskiy/Julija Boguna/Tomasz Rozmysłowicz (Hg.):
Translation und Exil (1933–1945) I. Namen und Orte. Recherchen zur Geschichte
des Übersetzens. 494 Seiten. ISBN 978-3-7329-0744-1

Bd. 54 Hildegard Maria Mader: Von Paris nach Kairo: Wissenstransfer im *Paris-Bericht*
Rifā'a Rāfi' aṭ-Ṭahṭāwīs. Ein Beitrag zur Übersetzungsgeschichte Ägyptens
im 19. Jahrhundert. 118 Seiten. ISBN 978-3-7329-0841-7

Bd. 55 Yafen Zhao: Take it or leave it? Notationstechnik beim Konsekutivdolmetschen
Chinesisch–Deutsch. 276 Seiten. ISBN 978-3-7329-0871-4

Bd. 56 Hannah Spannring: Lore Segal – Ein translatorisches Porträt im Kontext Exil.
238 Seiten. ISBN 978-3-7329-0901-8

T Frank & Timme